P9-DZA-025

Readings in
DEAF
EDUCATION

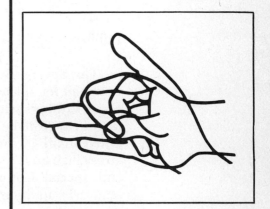

Special Learning Corporation
42 Boston Post Rd. Guilford, Connecticut 06437

Special Learning Corporation

Publisher's Message:

The Special Education Series is the first comprehensive series designed for special education courses of study. It is also the first series to offer such a wide variety of high quality books. In addition, the series will be expanded and up-dated each year. No other publications in the area of special education can equal this. We stress high quality content, a superb advisory and consulting group, and special features that help in understanding the course of study. In addition we believe we must also publish in very small enrollment areas in order to establish the credibility and strength of our series. We realize the enrollments in courses of study such as Autism, Visually Handicapped Education, or Diagnosis and Placement are not large. Nevertheless, we believe there is a need for course books in these areas and books that are kept up-to-date on an annual basis! Special Learning Corporation's goal is to publish the highest quality materials for the college and university courses of study. With your comments and support we will continue to do this.

John P. Quirk

©1979 by Special Learning Corporation, Guilford, Connecticut 06437

All rights reserved. No part of this book may be reproduced, stored, or communicated by any means--without written permission from Special Learning Corporation.

First Edition

2   3   4   5   141709

ISBN No.   0-89568-006-8

SPECIAL EDUCATION SERIES

Autism
* Behavior Modification
Biological Bases of Learning Disabilities
Brain Impairments
Career and Vocational Education
Child Abuse
Child Development
Child Psychology
Cognitive and Communication Skills
* Counseling Parents of Exceptional
Children
Creative Arts
Curriculum and Materials
* Deaf Education
Developmental Disabilities
* Diagnosis and Placement
Down's Syndrome
Dyslexia
Early Learning
Educational Technology
* Emotional and Behavioral Disorders
Exceptional Parents
* Gifted and Talented Education
* Human Growth and Development of
the Exceptional Individual
Hyperactivity
* Individualized Educational Programs

● Language & Writing Disorders
* ● Learning Disabilities
Learning Theory
* ● Mainstreaming
* ● Mental Retardation
● Motor Disorders
Multiple Handicapped Education
Occupational Therapy
● Perception and Memory Disorders
* ● Physically Handicapped Education
* ● Pre-School Education for the
Handicapped
* ● Psychology of Exceptional Children
● Reading Disorders
Reading Skill Development
Research and Development
* ● Severely and Profoundly Handicapped
Education
Slow Learner Education
Social Learning
* ● Special Education
* ● Speech and Hearing
Testing and Diagnosis
● Three Models of Learning Disabilities
* ● Visually Handicapped Education
* ● Vocational Training for the Mentally
Retarded

● Published Titles   * Major Course Areas

Readings in
Human Growth And
Development of the
Exceptional Individual
Special Learning Corporation

Readings in
Pre-School Education
For The Handicapped
Special Learning Corporation

Readings in
Vocational Training For
The Mentally Retarded
Special Learning Corporation

Readings in
Career And Vocational
Education For
The Handicapped
Special Learning Corporation

DEAF EDUCATION

CONTENTS

FOCUS

GLOSSARY OF TERMS

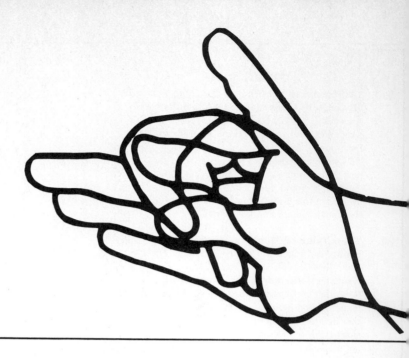

aphasia Inability to understand and/or use language meaningfully.

articulátion The movements of speech organs employed in producing a particular speech sound or consonant.

audiometer Instrument for testing acuity of hearing.

auditory closure The ability to recognize the whole from the presentation of a partial stimulus.

aural training Of or pertaining to stimulus training perceived by the ear.

autism A disorder characterized by early onset, lack of interest in social contacts, delay in language development, and ritualistic behavior patterns.

cleft palate A congenital defect due to a failure in development of the roof of the mouth.

cochlea A spiral tube of the inner ear resembling a snailshell and containing nerve endings essential for hearing.

conductive hearing loss A condition which reduces the intensity of the sound vibrations reaching the auditory nerve in the inner ear.

congenital Present in an individual at birth.

deaf A hearing impaired person whose auditory channel cannot or does not serve as the primary sensory means by which speech and language are received and developed.

decibel A relative measure of the intensity of sounds, zero decibel represents normal hearing.

intonation A manner of producing or uttering tones, especially with regard to accuracy of pitch as an element of meaning in language.

linguistic development Of or relating to language acquisition or linguistics.

lipreading A technique used by the deaf to understand inaudible speech by interpretation of lip and facial movement.

middle ear The space between the tympanic membrane and the inner ear which contains the auditory ossicles which convey vibrations to the auditory tube.

otosclerosis The formation of spongy bone in the capsule bone in the ear.

ototoxic Caused by poison or toxin creating damage to the ear.

phonology The science of speech sounds including phonetics, and phonemics.

profound deafness Penetrating beyond hearing impairment to the most far-reaching form of deafness.

residual hearing The quantity of remaining hearing left after damage by noise or injury.

sign language A system of communication by means of hand gestures.

soft palate The movable fold, consisting of muscular fibers enclosed in mucous membrane, that is suspended from the rear of the hard palate, which closes off the nasal cavity from the oral cavity during swallowing or sucking.

tympanic membrane The thin, semitransparent, oval-shaped membrane separating the middle ear from the external ear, also called the "eardrum."

velar-control Phonetics which are formed and controlled with the back of the tongue on or near the soft palate.

TOPIC MATRIX

Readings in *Deaf Education* provides the college student in special education a comprehensive overview of the subject. The book is designed to follow a basic course of study.

COURSE OUTLINE:

Education of the Deaf

I. Acquisition of Language Skills
II. Principles and Techniques with the Deaf
III. Development and Adaptation of Curriculum Materials
IV. Evaluation Instructional Needs of the Deaf

Readings in Deaf Education

I. Education of the Deaf: A Perspective
II. Research, Diagnosis and Assessment
III. Linguistic Development
IV. Educational Resources and Methodologies

Related Special Learning Corporation Titles

I. Readings in Special Education
II. Readings in Speech and Hearing
III. Readings in Mainstreaming

PREFACE

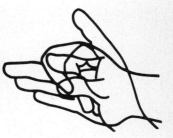

Without knowing a deaf person it is very difficult to understand the true meaning of deafness. Deafness is not only the handicap of not being able to hear. It encompasses emotional problems, discrimination, shame, learning disabilities, problems in socialization and the general day-by-day experiences only a deaf person can comprehend.

One might think of what a person misses when he cannot hear music, a mother's voice, laughter, or children singing. But it is not lack of hearing that constitutes the real problem. The real problem is learning how to deal with and get along with other people — many of whom cannot understand, appreciate or sympathize.

Helen Keller, herself deaf and blind, said of the handicap of deafness:

"The problems of deafness are deeper and
more complex, if not more important than
those of blindness. Deafness is a much worse
misfortune. For it means the loss of the most
vital stimulus—the sound of the voice that
brings language, sets thoughts astir, and keeps
us in the intellectual company of man."

Educational Resources and Methodologies

The truest challenge of the teaching profession is for those who work with the deaf. They must face the fact that the extreme barriers of communication must be neutralized in order to make a breakthrough for inroads of education.

First, who are the deaf? Deafness has been found to be a highly individual matter taking into consideration the amount of hearing loss, the child at onset, the cause and the type of loss — all these factors come together in order that an educational plan might be formed and acted upon. The degree of hearing loss must first be determined in order that a day school speech therapy program might be offered, that is if the child is individually capable of speech and speech reading. The purpose of the school then becomes a clinical rather than educational one, as classroom learning activities can be hampered by overzealous demands on the part of parents and educators on standards of performance. Therefore, speech development must become an integral part of the child's learning rather than the "subject matter."

How might education accomplish all this? Perhaps through implementation of lipreading. This process has been called a form of educational guesswork by some, as intensive training in the field can produce stronger lipreaders than others simply according to intelligence levels, situations of the environment, and accuracy of ability through practice. However, if the child is given the most positive attitudes, properly trained personnel, appropriate and up to date facilities, the latest equipment and educational resources, with balanced programs of education which should be based on the individual interests, needs and capabilities, he should become a contributing member of society at large who can possess a good education in order that he might make his contribution to life.

Successful education programs for the deaf have confirmed these facts to be valid. With emotional and positive support from the teacher and family of deaf children, frustration and problems can be overcome. Complete acceptance as he is can add dimension to his life in such a way as to bolster the knowledge of a loving attitude of guidance and direction, so that the goals of a deaf child might become more attainable when he reaches adulthood, as a result of his well rounded educational abilities.

BY THE DEAF FOR THE DEAF

THE DEAF ARE BEING TAUGHT TO TEACH THE DEAF IN AN APPROACH COMBINING SIGN LANGUAGE, LIPREADING, AND "BODY LANGUAGE"

Flashing the sign language, mouthing words, and using "body language" is "total communication" as practiced in a training program at Western Maryland College in which deaf teachers teach deaf youngsters. The children are students at the Maryland School for the Deaf at Frederick. The sophisticated electronic aids worn by the pupils supplement any remnant of residual hearing they may have.

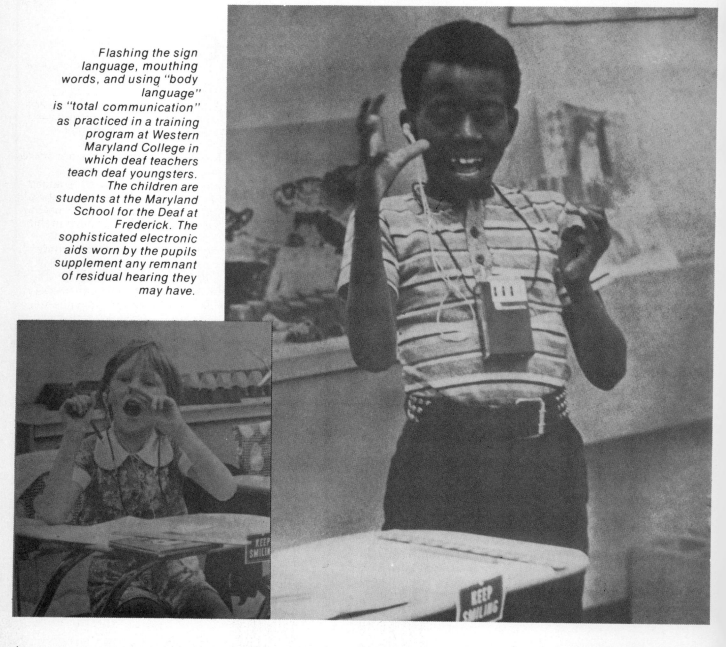

1. **By the Deaf**

There is no energy crisis in the classroom at Western Maryland College where McCay Vernon teaches "total communication." Energy is unrestrained among teachers and students alike. The atmosphere seems electrified by a special desire of the students to learn—and the teachers to show—new ways of breaking through a barrier of silence that obstructs their lives. And there is an energizing force also in the determination of the students to pass on the skills they are learning to other young people who, like themselves, have difficulty getting through to their fellow humans.

One basic characteristic of the young men and women in Dr. Vernon's classroom is deafness. A second is intense eagerness to become teachers of the deaf. McCay Vernon is showing them how.

Western Maryland, a small liberal arts college in the foothills of the Blue Ridge Mountains at Westminster, is unique in accepting deaf students to train as teachers and social workers serving the deaf. Moreover, it is one of the few institutes in the United States at which both hearing and nonhearing students work and study together. The goal is to help the deaf become integrated into the hearing community, to the extent that they wish and feel it is feasible.

The Western Maryland program, formally known as Teacher Preparation for Education of Deaf Children, is funded by the Office of Education's Bureau of Programs for the Handicapped. The object of the program is to prepare professionally outstanding teachers to meet what BPH officials describe as a critical need for teachers in deaf education throughout the United States.

The Western Maryland program, open to both undergraduate and graduate students, was begun specifically to meet the need for teachers and dormitory counselors at the Maryland School for the Deaf at Frederick (about 25 miles from the WMC campus), a need expanded by the recent opening of another campus of the Maryland School for the Deaf at Columbia (about 45 miles from WMC). More broadly, Western Maryland is seeking to respond to such trends as (1) the requirement by increasing numbers of schools that teachers of the deaf regularly return to the classroom to polish up their teaching skills, (2) the growing practice of filling vacancies only with fully certified rather than noncertified teachers, and (3) the emerging policy—in many cases set by new State legislation—of establishing classes for the deaf in schools attended for the most part by students with normal hearing.

Generally speaking, there are two schools of thought about how to educate the deaf: *oralism*, a method of instruction limited primarily to the use of speech, lipreading, and amplification; and *total communication*, which involves all of these techniques plus the use of the language of signs and finger spelling. There is a long-running debate between educators of the deaf as to which method may be the better. Western Maryland uses *total communication* and adds *body language*, a form of expression as old as the wink and as familiar as the nod.

"It was Charles Darwin," Dr. Vernon says, "who initially theorized the presence of universals in the 'body language' of man and animals. He found that persons of widely different cultures had no trouble in recognizing the emotions expressed in the drawings and pictographs of people from other cultures."

Dr. Vernon sees this phenomenon as having particularly important implications for the deaf. "Since they are denied adequate verbal communication with most persons with whom they have interaction," he says, "including many of their teachers and often their parents, they are almost totally dependent upon reading body language to perceive the basic effects, feelings, and essence of people while being denied the verbal cognitive."

As a start toward carrying out that principle, trainees at Western Maryland sit in as observers in classrooms at the Maryland School for the Deaf, seeing "total communications" teaching in action. Subsequently they begin to serve as teachers aides, putting to practice the methods and techniques they have observed. Outside regular school hours they work with parents in special classes for adults who are learning to communicate with their deaf children.

Throughout, the emphasis is on the proposition that the person—not a book, a chart, a film, or a teaching machine—is the most important medium in the language process. Thus though numerous teaching aides are available, the most important are lightweight sound amplification units provided each student.

These devices permit all but the most profoundly afflicted youngsters to hear at least partially the teachers and trainees as well as follow their lip movements, sign language, and gestures.

In many ways, the deaf student-teachers say, their handicap is an asset that gives an added dimension in developing teaching skills—enabling them to relate more readily with the deaf children's difficulties in learning new signs and new speech patterns and giving them a special understanding of the need of non-hearing students to penetrate the isolation of silence and dispel feelings of separation from the world around them.

A trainee assigned to observe teaching at the Frederick campus might be working with Linda Amato, who, as a graduate student completing requirements for her Master's degree in education of the deaf (MED) at Western Maryland, teaches an upper primary class for nine-to-eleven-year-old deaf children. Or, the trainee may be given a practice teaching assignment in the class for children of ages eight and nine, taught by Nancy Swaiko, who graduated last year from Western Maryland with a MED.

Mrs. Amato may be giving her students instructions in writing and spelling, using the device of having students write letters to their parents. Since most of the youngsters come from distant homes and live five days a week at the school, this exercise has the added advantage of keeping parents abreast of progress the students are making. A typical trainee assignment in this situation is to help the students translate signs into written words.

In Ms. Swaiko's classroom the trainee may find the students practicing total communication as they tell stories, a sort of show-and-tell for the deaf. At one point in his story, a nine-year-old boy comes to the part where he says in sign language that a certain experience was "really neat," an expression of youth for something especially pleasing.

At this point, the trainee would discover that the boy may not finger spell "r-e-a-l-l-y n-e-a-t." Instead he uses body language—a big smile and a twist—and makes the sign for "wow," the three-fingered "w" made with both hands.

The Western Maryland program requires teacher trainees to complete courses in speech, manual communication, language development in deaf children, auditory and vocal mechanism, speech-reading, and hearing and auditory testing and training.

Undergraduates and graduate students alike must take Dr. Vernon's

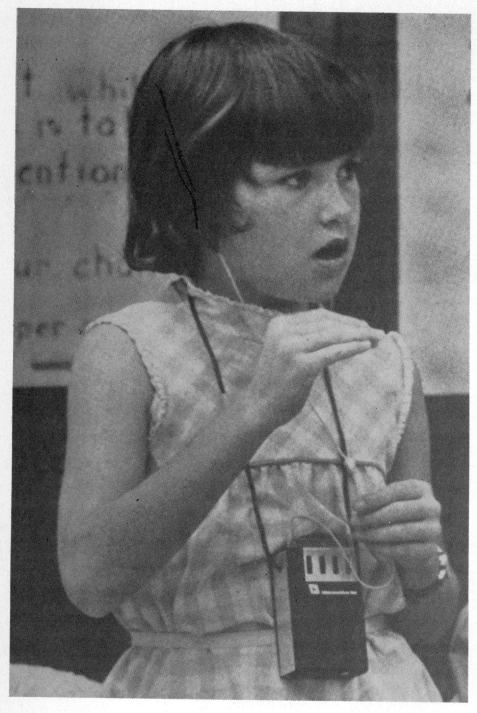

course in the psychology of deafness, which examines the effects of a lack of hearing on personality and behavior.

In the classroom Dr. Vernon is an animated example of his total communication concept. He simultaneously speaks aloud for students who read lips; flashes the sign language for those who know or are learning that skill; and buttresses both with whatever expressions or gestures suit the mood of his topic—a smile, a frown, a shake of the head, a grimace of discomfort. From time to time, he pauses while a student

interpreter, standing at his side, repeats the signs for those who have been unable to keep pace with their teacher.

A recent visitor to Dr. Vernon's classroom found the students and teacher discussing a documentary film which explored various psychological effects of deafness on children and on parents. The students had recently viewed the movie as part of their studies. The full-color production—presented with both sound-track and captions so that both the hearing and the non-hearing students can comprehend its

message—depicts case histories of deaf children whose parents can hear normally.

One important portion of the film focused on the problems arising from the difficulty encountered by parents not only in communicating with their deaf offspring but even in grasping the situation that confronts them. For example, in one of the families portrayed in the movie, it was many months before the parents discovered their infant was deaf. Meanwhile, they had tiptoed around its crib speaking to each other in whispers, mistakenly believing that if they had done otherwise they would have awakened the baby. Thus, the title of the film, "We Tiptoed Around Whispering."

In another episode in the film, it was six years before the parents learned their child was deaf. In both these cases inaccurate medical diagnosis was given as the reason parents were left thinking their children were suffering from some kind of mental retardation. The film tells the trainees that deafness is in some cases hereditary and in others may be caused by prenatal rubella or meningitis.

Using his total communication methods—forming the words with his mouth, signing them with his fingers, and emphasizing them by gestures—Vernon starts the discussion:

"The situations in the film were based on actual experience. The language was taken from interviews with parents and physicians. The problems are real. What is your reaction?"

In response, one of the graduate students, Paula Ammons Woodall, who has been deaf since birth, declares with rapidly flicking fingers—and with facial expressions that emphasize her point:

"The doctors made me mad. Discovering deafness is still a problem, especially in rural towns. The doctors should have had some training in medical school to recognize deafness in small children. The acceptance of a deaf child's difficulties by the parents, once the correct diagnosis was made, was one thing; but knowing what to do about it was another."

Paula's comment has a special ring of authority based on wide experience in dealing with handicaps of deafness. Her parents are deaf, she has two deaf sisters, and she married a deaf man. Because her parents made themselves aware of her lack of hearing while she was still an infant and *did* know "what to do about it,"

Paula received elementary education in the Kendall School on the campus of Gallaudet College in Washington, D.C.; secondary schooling at the National Technical Institute for the Deaf in Rochester, N.Y.; and a Bachelor's degree in sociology at Gallaudet. She and her husband are employed as dormitory counselors at the Maryland School for the Deaf.

"We Tiptoed Around Whispering" is one of a series of documentary films on deafness sponsored by BPH and produced in Western Maryland's Total Communication Laboratory to augment the teacher trainees' studies. The film-maker is L. Earl Griswold, a professor of sociology who made a movie production studio out of a milk shed on his dairy farm near Westminster. The series, produced jointly by the college and the Maryland Center for Public Broadcasting under the compendium, "They Grow in Silence," earned Griswold the Community Service Award, the equivalent of an "Emmy" in the Public Broadcasting Service. The films are available from WMC for public televising or organization viewing.

Now in the making is a new series which Dr. Griswold believes will help teachers to educate small deaf children much as "Sesame Street" is helping in the education of disadvantaged children with normal hearing. An important element in the series is a Rube Goldberg type of console, with flashing lights and spinning wheels, designed to transmit visually basic education lessons to the hearing-impaired youngsters. Other instruction, such as teaching finger spelling, will be provided by a teacher using sign language and costumed as a large kangaroo, a counterpart of Big Bird on "Sesame Street."

A good part of the energy that goes into Western Maryland's teacher training program is generated by Britt Hargraves, director of the graduate program, the audiologist in residence, and a champion of the idea of teaching by the deaf, for the deaf. And the message is getting through, he says, pointing as evidence to the several schools for the deaf that have recently started to cooperate in the Western Maryland program by making facilities available for classroom teaching experience, and in some cases offering internships.

As further evidence he notes that every one of the 34 full-time students who were graduated as teachers of the deaf last year were immediately offered positions, not only in

Beginning with the sign for "Y"—and communicating with his facial expressions as well as his fingers—this youngster is telling his classmates of an outing he enjoyed.

Maryland but in communities as far away as Canada. A summer program, which filled requirements for certification by the Council on the Education of the Deaf, trained 146 young men and women who either needed certification to teach the deaf, or who were seeking to renew their certificates. "At the close of the program in August," Hargraves says, "we had more requests for teachers than we could fill."

As the people at Western Maryland College see it, the practical payoff of the program is equaled by its symbolic benefits. By their example the deaf young teachers are showing the hearing-impaired that they can not only carve out successful careers but can in the process perform a service that commands the respect of their fellow citizens everywhere.

That the Deaf May Hear and Speak

Leo E. Connor, Ed.D.

The president of an organization is allowed during his tenure one final chance to voice the hopes and the dreams, the fears and the frustrations, the basics and the trivialities which have motivated his office. Like presidents of the A. G. Bell Association who have gone before me, I have prevailed upon your membership in the Association to invite you to this assemblage tonight, and I have used my waning influence with the program committee to schedule a presidential speech. I hope you find that it deals more with basics than fads and more with hopes than frustrations.

As your President, I want to do more than cheer you up or paint a rosy picture. However, I cannot succumb to recent irritants or discouraging setbacks. Rather, I wish to leave you an enduring set of statements that encompass a practical as well as an ideal set of objectives.

In my speech this evening, I would like to present a Bill of Rights for every deaf person. These are human rights, sacred to each individual, applicable to infants and children at an early age level, but vital to every stage of one's development, and specifically pertinent to the hearing impaired person growing up in our American culture.

The modern, mediated society of the 1970's has some peculiar overtones for all people. Today, the public relations experts sell "instant answers" and "scientific miracles" to life's problems. We have Action, Duz, Cold Tablets, Ice Milk, No-Doz, Sleepeze, One-A-Day, Instant Breakfast, imitation oleo, and even Total! We've got them all: the biggest, the best, the fastest, the cleanest, the cheapest! Most important, of course, is that each of these modern advances is exalted as working at breathtaking speed, with no effort, with little direction, without comprehension by the user, and with guaranteed results, or your money back.

Perhaps I am trying to swim against a flood, but my Bill of Rights has no panaceas or cures; it contains no quick results or *total* promises. It asks for dedication and consistency, daily and even minute-by-minute efforts, intelligent and creative endeavors, the highest level of professional help; and the delicate, complex, tough job of mutual cooperation and support between school and home over a period of many years.

The body of my Bill of Rights has five main provisions:

1. Every deaf child must begin his education at birth.

It is possible for many hearing impaired children to be identified in the hospital, within a few days of birth. We may not be able to describe the precise type of loss; but we can decide, with good to excellent certainty, that a child *has* a hearing loss. In all of our communities there are so many high-risk children who should be tested that you who are the parents and educators of deaf children must constantly preach to the medical profession that every baby's hearing should be evaluated in the first days of life before the baby leaves the hospital.

The otologists and audiologists, through their professional organizations, have adopted a current stance that testing infants' hearing is not advisable. That will not do! We, the educators, and you, the parents,

"That the Deaf May Hear and Speak," Leo E. Connor, Ed.D., *The Volta Review*, Vol. 74 No. 9, 1972. ©1972 The Alexander Graham Bell Association for the Deaf, Inc.

need universal infant testing at once (not in 1975 or 1978!). We are ready with our educational procedures for the babies, and their parents need counseling services as well as a knowledge of language and speech techniques *immediately*.

In particular, the hearing impaired babies cannot wait. I can tell you with certainty that there is an optimal physiological period in a child's life when he should learn speech and language skills as well as auditory awareness. It is before 2 years of age and, ideally, at six months of age when the hearing child is utilizing his speech and hearing within a normal developmental pattern to lay the foundation stones for his lifelong mastery of syntax and morphology and the ability to express himself verbally with facile complexity.

Research evidence is available from a variety of fields that, although developmental psychologists are not sure of specifics, their studies indicate the need for neonatal and infant stimulation, intervention, and parental support. I can summarize the growing trend of infant training by saying that all studies of these earliest years indicate significant achievement in specific developmental skills which are necessary for the future well-being of the hearing impaired child. Their conclusion is this: deafness is not a static condition but is cumulative—that is, it deepens and worsens the later in life that it is recognized and assisted.

II. Every deaf child should be able to use his residual hearing in a functional manner.

Let me illustrate this point with a case study. Laurie is a 7-year-old profoundly deaf girl. Currently, audiological tests indicate a hearing loss of 105 dB in the right ear and 115 dB in the left ear (ISO standards) at an average speech frequency. Probable cause of deafness was rubella. She was enrolled at the Lexington School for the Deaf when she was 19 months old. She attended school three days a week for two years and then daily until the end of the first grade. She was then transferred to a regular school second grade class in the New York City public school system. Although she has received daily tutoring from a resource room teacher and a private tutor during the past year, she spends all of her day in the regular class.

Laurie's *amplified* hearing loss is 42 dB in the speech frequencies and, at 7 years of age, she can use the telephone to carry on two-way conversations with her friends. She had a WISC IQ of 110 in January 1971.

Laurie is, in every respect, a child with a *profound* loss of hearing, who is functioning in what most people call the mildly hard of hearing category. She uses lipreading for reception of ordinary communications but can, if necessary, rely upon hearing alone to obtain verbal information from those around her. Basically, I repeat, she is mildly hard of hearing in her life activities and has developed normal, lilting speech patterns (with a slight tendency to drop her *s*'s), and has absolutely normal colloquial 7-year-old language patterns. Her tested unamplified ISO hearing loss, again, is 105 dB in one ear and 115 in the other.

Laurie is not unique. Since 1962 the Lexington School for the Deaf has had intimate experience with over 110 deaf children who started our program before 2 years of age. These children, who test in the profoundly deaf range (e.g., between 90 and 115 dB) at 6 to 10 years of age, show audiograms which, on the average, are 40 dB higher with amplification. In other words, the Lexington School for the Deaf has enrolled 110 children who would have been called profoundly deaf a few years ago, but who are currently using their residual hearing at a hard of hearing level in an everyday, functional manner. They are all expected to transfer to regular classrooms by their 12th birthday, irrespective of IQ, family background, or home community. Our records show a high correlation between their use of residual hearing and the following factors: 1) early age of entry into the program; 2) retention of the babbling and chattering syndrome from 6 months of age onward; 3) earlier fitting with binaural hearing aids; 4) interest and involvement of at least one parent; 5) frequency of attendance; and 6) self confidence or outgoing personality.

What I am saying to you is that even the most profoundly deaf child, if given an early start at 6 days, or 6 weeks, or at 6 months of age, will develop testable, consistent, functional usage of hearing by the time he is 4 to 6 years old. This, in turn, has resulted in the following verifiable skills of our Lexington students: subtle auditory differentiations can be demonstrated in both receptive and expressive speech by severely and profoundly deaf children who have received consistent early auditory stimulation. Receptively, these include voice and speech recognition and identification of emotional quality of voice. Expressively, they include imitation and use of speech temporal patterns; intensity, rate and stress; voice quality and intonation contours which convey meaning; rhythmic patterns and correct number of syllables; as well as phrases and sentences.

Hearing, then, is the key to normal language and speech development for the deaf child. I am aware that Whetnall and Fry, Murphy, Griffiths, the Ewings, and others in several countries have devised varying approaches, either unisensory or multisensory, to highlight the use of residual hearing. Whatever the specific techniques, Doreen Pollack's words, as she discusses one of the deaf children in her book *Educational Audiology for the Limited Hearing Infant*, highlight the key concepts that I wish to emphasize:

> If this particular girl [87 dB loss] were judged by the classification system . . . [still used in the vast majority of clinics and schools], and if her teachers approached her with the attitude that she is *deaf* . . . all kinds of limitations would be placed upon her—orally, educationally and vocationally. . . . I believe that the use of the term *deaf* with its connotations is outdated.*

John Dewey, the famous educator, has written that "education is primarily a public business, and only secondarily a specialized vocation. The layman, therefore, will always have his right to utterance on the operation of the public schools."

Two important concepts were being emphasized by Dewey: first that parents have a normal, natural, legal, intellectual, and emotional right to be involved with their deaf child's education; and, secondly, that if such an education is not satisfying to them and to the child, they should and must ask questions, present suggestions, criticize, and obtain change or, in the final act, remove their children from such unsatisfactory atmospheres and, through legal or political action, force the authorities to evaluate and to improve.

The heart of the curriculum in our classes is the deaf child who has a hearing, a speech, and a language problem. Poor results in a school program are like continuing sicknesses and deaths in a hospital; they are the failures of the institution which was founded to avoid such conclusions. If a school does not educate, then its teachers, its supervisors, and its curriculum are all at fault and need an evaluation and an objective statement of their faults.

Educators of the deaf must expect the deaf child to utilize his hearing in a functional manner, or else they will be forced to turn over his aural habilitation activities to other professional groups who can produce better results.

III. Every deaf child should be able to speak intelligibly.

At the Lexington School for the Deaf we have two graduations every June. At one of our graduations the traditional caps and gowns are worn by the 15 to 20 twelfth-graders, about half of whom are going out to job situations while the other half will go on to post-secondary programs at Gallaudet College, the National Technical Institute for the Deaf at Rochester, New York, the special junior colleges for the deaf in Denver, New Orleans, Pittsburgh, Seattle, etc., as well as to the New York City and State University junior colleges with their open admissions programs. A few of these graduates started their schooling about 15 years ago at Lexington, but most of them transferred into our program at 12 to 16 years of age from other schools for the deaf which terminated at the elementary or junior high levels.

These deaf young men and women are marvelous people—personable, sensitive, intelligent, and resourceful. They are the typical deaf persons whom we meet in the adult deaf world and who have been studied and written about by Helmer Myklebust, McCay Vernon, and

---

* Pollack, D., *Educational Audiology for the Limited Hearing Infant*. Springfield, Ill.: Charles C Thomas, 1970. Pp. 16-17.

others. You should realize that the currently available studies of deaf adults usually conclude just what any intelligent person would guess: that the typical deaf child, who has been raised in a closed society of values, understandings, and aspirations, at adolescence or adulthood exhibits characteristics of emotional backwardness and social immaturity, as well as academic and language deficits. The overwhelming group of survey studies which you hear quoted are the results of education in state residential schools which have always had a traditional and conservative curriculum, a combined methodology, and an administration dedicated to promoting a closed society for the deaf.

The other graduation from the Lexington School, with diplomas presented, parents and friends attending, and all the paraphernalia as well, is held to honor the 20 to 30 deaf students between 5 and 13 years of age who are transferring from the Lexington School to full-time educational programs in regular schools. These are our most successful graduates, those who leave a special education program early in their educational careers, who are "lost" to the deaf world, and who are never researched or reported in the literature of our field.

What is the essential difference between the deaf child who integrates and those who must spend their educational careers in a specialized school for the deaf? It is invariably their speech skills. If a deaf child has understandable speech by 8 or 9 years of age, I can find a regular school in the New York metropolitan area that will accept him in a regular class. These can be private, parochial, or public programs; large classes or small; progressive or conservative—you name it and I can locate it and convince the principal and teachers to try out your deaf child if he or she has understandable speech. Less than 5% of the Lexington School's profoundly deaf students ever return to our school or to another special program for the deaf once they have been integrated. And, since we follow them for two to three years by actual visits, we know they are "making it" comfortably.

Is intelligible speech for the deaf such an impossible dream, or have we created in most of our educational programs in this country the conditions for its inevitable failure? When we isolate deaf children from hearing children through special schools and classes, when we start speech tutoring at 4 or 5 years of age under teachers who are typically untrained or who are convinced that speech for the deaf child is not important or is too difficult for him to attain, then we have created for ourselves as professionals and parents a closed system which says that the deaf always have monotonous or strained vocal tones, unrhythmic patterns, or missing phonemes which result in lack of intelligibility and of desirable voice quality. What we are really saying is that we have proven that when a person sits in his wheel chair for 15 years, research studies will show he lacks the walking characteristics and achievements of persons who have no leg or body problems.

May I suggest some other models more worthy of your consideration and emulation:

Item—Why can Japanese profoundly deaf children at 10 to 12 years of age lipread and speak intelligibly in two languages (Japanese and English) when the average American deaf child cannot speak and lipread in one?

Item—Why can Dutch and German educators of the deaf require their prelingually deaf students to be able to lipread and speak intelligibly in two or three languages, one of which must be English?

Item—Why do Latin American deaf children exhibit pleasant voice quality in Spanish with almost none of the strained muscular efforts exhibited by many American deaf children?

Item—Why do some American profoundly deaf children with the same or more profound hearing losses than other deaf children develop such understandable, useful, and natural speech patterns?

Item—Why do profoundly deaf children who have had a very early and persistent speech development almost always have pleasant voice quality and intelligible speech?

Item—Why can profoundly deaf children who have had infant auditory training and consistent speech and language input in normal settings have vocabularies of thousands of words at age 7 and reading skills of second and third grade reading level at 8 or 9 years of age?

May I propose that we stop looking to the practices of segregated educational programs or to the self-defeating philosophies which openly state that intelligible speech for the deaf is not important enough to work for as a major objective. Why should we look to the professional leaders in this country who do not believe in intelligible speech for the deaf for our speech advice? It does not seem reasonable to me that anyone who wants to know what McGovern says would be good for the country would ask Nixon for advice on how to vote in November.

If my premise is correct—that it is speech intelligibility *alone* that makes the difference between deaf children who are acceptable in regular school programs and those who are segregated into special classes and schools—then the same principle will hold true at the adult level. Think of your own experience, limited or extensive. Is the deaf person who has intelligible speech more acceptable to hearing persons in the working or social circles that you know of? Does the deaf person who has intelligible speech spend more time with hearing people; is he, in many cases, the spokesman for other deaf adults; do you feel more comfortable in his presence than you do with the unintelligible deaf adult? In short, is not my premise correct—that deaf children and adults are mainly segregated or integrated on the basis of their speech development alone and not their IQ, their educational attainments, their language facility, or their hearing loss? Will reading or language mastery, without intelligible speech, ever help the deaf child or adult to be comfortable in the hearing world?

IV. The concept of "deafness" is outmoded.

Is severe loss of hearing an unchanging condition? Can hearing be improved? Can prelingually, severely deaf young children with amplification utilize their hearing in a functional manner? How many profoundly deaf children can be "reached" with modern amplification and can functionally hear like a traditionally hard of hearing person?

When the word *deafness* is used, one usually thinks of a permanent handicapping condition. The medical implications of deafness deal with lifelong nerve damage and irreversible severe or total hearing loss. A few years ago, most educators of the deaf also had adopted the term *deafness* to indicate a stable hearing condition and consequent major barriers of speech problems, language immaturity, and academic retardation.

It is a remarkably well-kept secret that, in this year of 1972, none of these "facts" is necessarily true. Only when educators of the deaf accept speech, language, and academic limitations as irreversible in their teaching and rehabilitative programs do these so-called "facts" assert themselves and become dominant in the life of a deaf child. I believe that the concept of deafness as a permanent, immutable hearing loss can be challenged and that under modern methods of education from infancy, a child's hearing loss can be functionally changed! A deaf child can live his life with a use of hearing that moves him from the status of a "visually oriented" human being to that of a functional "hearing loss" person.

At the Lexington School, where we have watched hundreds of profoundly deaf children develop, we are saying that for most, and perhaps all, of our profoundly deaf students who start early enough, it is possible to *change* their hearing usage. We can prove such hearing utilization by objective audiological test data, and our teachers can see this functional use of hearing every day in the classroom. The concomitant effect upon speech acquisition and development, language skills, and academic progress is equally encouraging and realistic.

The truth that must be faced in the education of deaf children is that a few clinics and schools *are* willing to make the complex and sustained efforts necessary to produce profoundly deaf children who are auditorily oriented and who can use their hearing in functional ways so that language and speech skills are attained in a normal pattern. It no longer remains true that deaf children must learn visually or even depend upon lipreading for the majority of their language input.

The question that should be answered for the future is, "Which way the deaf child?" The words we use to discuss such children do express our attitudes. Our attitudes as educators and parents do shape behavior and

2. **Hear and Speak**

change our children's lives. Whether a child with a disability becomes a handicapped adult is usually the work of the people in the child's environment.

Whether the deaf child grows up to be deaf or can live his life with a hearing loss is really what the education of deaf children is all about. It is why there is so much heat and seriousness about this question of teaching methodology. We are not debating a method for classrooms; we are deciding as an administrator or an educator or as parents whether a handicapped child shall be a member of a deaf subculture or a hearing impaired person whose philosophy and life objectives are as wide as those of the rest of the human race.

V. Every deaf person must live and develop in the mainstream of society.

Like every other American person, the deaf child grows up as a member of several different minority groups. He is an Italian or a Protestant or a Southerner or an adolescent, or he's short or strong or gifted or black or rich or has big feet or pimples or needs glasses. I'm a terrible combination of minorities: Irish, white, middle-aged, middle-class, a teacher, short arms, thick fingers, and legally blind (without my glasses)!

A deaf child may always remain a member of some of his minority groups. Some of his minorities will change as he grows up; some he can change any time he thinks it's worth the effort. Some must be changed for him by his parents and teachers. Unfortunately, most of us have accepted the "big lie" that he always will remain *a deaf person!* This is the crux of my credo and hope: that every deaf child should understand and be understood by the hearing world not as a deaf person, but as a human being who has a hearing loss.

Into the life of everyone at some time creeps or stalks that psychological state of "us" versus "them." It occurs in the earliest years for some humans; it seems to be increasing during recent times in a deeper form and permeating most areas of the daily experiences of almost all people. For parents of deaf children and for deaf persons it inevitably must be faced more often, more deeply, and with more profound consequences than for the non-handicapped or those without severely handicapped family members.

What is this hearing world which some deaf persons fear and avoid while many parents and educators of the deaf hold it out as an ideal goal to be attained?

To answer this question we should look below the surface of minority minded concepts. Psychologists state that stigma is a self-induced wound of the psyche or the self. They look at a person who thinks he's different and call this "avoidance of reality." The psychiatrists say that not much research has been done concerning the development and maintenance of self-esteem, and about the development of attitudes toward the handicapped. The one thing they are sure of is that much study of these conditions needs to be done, but not by those so handicapped! If physicians are asked not to treat their own family because of close emotional ties, mental health experts know even more how biased can be the perspective of a handicapped person who tries to define his own social identity.

I believe that deaf persons must have identity norms like everyone else and that schools and society have, up to the present, created a subculture for the deaf which feeds upon its own frustrations and satisfactions. But, parents and educators of the deaf who wish to break out of this cycle must assume that deaf children have the same mental make-up as any non-handicapped child and that the difficulties they will face are the learned differences which any child acquires as he grows up.

If the normal differences which hearing loss imposes on deaf children are acquired in the context of a confident self-belief, family and educators' support, consistently reasonable explanations, and incessant rapport and interactions with the "majority" of the hearing world, then each deaf child will have the opportunity to keep his differences within the realm of normal reactions and mental sets. He will not become the isolated and suspicious caricature of the "deaf-mute" or the overly aggressive and radical demander of the "deaf power" movement.

1. A PERSPECTIVE

Educators, parents, and deaf children must be assured of the most important fact of all concerning the minority group of the deaf: that a handicapped person is like everyone else and that his own and the majority's viewpoint of his handicap fundamentally agree. If abnormal differences and difficulties arise, they are so because someone, early in the deaf child's life, was not convinced of this fundamental sameness or failed to prepare the deaf person with the communication and social skills necessary for any human person to get along with his family and the majority world of the hearing in which we all live.

Many deaf people in the United States regard themselves as a handicapped, minority group; but many other severely hearing impaired persons live and think of themselves as members of the "hearing world." We should hope and work for the day when there is no subculture of the deaf but rather differences which are acknowledged, understood, and accepted by everyone, including the deaf.

In the United States the deaf children in most residential schools for the deaf have had decisions made for them by their parents and/or educators which will result in their being prepared to live in the minority "world of the deaf." This is a sad state of affairs because anything less than commitment to total integration into a hearing society is a goal that cannot be acceptable to parents of deaf children.

A letter of June 12, 1972, to the *New York Times*, titled "English, not Dialect," provides a remarkable illustration that deaf people are not alone in facing the problems of modern-day minority living. T. J. Sellers, a former editor of the *Amsterdam News* (a Harlem, New York City, newspaper) wrote the following excerpts:

> Bright young white teachers, from good schools and financially secure homes, often play down the importance of teaching reading and the other basic tool skills to the poor black kids in the ghetto. . . . Black teachers and black poets and black editors have joined the crusade to make little black boys and girls happy in their hang-up with the classroom.
>
> Black dialect language should be accepted for what it is, a method of communication between some human beings. Black dialect should not be regarded as an index to intelligence . . . however, when the dialect of inner city children is projected as the "language of their culture" and a determined effort is made to justify the teaching of the basic structure of distorted English in the formative years, this linguistic approach becomes another innovative nightmare that retards the progress of generations of poor black school children . . . this is an academic trap which should be challenged by the parents of the children involved and discouraged by dedicated teachers everywhere.
>
> The advocates of "do your own black thing" may really want to help disadvantaged boys and girls develop a positive self-image and race pride, but this thrust for black dialect actually seems another way of saying that since black children cannot be educated to become literate Americans, a substitute method must be found and accepted—a method, incidentally, which takes black and white teachers off the hook for inferior pupil performance in reading and oral and written communication.

With Mr. Sellers, I would say to you about *our* minority of the deaf that there just isn't anything wonderful about manualism, which is simply an esoteric method of communication; there isn't anything exciting or thrilling about telling deaf people they are condemned to continued failure in speech, reading, and language development; there is cowardice and failure inherent in anyone's avoidance of the primary problems which deaf people face: speech intelligibility, reading achievement, and social maturity.

Let me quote Mr. Sellers again as he concludes his letter about black children:

> The black kids who are in school now have to compete for jobs with people who have been educated in the accepted culture that prevails in this country. And it is a cruel hoax for teachers or poets or editors or leaders to make children feel that a romantic excursion in distorted grammar will help them with this overwhelming task.

I do not believe that the social problems facing deaf people in today's world are exclusively concerned with an esoteric method of communication; rather, they are wrapped up in the basic nature of our modern society. The modern freedom in mores and customs, our throwaway culture, the demise of geography, emphasis upon the success syndrome, and the resulting disillusionment of high expectations—all these add up to the deaf person's impatience with his own problems and, more important to us, the deaf person's condemnation of those around him who have not produced instant answers for his difficulties with speech and language and hearing and reading.

In the context of our modern society and faith in progress, the deaf person is right. He must assert his needs; he must demand better answers, higher pay, and educational opportunities. In today's world of "future shock," it was inevitable that "deaf power" would arise. Its appearance, and its rational use up to the present, are high praise to the deaf persons of this country who want to be helped to achieve success, recognition, leadership, independence, and acclaim.

But, as minority groups have learned before and are learning again, most revolutions must be created from within the system through long and difficult struggles. Whatever the battle cry of any revolt, a motto seldom solves reality problems. Only allies, luck, intelligence, resources, planning, and success can carry a group down that long path of change to some satisfactory solutions.

The deaf person and the deaf community and the parents and the teachers and the audiologists and the engineers and the government officials and all those who wish to work successfully for the deaf of this country must ask the ultimate question: what kind of person are we trying to help to help himself? All other problems are but different versions of this fundamental one which poses the ultimate issue of the deaf person's goal in this life and world.

Is the deaf person to solve his problems within his own group or as a fundamental part of the human society? Is the deaf child to be educated in a segregated environment or as an intimate part of regular education? Is he a human person with a hearing problem or a truncated person with a misshapen view of reality? Does he experience the world the way that hearing people do or are his sensory inputs and mental functions altered by his hearing loss? Does the deaf person think well of hearing persons or does he reason that hearing people can never really know or understand him? Is deafness a subculture or a part of the mainstream?

The answers to those questions can only add up to a view of the deaf person as a normal human being; or the answers will inevitably lead to the conclusion that deafness is just too big and complicated ever to be overcome and, therefore, deaf people should retreat from human society to live in their own safe ghettos. It is tragic that those who may be deeply disturbed about the problems which deaf people face have concluded that the only way out is to give up the fight for full humanness. They say, in essence, that deaf people should be taught to be different and must be allowed to be sheltered and segregated throughout their lifetime.

Short-term solutions or failures to face life's realities are a disservice to the deaf. The human child who is deaf is faced with a hearing problem, a speech problem, a language problem, and a reading problem. These obstacles must be alleviated by a direct attack on their causes and by solutions which will overcome the problem. The goal is to guarantee all deaf persons the achievements and satisfactions as a human being which will allow him to live continuously in the mainstream of American society.

A Position Paper of the American Organization for the Education of the Hearing Impaired, May 1, 1975

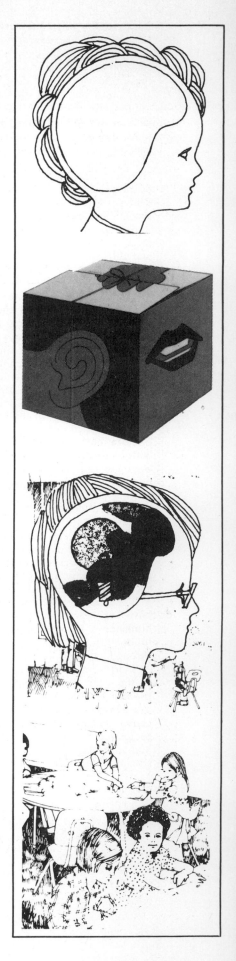

The American Organization for the Education of the Hearing Impaired (AOEHI) recognizes the reality that there is no *one* educational philosophy applicable to *all* hearing impaired children. However, concern is voiced that many deaf children are not reaching optimum educational, social, or vocational potentials as they are currently programmed. The auditory-oral philosophy endorses the proposition that all hearing impaired children should have the opportunity to learn to speak and understand spoken language. The manual philosophy asserts that the hearing impaired child cannot be expected to develop adequate auditory-oral communication and that a visual-manual method is necessary. A variation of the manual philosophy, known as total communication, advocates the use of both manual and oral methods at the same time.

methodological differences

The methodologies stemming from the two philosophies are quite divergent. The auditory-oral method involves the optimal use of residual hearing through early amplification and auditory training, speech, and speechreading. It is based on the premises that English is a phonetic language and that speech is the basic means of communication and an essential tool for interaction in human society. A major objective of this approach is the development of verbal concepts and an understanding of spoken language. Furthermore, the auditory-oral method seeks to build on this linguistic foundation by providing the training necessary to develop intelligible spontaneous speech (Griffiths, 1967, Pollack, 1964). The goal of the auditory-oral approach is to provide the hearing impaired person with the ability to move as freely as possible as early as possible in a variety of instructional and social settings (Lunde & Bigman, 1959).

Advocates of total communication insist that in addition to the oral and auditory experience, the hearing impaired child needs the supplemental, nonambiguous information provided by manual modes of communication (Alterman, 1970). They also assert that most (if not all) profoundly deaf children are incapable of acquiring functional auditory-oral skills. The particular types of manual communication systems utilized by total communication educators may vary widely in their relationship to spoken English (Bornstein, 1974). In addition, within the total communication methodology there is much variation in the quality of and emphasis on the oral, auditory, and manual aspects of the combined system. Many advocates, in fact, practice an approach in which the auditory-oral components are severely neglected and total communication becomes a substitute label for manualism (Lloyd, 1973). In the application of such a method, the relative ease of teaching a hearing impaired child a manual communication system and the use of this form during academic instruction and nonacademic activities take precedence over the difficult task of teaching and maintaining auditory-oral abilities (Hanners, 1973; Babbidge, 1965).

It is the position of the American Organization for the Education of the Hearing Impaired that spoken expressive language and academic achievement relative to normal children are the criteria by which the hearing impaired child is to be judged in society. Many more educational, vocational, and social opportunities are available to the hearing impaired individual (Lunde & Bigman, 1959) who can talk and understand speech than are available to the hearing impaired individual who is dependent primarily on visual-manual communication (Vernon, 1970; *More Jobs for the Deaf,* HEW, 1974). The effort and expense necessary to assist the hearing impaired child in achieving success in auditory-oral communication are overwhelmingly justified.

Scientific data in support of the various methodologies are limited (Moores, 1973), and results of investigations dealing with unisensory versus multisensory stimulation are conflicting (Gaeth, 1962; Gaeth & Lounsbury, 1966; Klopping, 1972). Studies of the early introduction of manual communication suggest that academic skills are enhanced (Stevenson, 1964; Stuckless & Birch, 1966; Meadow, 1968; Vernon & Koh, 1971; Moores, 1973). The significant factor in these investigations was that they occurred in residential schools where there was no chance of finding truly oral children because 1) signing was permitted in the dorms and outside the classes, and 2) the most oral and verbal children were probably programmed elsewhere. At present, the major factor affecting these skills appears to be the emphasis given to them in a particular program (Moores, 1973).

maximizing residual hearing

It is extremely rare to find even a profoundly hearing impaired individual who does not possess some residual hearing. Advancements in technology and technique make it possible to test very accurately the extent of any hearing loss within the first year of an infant's life. Early identification and assessment of a hearing loss, the immediate use of appropriate amplification, and a program which involves the parents during the earliest years of the child's life can provide the structured verbal input and encouragement of output necessary for linguistic functioning. The early, continued, and consistent use of amplification is an important factor in enabling children with severe and profound losses to develop expressive language superior to that of children who have been exposed to total communication programs (Hanners, 1973). Nearly all children who have had the benefits of a comprehensive and high quality auditory-oral program can compete successfully with their hearing peers in further educational and vocational pursuits (Blish, 1967; Northcott, 1973 b; Rister, 1975).

Educational programs with an auditory-oral emphasis in the early school years can assist hearing impaired children in continuing the development of oral skills established in the preschool stage; whereas programs that do not continue the strong emphasis on oral communication have deleterious effects on oral communication skills (Walton, 1964). While the number of programs which provide the supportive services necessary to enable a child to develop an auditory-oral communication system in his preschool years and to integrate into the educational system of the majority is limited, there are such programs available to serve as models (Griffiths, 1967; Knox & McConnell, 1968; Simmons, 1967; Northcott, 1974; Castle, 1974). It is the position of AOEHI that more programs of this nature need to be developed and that the educational opportunities for continuing a strong auditory-oral approach must be made available from the infant years in order to ensure the successful integration in later stages of the educational process.

1. A PERSPECTIVE

The American Organization for the Education of the Hearing Impaired considers the simultaneous teaching of auditory-oral skills and manual skills to be incompatible with the maximization of auditory-oral communication skills. To successfully implement the auditory-oral philosophy, the hearing impaired individual must be placed in an atmosphere in which spoken language is the normal and required means of communication. He must be taught by capable teachers who are skilled in developing maximum auditory-oral communication competencies. Reading and writing skills should also be developed as an integral part of the communication process while academic areas are keeping pace. High but reasonable standards should be set for the student not only by the teachers during the academic day but by everyone with whom the child comes into contact outside the classroom.

parents' right to make a choice

Every parent should have the right to choose the educational philosophy and methodological approach for his child. Professionals, including clinicians and educators, have the responsibility to consider each child as an individual and to assist the parents in making their choice. The educational system must develop high-quality programs encompassing a set of options so that the parent and, later, the hearing impaired individual himself can make a choice. Every parent also has the right to demand maximum development of auditory-oral skills regardless of the philosophy of the chosen educational program.

It is the position of the American Organization for the Education of the Hearing Impaired that the majority of hearing impaired children have the potential to participate in the hearing-speaking world. The opportunity to develop that potential must be provided by educational programs starting at infancy and stressing the continued development and utilization of auditory-oral skills.

Additional copies of the AOEHI Position Paper are available on request. Write: AOEHI, The Volta Bureau, 3417 Volta Place, N.W., Washington, D.C. 20007.

REFERENCES

Alterman, A. Language and the education of children with early profound deafness. *American Annals of the Deaf,* 1970, **115,** 514-521.

Babbidge, H.D. (Ed.) *Education of the deaf: A report to the Secretary of Health, Education, and Welfare by the Advisory Committee on Education of the Deaf.* Washington, D.C.: U.S. Dept. of Health, Education, and Welfare, 1965.

Blish, S. A survey of the results of the educational and guidance program of the Clarke School for the Deaf. *Proceedings of the International Conference on Oral Education of the Deaf.* Washington, D.C.: The Alexander Graham Bell Association for the Deaf, 1967. Pp. 329-344.

Bornstein, H. Signed English: A manual approach to English language development. *Journal of Speech and Hearing Disorders,* 1974, **39,** 330-343.

Castle, D.L., & Warchol, B. Rochester's demonstration home program. A comprehensive parent-infant project. *Peabody Journal of Education,* 1974, **51,** 186-191.

Gaeth, J., & Lounsbury, E. Hearing aids and children in elementary schools. *Journal of Speech and Hearing Disorders,* 1966, **31,** 283-289.

Gaeth, J. Verbal learning among children with reduced hearing acuity. *Report of the Proceedings of the Fortieth Meeting of the Convention of American Instructors of the Deaf,* June, 1962.

Griffiths, C. Auditory training in the first year of life. *Proceedings of the International Conference on Oral Education of the Deaf.* Washington, D.C.: The Alexander Graham Bell Association for the Deaf, 1967. Pp. 758-772.

Hanners, B.A. The role of audiologic management in the development of language by severely hearing impaired children. Paper presented at the Annual Meeting of the Academy of Rehabilitation Audiology, Detroit, Michigan, October 12, 1973.

Klopping, H.W.E. Language understanding of deaf students under three auditory-visual stimulus conditions. *American Annals of the Deaf,* 1972, **117,** 389-396.

Knox, L., & McConnell, F. Helping parents to help deaf children. *Children,* 1968, **15,** 183-187.

Lloyd, L.L. Mental retardation and hearing impairment. *Deafness Annual,* 1973, **3,** 45-67.

Lunde, A.S., & Bigman, S.K. *Occupational conditions among the deaf.* Washington, D.C.: Gallaudet College, 1959.

Meadow, K.P. Early manual communication in relation to the deaf child's intellectual, social, and communicative functioning. *American Annals of the Deaf,* 1968, **113,** 29-41.

Moores, D. Early childhood special education for the hearing impaired. Occasional paper #13, February 1973.

More jobs for the deaf. In *Social and rehabilitation record.* Washington, D.C.: U.S. Dept. of Health, Education, and Welfare, March 1974.

Northcott, W.H. A family oriented infant/preschool program. *Peabody Journal of Education,* 1974, **51,** 187-191.

Northcott, W.H. Competencies needed by teachers of hearing impaired infants, birth to three years, and their parents. *The Volta Review,* 1973, **75,** 532-544 (a)

Northcott, W.H. (Ed.) *The hearing impaired child in a regular classroom: Preschool elementary, and secondary years.* Washington, D.C.: The Alexander Graham Bell Association for the Deaf, 1973 (b)

Pollack, D. Acoupedics: A uni-sensory approach to auditory training. *The Volta Review,* 1964, **66,** 400-409.

Rister, A. Deaf children in mainstream education. *The Volta Review,* 1975, **77,** 279-290.

Simmons, A.A. Home demonstration teaching for parents and infants at Central Institute for the Deaf. *Proceedings of the International Conference on Oral Education of the Deaf.* Washington, D.C.: The Alexander Graham Bell Association for the Deaf, 1967. Pp. 1863-1873.

Stevenson, E.A. *A study of the educational achievement of deaf children of deaf parents.* Berkeley: California School for the Deaf, 1964.

Stuckless, E.R., & Birch, J.W. The influence of early manual communication on linguistic development in deaf children. *American Annals of the Deaf,* 1966, **111,** 452-460. 499-504.

Tervoort, B.T. Development of children's language. Unpublished lectures. San Francisco State College, 1967.

Vernon, M., & Koh, S.D. Effects of oral preschool compared to early manual communication on education and communication in deaf children. *American Annals of the Deaf,* 1971, **116,** 569-574.

Vernon, M. Early manual communication and deaf children's achievement. *American Annals of the Deaf,* 1970, **115,** 527-536.

Walton, J. A study of the post-preschool level of oral language functioning in a group of hearing impaired children. Thesis for master's degree, Vanderbilt University, 1964

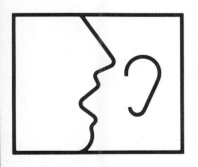

The Missing Vital Dimension in Successful Integration

Geraldine Porter

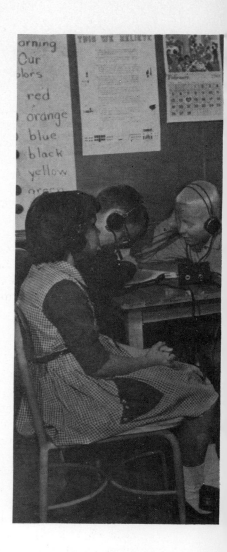

Oralingua School for the Hearing Impaired in Whittier, California, has developed an integration program which focuses on developmental preparation of the classroom teacher and administration. The regular classroom and teacher are selected for each child, only after careful scrutiny. An ongoing program of cooperative teaching and discussion between Oralingua and the classroom teacher is then undertaken to insure the continued growth of the hearing impaired child.

The trend throughout the nation in special education is to attempt to have the exceptional child learn within the regular classroom. It is agreed that preparation for such a placement must be carefully sequenced: providing growth for each child's individual needs; insuring his ability to verbally express his ideas and feelings; and stimulating his ability to think and learn within a new educational setting. But does the preparation lie with the child alone? Many programs and placements provide only for this limited dimension with the addition of possible occasional tutoring for the child. It is felt that many failures have been seen as a consequence. In a cooperative program, Oralingua School for the Hearing Impaired has added another vital dimension in placements for children—the *continual preparation* of the classroom teacher and administration.

The following factors are essential if an optimum placement is to be made: early survey and selection of teacher and classroom; orientation and education of administration and staff; an on-going education and orientation of the classroom teacher throughout the year; and continual participation of a trained liaison person (cooperative teacher) from Oralingua within the regular classroom.

To acquire the proper perspective, a brief examination of Oralingua's cooperative classroom framework is necessary. The progression levels at Oralingua help to better prepare the child, the regular classroom teacher, and the schools for such placement.

preparation for integration

Progression Level 1: (Preschool age)
Instruction within a self-contained classroom where social and emotional needs are stabilized and growth in language, speech, and general ability to verbally communicate is developed.

Progression Level 2: (Preschool age)
Interaction with other preschool age hearing peers on the Oralingua campus. A combined class of about seven hearing and six hearing impaired children is team taught by a regular elementary teacher and teacher of the hearing impaired. Together they strive to make

"The Missing Vital Dimension in Successful Integration," Geraldine Porter, *The Volta Review*, Vol. 77 No. 7. ©1975 The Alexander Graham Bell Association for the Deaf, Inc.

each communicative exchange meaningful—building confidence, planting success. The behavior of hearing children is ever present; expectancy in language and social/emotional behavior is high.

Progression Level 3: (Preschool and up)
Partial or full placement, for social or academic reasons, into a school within the Whittier area; insuring close contact between the cooperative teacher and the child, administration, and teachers. There is one hearing impaired child per class. This helps to develop the child's interdependence with his hearing peers.

Progression Level 4: (Elementary age)
Full placement into his neighborhood school.

Each step is flexible and the child moves along at his own rate of growth; perhaps spending two years in a self-contained class and two years at a school within the close influence of Oralingua before he is sufficiently prepared to function independently within his neighborhood school.

cooperative teacher's role

It is Progression Level 3, involvement within schools in the Whittier area, that we find to be one of the most beneficial for the child and the regular classroom teacher. Since the child's placement is within a 5-mile radius of Oralingua, it is possible for a cooperative teacher to be available and work in close contact with the child, classroom teacher, hearing children, and administrator. In a sense, she is integrated into the classroom; creating an atmosphere for cooperation and an exchange of ideas and feelings. Her degree of involvement is dependent upon the needs of the child and the classroom teacher. Daily involvement has been necessary at a preschool/kindergarten level. First and second grade students have required less involvement—2 or 3 days a week for portions of the day. Flexibility is an integral part of our program which must be reevaluated constantly to meet the needs of each child.

classroom teacher's opportunities

As a part of the program, the classroom teacher is given the opportunity to:
a) partake in on-going discussions of children (both hearing and hearing impaired) in order to evaluate the progress of each child.
b) deepen awareness of listening skills to be developed in all children.
c) witness attitude growth of the children in the classroom.
d) observe the cooperative teacher handle communicative experiences successfully.
e) answer questions in on-going situations.
f) observe the child's functioning in a variety of academic/social settings.
g) better understand hearing loss.
h) receive continual in-service education pertaining to hearing impaired children.

The hearing impaired child is given the opportunity to:
a) learn from a variety of people and friends not always available in a special classroom.

b) be accepted by his peers as another child.

c) experience and handle early some of the social buffings he may receive as a child in a larger social environment.

d) build his self-confidence in his language/academic abilities.

e) acquire natural or colloquial expression of language.

f) feel good about himself.

The children within the classroom are provided the opportunity to:

a) develop a better understanding of hearing impairment.

b) realize that all people have strengths and weaknesses and learn to appreciate other children for their individual strengths.

c) become aware of the need for listening skills for all children.

administrative groundwork

To create a cooperative atmosphere, groundwork must be laid. The procedure begins six months prior to the fall placement with a survey of schools nearest Oralingua. A cooperative teacher serves as a link between the school, the administration, and each child expected to participate.

There is a sequence involved if full administrative support is to be gained. First, the administrator of Oralingua meets with the superintendent of the schools within the immediate area to discuss the suggested program and its benefits for the participating teacher, the hearing impaired child, and the hearing children. They also discuss which schools are available for observation. The superintendent then contacts the administrators of those schools, requesting participation. After the initial contact is made, the cooperative teacher meets with each administrator to give an explanation of the program in detail and to look for classrooms and teachers that would meet the needs of particular hearing impaired children. It is important to discuss the idea with the classroom teacher. Her interest and cooperation are essential from the beginning if an honest rapport is to exist.

teacher selection

Since the teacher will be the nucleus of the child's educational framework, her selection is very important. It is felt that the integration of the hearing impaired child has to be more than just a physical placement. It is a meshing of personalities (child to child, teacher to teacher, child to teacher), of environments, and even curriculums. Some areas to be considered in choosing a teacher are:

Her attitude toward children: Does she indicate that she enjoys working with children and show an interest in understanding the hearing impaired child? Does she encourage freedom of participation? Is she receptive to the needs of the individual? Does she respect the ideas of the child?

Her teaching style: From where in the room does she generally teach? Does she stand while teaching, sit down, walk around, or teach behind a desk? Does she encourage discussions? Does she include repetition of ideas and questions when children are having difficulties? Does her voice project?

Her openness to ideas: Does she seem interested in the concept of the program? Does she feel comfortable with the presence of the cooperative teacher? Is she open to suggestions?

selection of classroom environment

The selection of the child's classroom environment depends greatly on his educational as well as his social and emotional needs. In general, the cooperative teacher looks for a creative environment which utilizes audio-visual materials and stimulates independent learning. The curriculum should offer a balance of language, math, and social studies. Children's work should be in evidence around the classroom and the children in the class should show an enjoyment of their situation and be able to communicate with each other and the teacher.

teacher orientation/education

After many observations of the classrooms and teachers, selections are made. The interested teachers are invited to an Orientation Tea held in June. The orientation is designed to educate and familiarize the regular classroom teacher with the oral deaf child's social, emotional, and educational background and projected needs. Prospective and former teachers are present to enable immediate feedback of experiences. The program format consists of: a discussion of the purpose of placement that explains how a hearing loss may affect the speech and language of an impaired child; demonstrations of audiograms and hearing aids; and an explanation of how language/speech is taught. Video tapes are shown of the children to be placed in the regular classrooms. This enables the teacher to feel acquainted with the child, his abilities and functioning level. Encouragement is also given to visit actual classrooms at Oralingua to see the school's program in action. An educational exposure and discussion, such as this, does much to alleviate misconceptions and apprehensions.

The classroom teacher needs and wants some preparation and continued guidance. The cooperative teacher provides these services; she is actually considered an additional member of the staff. In addition to academic tutoring of the hearing impaired child, she teaches a variety of curriculum subjects to portions of the class. Her involvement provides on-the-spot demonstrations of handling activities effectively in groups mixed with deaf and hearing children. By becoming personally involved with the children, she is considered by them an approachable teacher figure. She is able to candidly observe behavior and academic performance of the hearing impaired child, which enriches her insight to his needs. (See cooperative teacher schedule)

Weekly discussions are held to maintain the continued growth in attitude and expansion of the teacher's education regarding the hearing impaired child. The classroom teacher is given details of the child's particular hearing impairment. She is shown his audiogram and taught how his hearing aid functions and how to make minor adjustments and repairs. The child's academic abilities and his adjustment to the classroom situation are also discussed. An exciting bonus is gained from this type of personal involvement and training. It is the exchange of curriculum ideas between programs and the opportunity to educate in a variety of settings.

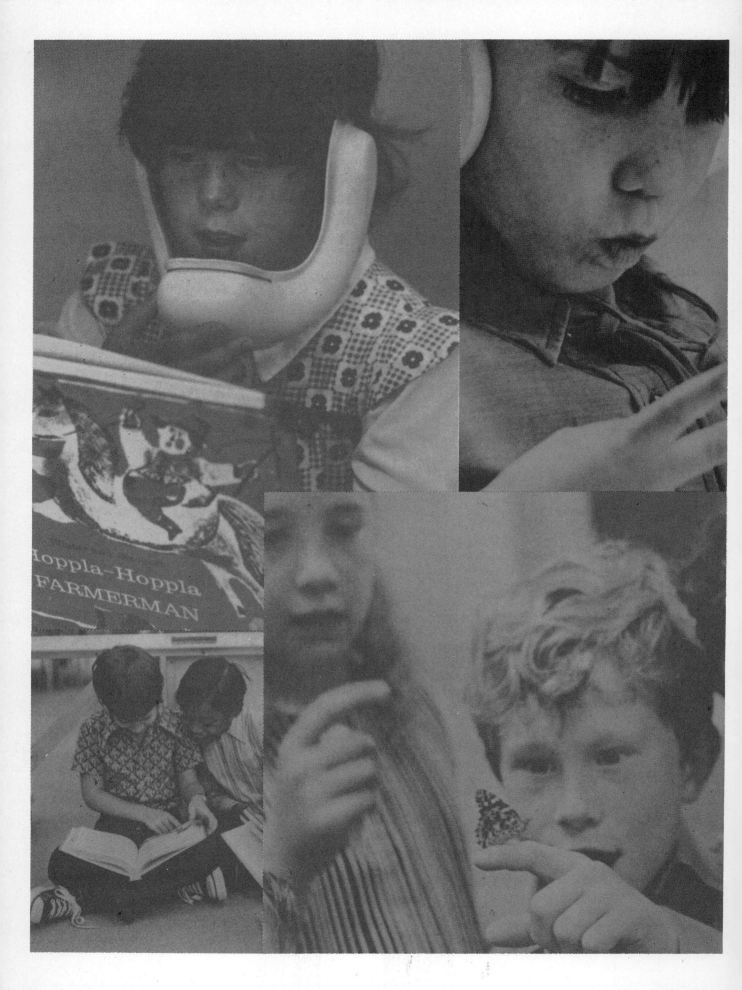

Research, Diagnosis and Assessment

Materials and experiences which employ the use of sight can provide the greatest form of stimulation and motivation for the deaf child. Proper forms of integration, reaction time, and perception must all be considered in the overall assessment of each individual, in order that proper diagnosis be obtained.

Prelingual deafness has been diagnosed to be present at birth, or can take hold before the acquisition of language. Postlingual deafness can be incurred after the attainment of speech and language through regular channels of hearing. From this point it can be determined as to whether the child is to be assessed as "hard of hearing" or "deaf". This typing process will determine the degree of hearing impairment. The hard of hearing will experience mild to severe hearing loss and will be able to acquire language and speech without the use of a hearing aid. The child with less hearing ability will be diagnosed to have needs which are very individual due to the fact that the best amplification will not allow him to develop spontaneous speech and language abilities.

The overall diagnosis of "hearing impairment" can denote most any degree of loss of hearing from mild to profound in nature. Research is then implemented in order that special services might be designed around the degree of hearing loss. These might include placement in day school programs for deaf children or carefully laid out speech therapy programs. Thus far, the medical profession has offered no one cure for deafness — be it profound or sensori-neural. Causes can be congenital in nature or adventitious after birth. Congenital deafness can result from the problems of genetics, Rh blood factor, premature birth, and German measles. Adventitious deafness has been diagnosed as being caused by childhood diseases such as accidents, encephalitis, spinal meningitis and damage to vital parts of the central nervous system which enable one to hear.

Audiologists will then conduct specially constructed tests through an audiometer to record the amount of hearing in decibels and frequencies through pure-tone response tests to determine the depth of hearing loss. Research has developed the EEG which can measure sound waves which are transmitted to the brain. It will then be determined if any amount of hearing remains functional. This is called "residual hearing" and can be most valuable for the purpose of auditory training to gain development of speech. Then and only then can goals and expectations be set through clinical assessment, taking into view individual goals and abilities which monitor environmental sound, to set meaningful developmental patterns for speech acquisition.

Use of hearing aids, multisensory approaches, lipreading and stimulatory reinforcement and therapy have been most useful in providing grounds of support and encouragement, so that the deaf child might gain a positive sense of self-concept and self respect in order that he can become a well adjusted and productive member of society.

An Experimental Study of the Semantics of Deafness

Gary B. Wilson, Mark Ross, Ph.D.,
and Donald R. Calvert, Ph.D.

In their 1967 article, "The Semantics of Deafness," Drs. Ross and Calvert presented the thesis that use of the term "deaf" to describe a person with hearing loss sets into motion the dynamics of a self-fulfilling prophecy which results in behavioral attributes in the direction connotated by the label. For example, since "deaf" people purportedly *cannot hear*, residual hearing may be dismissed as an irrelevant consideration, and the child's resulting communication behavior and achievement may become consistent with the hypothesis of "deafness."

basic premises of the self-fulfilling prophecy

This thesis is based on three premises. First, there is considerable variability in the type, degree, and configuration of the hearing losses among a group of children. Thus, any single label applied to such a group is bound to be an oversimplification. This is significant because differences in function are related to the degree of residual hearing (Montgomery, 1967; Watson, 1967; Ross, Kessler, Phillips, & Lerman, 1972, Quigley & Thomure, 1968; Boothroyd, 1972).

The second premise is that different labels used to denote a hearing problem are not truly synonymous. Rather, they connote significantly different information regarding the background and potential of hearing impaired persons as well as the attitudes toward hearing loss. Third, expectations and treatment are biased by these connotations and thereby exert differential effects on performance. This third premise is supported by studies in education and psychology which have directly investigated the dynamics of the self-fulfilling prophecy (Rosenthal, 1966; Rosenthal & Rosnow, 1969).

a discussion of terminology

When referring to individuals with hearing losses, both general and specific terminology are needed. "Impairment" in a general sense has been commonly used to denote "a deviation or a change for the worse in either structure or function, usually outside the range of normal" (Davis & Silverman, 1970, p. 263). Accordingly, the term "hearing impaired" has been applied to any person whose auditory skills fall below normal (Northcott, 1971; Frick, 1973; CED, 1972). It is not a substitute for the terms "deaf" or "hard of hearing," which have more specific connotations and can be made even more explicit with qualifying adjectives.

The word "deaf" is reserved for a hearing impaired person whose auditory channel cannot or does not serve as the primary sensory means by which speech and language are received and developed. The converse meaning is associated with "hard of hearing." Thus, a vast difference is recognized in function and prognosis between someone who is "deaf" and one who is "hard of hearing." Most hearing impaired persons do not fall neatly into one category or the other regardless of the criteria used (hearing level, uni- and bi-sensory intelligibility scores, speech development, auditory self-monitoring, etc.). It is therefore important to refrain from applying the label "deaf" to a child who is, or is potentially, "hard of hearing."

Concern with the "semantics of deafness" would be unnecessary if people did not make semantic distinctions between the various terms used to describe a hearing loss. If such terms as "deaf," "hard of hearing," and "hearing impaired" carried similar meanings for those who use them, differential expectations would not be developed and, consequently, differential performance might not be observed. The purpose of the present study was to investigate whether there is an objective basis for our second premise above: namely, that people do make semantically separate distinctions regarding the terms used to denote a hearing loss, and furthermore, that these distinctions necessitate use of a generic term, i.e., "hearing impaired."

methods of investigation

This study consisted of four stages or phases. In the first three, a methodology was developed for adequately tapping the psychological dimensions used by lay audiences to evaluate a person having some degree of hearing deficiency. In all phases of the study, the population consisted of students enrolled in the basic communication theory course at the University of Connecticut. These students had had no courses in speech or hearing pathology and were assumed to be relatively naive in those areas. The study was conducted over a period of three semesters.

Phase I. The purpose of the first phase was to develop a list of words and phrases which people unfamiliar with speech and hearing sciences might use to describe individuals having some degree of hearing deficiency. A total of 21 bipolar scales was then developed from the most common words and phrases generated by the students (N=60) and supplemented with word pairs reported in Osgood, *et al.* (1958).

Phase II. To investigate the possibility that the general context in which a label is used might affect the impact of the label itself, each label signifying hearing loss was inserted in a brief (20- to 25-word) description of an individual to be rated. The descriptions characterized the person as being either generally intelligent and pleasant, generally dull and negative, or average with no outstanding characteristics. A sample of 271 students were given a sheet of paper containing one of the descriptions and the 21 bipolar scales generated in Phase I. They were each instructed to rate the individual described in the brief paragraph on each of the 21 scales. The data indicated that these descriptions did significantly affect the ratings as predicted. However, there was no evidence that the handicap label operated differently within the various contexts. That is, the effect of a particular label was generally the same regardless of what the rest of the description contained.

The data generated in this phase were factor-analyzed using a varimax rotation of an orthogonal solution to obtain independent factors of judgment. The five-factor solution seemed to yield the most meaningful description of the data. Four of the original scales were dropped from further use because they had no factor loading above .50 on any of the five factors. Discussion with some of the participants in Phase II led to the addition of the bipolar scale "Intelligent-Unintelligent" to the 17 scales that were retained.

Phase III. As a test of the factor structure obtained in Phase II, the list of 18 bipolar scales was submitted to a new sample of 78 students naive in the area of speech pathology and audiology. The subjects were instructed to rate the individual described in the neutral paragraph, with or without a handicap label, on the 18 scales provided. The final factor structure that was accepted and the constituent scales appear in Table 1.

Phase IV. The fourth and last phase consisted of submitting the final 18 scales and 11 labels (selected by the authors to represent the range of labels being used) to a new sample of 69 students from the basic communication course at the University of Connecticut. Each subject received a 12-page booklet. The first page consisted of instructions on how to complete the bipolar scales, and each of the next 11 pages contained one of the audiological terms and all 18 bipolar adjectives. The order of the presentation of the audiological terms was randomly varied. The bipolar scale ends were reflected to help control for response set. Each of the 69 subjects rated each of the 11 terms on each of the 18 bipolar scales.

Data analysis consisted of summing the scales within each of the five factors or dimensions of judgment presented in Table 1. Individual labels were compared via correlated *t* tests.

Table 1. The five factors and their constituent scales used in the final study.

Factor 1	Factor 3
Interpersonal Effectiveness	*Mental Agility*
Competent-Incompetent	Intelligent-Unintelligent
Organized-Disorganized	Active-Passive
Attentive-Inattentive	Fast-Slow
Friendly-Unfriendly	Strong-Weak
Factor 2	Factor 4
Interpersonal Affect	*Benevolence*
Intimate-Remote	Good-Bad
Warm-Cold	Kind-Cruel
Cheerful-Gloomy	Nice-Awful
Extrovert-Introvert	
Sociable-Unsociable	Factor 5
	Speech and Language Effectiveness
	Verbal-Nonverbal
	Articulate-Inarticulate

results of the study

Table 2 presents the means and standard deviations of the ratings for all five factors of judgment. The first factor or dimension, Interpersonal Effectiveness, had a range of scores of from 4 to 28 (four bipolar terms, each scored on a 1 to 7 scale). As indicated in the table, the term "hearing impaired" generated the least negative affect on this dimension. The mean of 19.09 was significantly higher than 7 of the other 10

Table 2. Rating scale means and standard deviations for the five dimensions of judgment.

Factor		Deaf	Deaf Mute	Deaf & Dumb	Hearing Impaired	Hard of Hearing	Hearing Loss	Partially Hearing	Partial Hearing Loss	Limited Hearing	Hearing Handicapped	Partially Deaf
1	$\bar{X}$	18.44	16.61	15.68	19.09	17.87	18.33	17.96	18.81	17.62	17.94	17.23
	SD	3.84	4.62	4.50	3.95	3.94	3.88	4.35	3.77	3.76	4.23	4.20
2	$\bar{X}$	19.68	18.36	17.93	21.56	20.45	19.65	20.39	21.00	20.64	20.32	20.46
	SD	4.63	5.56	5.16	4.91	4.06	4.92	4.90	4.80	4.38	4.52	4.53
3	$\bar{X}$	15.67	14.51	13.86	17.58	17.14	16.91	16.71	17.70	16.96	16.58	16.38
	SD	3.62	3.83	4.36	3.62	3.14	4.03	4.00	3.79	3.75	3.75	3.66
4	$\bar{X}$	12.16	11.80	11.41	12.32	11.87	11.09	12.13	12.04	11.86	11.90	11.75
	SD	2.76	3.09	3.13	2.59	2.53	3.40	2.83	2.77	2.54	2.77	2.57
5	$\bar{X}$	6.71	4.65	4.96	9.30	8.64	8.19	8.51	8.80	8.36	8.17	7.88
	SD	2.93	2.55	2.62	2.52	2.59	2.77	2.58	2.57	2.33	2.36	2.35

means at the .05 level. These results tend to support use of the term "hearing impaired" where one desires to avoid possible generation of prejudicial expectations. On the other hand, it is evident that the labels "deaf and dumb" and "deaf mute" are significantly more negative in affect than the simple term "deaf."

The second dimension, Interpersonal Affect, had a possible range of scores of from 5 to 35. Again, the label "hearing impaired" was the least stigmatizing and differed from 6 of the other 10 labels beyond the .05 level. Again, the term generating the least negative prejudice would seem to be "hearing impaired."

The third dimension, Mental Agility, had a potential range of scores of from 4 to 28. Here, the label "partial hearing loss" showed a small, nonsignificant advantage over "hearing impaired." The term "hearing impaired" however, remained superior to the other 9 labels—6 of the 9 beyond the .05 level. As in the first two instances, the terms "deaf and dumb" and "deaf mute" continued to generate the most negative affect.

The fourth dimension, Benevolence, had a potential range of scores of from 3 to 21. "Hearing impaired" again showed the highest mean score. However, the difference is significant in only 3 of the 10 possible comparisons. The same ambiguity remains at the low end of the scale. The term "hearing loss" generated the most negative affect with a significantly lower score than 9 of the other 10 possibilities beyond the .05 level.

On the final dimension, Speech and Language Expressiveness, scores could range from 2 to 14. Again, "hearing impaired" generated the highest mean rating among the 11 terms tested, being significantly higher than 9 of the other 10 labels at beyond the .05 level. "Deaf and dumb" and "deaf mute" also repeated as the most negative terms. "Hearing impaired" was rated significantly higher than 9 of the 10 terms, thus indicating that it generates less negative affect. Also, as in previous dimensions, the terms "deaf and dumb" and "deaf mute" are significantly more negative than any of the other terms tested and thus should probably be avoided when describing an individual.

discussion and conclusion

The results of the study clearly demonstrate that for this group of subjects, the label "hearing impaired" evoked fewer negative semantic associations than any of the other common terms and phrases used to denote a hearing deficiency. Thus, in respect to the dynamics of the self-fulfilling prophecy hypothesis, it appears that utilization of this term would generate fewer negative expectations and, therefore, better performance from children to whom the label is applied.

These results do not agree with Vernon's statement (Vernon, 1972, p. 532) that, "To change the word deafness, which objectively describes the problem, to a euphemism or to a softer sounding word such as 'hearing impaired' is ultimately harsh and cruel." The point is not the labeling itself, but how appropriately it is applied in a particular case. Certainly there are "deaf" children, who should be labeled and treated as such. But since the category is a more functional than physiological one, and since differentiation between a "deaf" child and a "hard of hearing" child is quite difficult with very young children, we need and can properly apply the generic term "hearing impaired" until we have some assurance of the particular category to which a child belongs. Then, too, when referring to *groups* of children with auditory deficiencies, it is necessary to invoke a general term to avoid misapplying the labels "deaf" and "hard of hearing" to particular children in the group. Referring to a "deaf" child as "hard of hearing" may do him an injustice; but it is equally damaging to misapply the label "deaf" to a "hard of hearing" child. The results of this study indicate that the term "hearing impaired"—as it is generally used—is not synonymous with "hard of hearing" or "deaf" and, consequently, that there is merit in utilizing the generic term "hearing impaired" until more precise labeling can be applied to a particular individual.

REFERENCES

Boothroyd, A. Distribution of hearing levels in Clarke School for the Deaf students. *SARP #3,* Clarke School for the Deaf, Northampton, Mass., 1972.

CED Standards for the certification of teachers of the hearing impaired. Rochester, N.Y.: Council on Education of the Deaf, 1972.

Davis, H., & Silverman, S. R. (Eds.) *Hearing and deafness* (3rd edition). New York: Holt, Rinehart, & Winston, 1970.

Frick, E. Adjusting to integration: Some difficulties hearing impaired children have in regular schools. *The Volta Review,* 1973, **75**, 36-46.

Montgomery, G. W. G. Analysis of pure-tone audiometric responses in relation to speech development in the profoundly deaf. *Journal of the Acoustical Society of America,* 1967, **41**, 53-59.

Northcott, W. N. Infant education and home training. In Conner (Ed.), *Speech for the deaf child: Knowledge and use.* Washington, D.C.: The Alexander Graham Bell Association for the Deaf, 1971, pp. 311-334.

Osgood, C. E., Suci, G., & Tannenbaum, P. *The measurement of meaning.* Urbana: University of Illinois Press, 1958.

Quigley, S. P., & Thomure, F. E. *Some effects of hearing impairment upon school performance.* Urbana: University of Illinois, Institute for Research on Exceptional Children, 1968.

Rosenthal R. *Experimental effects in behavioral research.* New York: Academic Press, 1966.

Rosenthal, R., & Rosnow, R. L. *Artifacts in behavioral research.* New York: Academic Press, 1969.

Ross, M., & Calvert, D. R. The semantics of deafness. *The Volta Review,* 1967, 69, 644-649.

Ross, M., Kessler, M.E., Phillips, M. E., & Lerman, J. W. Visual, auditory, and combined mode presentations of the WIPI test to hearing impaired children. *The Volta Review,* 1972, 74, 90-96.

Vernon, M. Mind over mouth: A rationale for "total communication." *The Volta Review,* 1972, 74, 529-540.

Watson, T. J. *The education of hearing-handicapped children.* Springfield, Ill.: Charles C Thomas, 1967.

Help for Deaf Babies

—MATT CLARK

About one in every 2,000 babies in the U.S. is born with a significant degree of deafness. But diagnosis with conventional audiometric testing is difficult in such cases because a baby can't describe how noises sound to him. At the University of California in San Diego, however, a team of neuroscientists is detecting hearing problems in infants by measuring the electrical impulses produced by sound as they travel from the ear to the higher auditory centers of the brain.

The team's leader, Dr. Robert Galambos, says there are two main types of deafness in children: first, conductive hearing loss, often involving damage to the bones of the middle ear that conduct sound waves from the eardrum to the inner ear; second, sensory-neural deafness, caused usually by a lack of hairlike cells in the cochlea of the inner ear that carry sound to the auditory nerve.

Many of these hearing problems can be corrected—by surgery, medication or the use of hearing aids. But because of the difficulty of testing hearing in small children, deafness often isn't detected until the child is around 2. Deprived of normal hearing perception for such a period, Galambos says, a child will suffer a lag in the development of speech and language skills that may lead to a permanent handicap—even after the hearing disorder is eventually diagnosed.

The new test was developed by Galambos and his colleagues at several other laboratories over the past eight years. It involves the measurement of electrical activity generated in response to sound by the brain stem, a short structure between the top of the spinal cord and the base of the cerebral cortex to which the auditory nerve is connected.

Signals: By means of earphones, the infant is presented with a series of clicking sounds that stimulate the auditory nervous system. The electrical activity evoked by the sounds in the brain is picked up by electrodes placed behind each ear and on top of the head. These electrical signals are amplified, fed into a computer and printed out in the form of waves on a graph.

Within 12.5 milliseconds of a click, the graph of a normal baby will show seven distinct peaks, each representing a point along the path the sound has taken from the auditory nerve to the hearing centers of the cerebral cortex. For a baby with impaired hearing, the peaks take longer to appear. Different types of hearing defects, moreover, will produce wave patterns that deviate from the normal in characteristic ways. For example, absence of all seven waves indicates total sensory-neural deafness, which is usually untreatable. In conductive deafness, on the other hand, wave patterns will emerge if the intensity of the sound is increased. Hearing aids are frequently sufficient to correct this problem.

Galambos, his wife, Dr. Carol Schulman Galambos, and Dr. Kurt Hecox have been testing infants as young as a day old who are suspected of having a hearing defect because of a family history of deafness or because of exposure to certain toxic drugs or infections. On the basis of the test results, about a dozen of the children have been outfitted with hearing aids. One child, a month-old boy whose mother was deaf and mute, was found to have a severe genetic hearing loss, but could perceive sounds at high intensities. Accordingly, he was given a hearing aid and is receiving special training for speech development.

Ted Lau

Hearing test: Hear those clicks

Tactual Hearing Experiment with Deaf and Hearing Subjects

SIEGFRIED ENGELMANN
ROBERT ROSOV

Siegfried Engelmann is Professor of Special Education, University of Oregon, Eugene, and Visiting Research Associate, Oregon Research Institute, Eugene; and **Robert Rosov** is Research Associate, Oregon Research Institute, Eugene, Oregon. This research was supported by Siegfried and Therese Engelmann, Linda Youngmayr, Laurie Skillman, Carol Witcher, Milly Schrader, The Collins Foundation, The Oregon Research Institute (Paul J. Hoffman, Director), and in part by National Institute of Health General Research Support Grant No. MH-05612.

Abstract: In two experiments with a tactual vocoder it was discovered that both hearing and deaf subjects could learn to discriminate between words that were minimally different and could attend to other prosodic features of language such as pitch and stress. Subjects were tested regularly on word identification. During the tests, the subjects neither looked at the trainer nor received any information other than that transmitted through the tactual vocoder. One deaf subject achieved a tactual vocabulary of 150 words and had a new word mastery rate increase of 46 times during the 48 week training period.

For over four decades investigators concerned with the problems of the deaf child have tried to develop a device that would function as an external ear. Such a device would provide information about pitch, loudness, and the characteristics of each phoneme. The deaf child would then receive the feedback information needed to begin matching his own utterances against those of an outside model.

Investigators have taken two different approaches: the visual approach and the tactual approach. The visual approach is characterized by the use of an oscilloscope. The child looks at the patterns that appear on the oscilloscope and matches them by saying something to produce a picture like the model picture. The problem with this approach is that the analogy between the oscilloscope and the ear is poor from a psychological standpoint. While it may be possible for an oscilloscopic presentation to provide information about phoneme struc-

ture, loudness, and pitch, the device involves volition. The subject chooses certain features to attend to, possibly irrelevant details.

For a device to be more analogous to an ear it would have to ensure that:

1. The subject receives the sound information whether or not he chooses to receive it.

2. All relevant aspects of each sound are presented as discriminable details that are felt by the subject. For example, something loud would *feel* different from something not loud.

3. The subject would be able to receive sound information in the range of situations that a hearing subject receives the information. The information would not be restricted to situations in which the subject looked at another person or looked at a device.

The tactual-vibration approach would allow for the construction of an external mechanical ear that is consistent with the psychological characteristics of hearing. The device would convert words or sounds into vibration, which would be delivered to the subject. Ideally, it would contain information needed for the subject to identify what is said, how it is inflected, how loud it is, and so forth. Hopefully, the nervous system would be adequate to handle this information and allow for accurate perception of what is presented in the form of vibration.

Tactual Displays

The first tactual device was reported by Gault and Crane in 1928. This device amplified sound from a speaker and presented it

to a subject as vibration. The device was crude and investigators did not find the results encouraging. During 1949 and 1950, Wiener, Wiesner, David, and Levine briefly experimented with a tactual glove, Felix, that was connected to a vocoder. Vocoders were first developed to transmit speech over long-distance telephone cables. Vocoders divide the speech spectrum into frequency bands or channels. For example, one channel might cover the frequency range of 200 to 240 Hz. Every time energy is present in this range, the channel is activated. The more energy present in the channel the stronger the signal becomes. At the other end of the long-distance line, the signals from all of the channels are reconstructed as speech.

Felix was designed so that different parts of the speech spectrum were displayed on different parts of the hand. The energy from the one part of the spectrum activated vibrators on one finger, while energy from other parts of the spectrum activated specific vibrators on other fingers. Apparently Felix was used only a few times before the investigators abandoned it. Later attempts to construct a vibratory prosthesis also ended in discouragement (Guelke & Huyssen, 1959; Kringlebotn, 1968; Pickett & Pickett, 1963).

The present experiment was based on the idea that the vocoding devices used in the past were adequate to provide a suitable display of speech. However, adequate *training* was lacking. Analysis of the training provided with previous vocoder devices disclosed that the investigators seemed to assure that if the display provided the information needed for adequate speech perception, the subject would learn quickly, if not instantly. The assumption underlying the present study was that a great deal of practice would be needed (probably at least 1,200 corrected trials) before a healthy subject could be expected to perform consistently on each of the early words to be discriminated.

Construction of a Tactual Vocoder

The tactual vocoder constructed at Oregon Research Institute (the site of the training experiments) incorporated several new features but was not radically different from previous tactual vocoders. The final version used with hearing and deaf subjects employed a 23 channel vocoder. The frequency range from 200 Hz through 4,000 Hz was divided into equal logarithmic intervals and transmitted through 15 channels. Four low frequency channels extended the lower range to 85 Hz, and four high frequency channels extended the upper range to 10,000 Hz. The purpose of the low frequency channels was to provide information about fundamental pitch of speech (Flanagan, 1972). The high frequency extension allowed for discrimination of fricatives (*sh, ch, s, f*), which are not adequately discriminated at the 4,000 Hz level for some speakers (Hughes & Halle, 1956; Heinz & Stevens, 1961).

To receive tactual information through the system, a subject attached five metal boxes (each about 3 inches long) to the surface of his skin (using elastic bandages to hold the boxes in place and upright). The boxes contained 23 vibrators, 1 for each channel. Three boxes held 5 vibrators each; two held 4 vibrators each. The vibrators consisted of miniature solenoids which drove 1 mm diameter metal plungers. The plungers were spaced at half inch intervals and protruded slightly through the base plate of the boxes. When speech energized a vocoder channel, that channel's solenoid was activated at 60 Hz and its plunger vibrated against the skin. Two microphones were attached to the system, so that a trainer could talk into one and the subject could respond into the other (see Figure 1).

Training Hearing Subjects

The hearing subjects were four female instructors employed by the Engelmann-Becker Follow-Through Program at the University of Oregon. All were in their 20's. Training began in September 1972 and terminated in August 1973. Subject 1 received 80 hours of training, subject 2 received 70 hours, subject 3 received 50 hours, and subject 4 received 20 hours.

The basic procedure used in all training sessions was for the trainer to sit next to the subject. The trainer spoke words into a microphone, and the subject responded by identifying the word. The subject did not look at the trainer during the word or sentence drill. Furthermore, the subject wore headphones that transmitted about 85 dB of white noise, rendering the subject artificially deaf. Since the subject neither looked at the trainer nor was able to hear the trainer, the only source of information about the words presented came through tactual vibration.

Training sessions lasted 20 to 60 minutes (usually 30 minutes). Although there was an attempt to schedule daily sessions, the subjects' university training activities took them out of town regularly, often resulting in absences of 1 or 2 weeks at a time in the training. The training time was divided roughly in the following ways:

1. Isolated words presented randomly (70% of available training time).
2. Vocabulary words presented in connected sentences (15%).
3. Inflection copying (5%).
4. Rhyming (2%).
5. Face to face work (3%).

The Word List

The isolated words presented to the hearing subjects and those used to compose the sentences they identified were taken from a list of 60 words. The word list contained samples of the following word types:

1. Words that are minimally different, that is, different in only one phoneme.
2. Single syllable words beginning with either consonant sound or vowel sound.
3. Two, three, or four syllable words.
4. Words occurring frequently in statement tasks and instructions used with deaf children (words such as *what, is, that, not, touch, why*).

Performance Tests

The subjects were regularly tested on the words in isolation. Words were presented in random order. If the subject correctly identified a word on the first run through of the list, that word was dropped and the subject received a score of "1" (first trial). If the subject misidentified a word, she was told the word; the word was set aside until the end of the first run through. All words not correctly identified on the first trial were then presented in random order in a second run through. If the subject then correctly identified a word, a "2" was entered on the score sheet for that word and the word was dropped. The procedure was repeated until all words had been correctly identified or until the subject had received three trials.

Results with Hearing Subjects

Isolated Words

Although the subjects often received no training for periods of 2 or more weeks at a time, the number of words they identified on first trial generally increased with additional time. Subjects 1 and 2 (who received training for the longest period of time) frequently achieved above 90% correct on the first trial when working with the complete list of 60 words. The relative degree of difficulty of different words diminished with training. During the first month of training, 18% of the words were not identified after the second trial. After the first 2 months, however, only 1% of the words were not correctly identified on either the first or second trial. Also, the more quickly a subject mastered a new word, the better she remembered that word.

The rate of acquisition seemed to be associated with the criterion used for introducing new words. The lower the criterion, the faster the subject mastered new words. Subject 4 was on a 60% new word criterion. After 2 months, she outperformed the other subjects. Subjects 1 and 2, who progressed fairly rapidly, were on a new word criterion of 70%. Subject 3, who progressed the slowest, was on an 80% new word criterion.

Words in Sentences

Over half of the arbitrarily constructed sentences presented to the subjects were correctly identified on the first trial, even when these sentences were quite elaborate. The most frequently missed word in the sentence was the first word. In longer sentences, the subjects would sometimes fail to identify the last words; however, actual misidentifications did not frequently occur near the end of the sentence. A possible explanation is that the first word of the sentence is presented against a baseline of silence. The word appears suddenly. The remaining words in the sentence, on the other hand, are presented against the characteristics of the preceding words. The performance of the subjects on sentences and the relatively small amount of time devoted to sentence identification implies that the perception of connected speech is easier than the perception of individual words.

Voice Pitch Patterns

With a minimum of training, subjects 1 and 2 could not only copy the relative pitch of a complex pitch pattern but could also imitate the pattern precisely, varying no more than a quarter tone from each pitch produced by the trainer. This performance was achieved on over 90% of the trials in which the subject responded to a female speaker whose voice fell in the same register as the subject's voice. When a male speaker presented pitch samples, the subjects copied the relative pitch but with diminished accuracy.

A minimum degree of facility with the vocoder seemed to be required before subjects could perform on pitch discrimination exercises. Attempts to train subjects 3 and 4 on pitch discriminations after they had received between 12 and 20 hours of instruction produced only modest results. Subjects 1 and 2, however, spontaneously began to match inflections of the trainer after they had received around 60 hours of instruction. Possibly attention to pitch assumes a familiarity with the other speech variables which are transmitted through the vocoder. This familiarity may be attainable only after so many words or types of words have become familiar.

Placement of Vibrators

Subject 2 worked with the vibrators attached to her fingers. The other subjects had vibrators attached to their forearms. No difference in performance seems attributable to the placement of the vibrators since subject 1 performed at least as well as subject 2. Subjects 1 and 4 performed as well when the vibrators were transferred to their legs. The same relative position of the vibrators was maintained, and the transfer was instant, which would indicate that performance observed was a function of mastery of the patterns, not of any neurological adaptation or increased sensitivity of particular body parts.

Training Deaf Subjects

In August 1973, training of the hearing subjects was terminated and work with three deaf subjects began. A fourth subject was added in November 1973. Subjects were young males, each with a bilateral hearing loss exceeding 85 dB in the range of 250 to 8,000 Hz.

Subject 1, an 8 year old boy, was alert but at the beginning of training lacked all except the most rudimentary speech behaviors. He was substantially behind in academic skills and tended to "act out" in school.

Subject 2, a 14 year old boy, was verbal and articulate on phrases used in everyday exchanges. At the beginning of training his verbal performance when reading a third grade book, however, was largely incomprehensible. With this hearing aid, he was able to hear voices and identify some words when he was not facing the speaker.

Subject 3 was a 13 year old boy who had a history of behavior problems. He seemed eager and cooperative, although his speech behavior (as well as written communication skills) were grossly deficient.

Subject 4 was an 8 year old boy who lacked all but the most elementary speech behaviors.

Subjects 1, 3, and 4 were prohibited from using hearing aids during training sessions with the tactual vocoder. During most of the experiment subject 2 was allowed to use the combination of tactual information and what information he could secure through his hearing aid.

Although the procedures used in the training session were similar to those used with hearing subjects, there were differences. Specifically:

1. Vibrators were placed on the subjects' thighs (three boxes on one thigh, two on the other) so that the subjects' hands would be free to touch objects or pictures.

2. Particularly during the first 2 weeks of training the subjects responded by touching rather than by producing verbal responses.

3. Some time was spent during each period to work on articulation (both to prepare the children for verbal responses and to break up the period).

4. Because of the need to teach basic speech skills in connection with the perception of speech patterns, longer periods were introduced (initially 1 hour a day for 6 days a week and later 1 hour a day for 5 days a week).

5. A reinforcement system was introduced to "turn on" the subjects and keep them on task. Children worked for pennies or nickels. The rules for earning these rewards varied with each child's proficiency.

6. The emphasis of the training sessions was on the identification of words contained in sentences. The goal was to provide the deaf subjects with as much "imprinting" of syntax as possible. To achieve this goal, the various tasks were designed so that all work, including word identification tasks were presented in a syntactical context, for example, "Get ready . . . touch the glass." "Get ready . . . say the word (pause) *glass*. Glass."

7. A variety of "phrases" was introduced so that work on word identification could be conducted in different syntactical contexts. Each subject was taught five or more phrases, such as "pick up . . .," "touch . . .," "hand me the . . .," "this is a(n) . . .," "I am a . . .," "this is not a(n) . . .," "I am not a(n) . . ."

The Training Sessions

Our rationale for each activity presented during the training sessions follows.

Face to face work on articulation (15% of available training time). We were faced with a difficult trade-off in terms of showing results with the vocoder. Perhaps the greatest potential of the system lies in the area of helping a deaf child speak in a conventionally acceptable manner. Since the perception of speech is a prerequisite to sophisticated articulation training, the investigators established *speech perception* as the highest priority.

The content of the face to face articulation work varied with each child. The rule followed by the trainers was this: If the child is to give a verbal response to any of the tasks presented, work on the articulation of those responses. Make sure that the subject

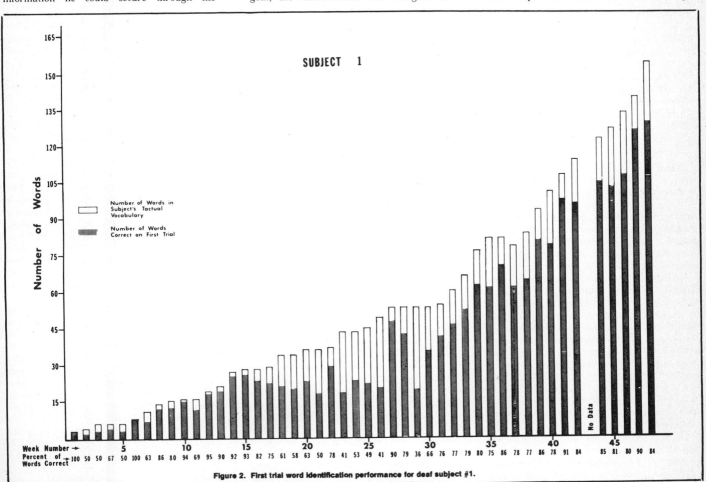

Figure 2. First trial word identification performance for deaf subject #1.

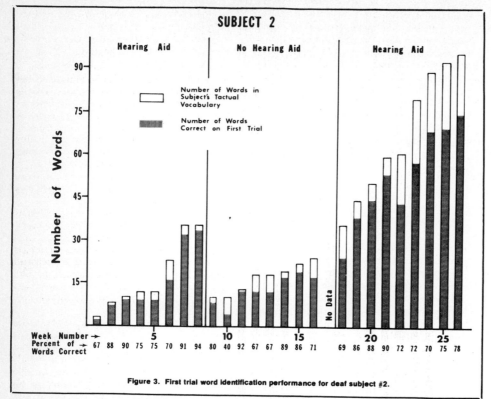

Figure 3. First trial word identification performance for deaf subject #2.

can produce an acceptable, if not perfect, response. Limit the amount of time spent on face to face work to no more than 8 minutes a session.

The initial face to face work concentrated on the production of basic sounds. For example, subject 1 initially could not say words beginning with an "m" sound. He stopped the "m," saying "mmbe" instead of "me." Subject 2 had a similar problem with "s" saying "s(t)itting" instead of "sitting." Later face to face work focused on more advanced skills, such as saying a sentence without stopping between each word, for example, saying, "Iamuman," rather than "Iyn amm oay monn."

Words and sentences (65% of available time). As noted above, the goal was to introduce words in a syntactical context as early as possible. Because of the management and articulation problems of the first days of training, however, the trainers had to present a series of "touching tasks." A display of three or more objects was placed in front of the child. The trainer sat slightly behind the child so that he could not see her face. The trainer would say, for example, "Get ready . . . touch the (pause) monkey . . . Monkey." The child was not required to produce a verbal response. He was required simply to touch the appropriate object. After perhaps 6 hours of training a format requiring a verbal response from the child was introduced, for example, "Get ready . . . touch the (pause) monkey . . . Monkey." The child was now required to touch the appropriate object and say the appropriate name, "Monkey."

As part of the work on words and sentences the children were tested at least twice a week. A test consisted of the presentation of all the words in the child's vocabulary.

Words were presented only one time, in random order. Trainers recorded the first trial performance for each word. During the tests, the words were presented in sentence contexts, using a format familiar to the child ("say the word. . ."). The convention of using the same phrase for all words was introduced to simplify the recording of data.

Isolated sounds and rhyming (10% of available time). During the early training sessions, work with letter identification was implemented with subjects 1, 3, and 4. The children identified letters by their sound (the letter *s* being identified as "ssss," for example).

Deaf subjects who received training for at least 20 weeks were introduced to rhyming tasks. For example, the trainer says "rhymes with at . . . mmm." The child responds, "mat". The rationale for work with rhyming was that it could be a useful source of information about the individual sounds within words (and that the words are composed of individual and different sounds). The rhyming tasks rarely exceeded 4 minutes during a session and usually involved the presentation of these sounds: "rrr," "mmm," "sss," "shhh," "c," and sometimes "lll."

Language action tasks (10% of available time). The work with language action tasks involved a less structured format. The trainer would present tasks from a book. The subject was not prohibited from looking at the trainer; however, the trainer pointed to illustrated matter on the page and often presented tasks while the child was looking at the page. The trainer would typically present tasks such as: "What is this?. . . Is this a man?. . . Say the whole thing. . . . What is the girl doing?. . . Say the whole thing. . . . Is the girl sleeping?. . . Is the girl riding a horse?. . . Is the girl sitting?. . . Is she climb-

ing a tree?"

The child was not required to repeat the questions presented by the trainer; however, from time to time the trainer would follow a question by saying, "What did I say?" The child received points for correct responses.

Language action tasks comprised as much as 20% of the early training periods. They were used as a change of pace to reduce the high degree of concentration required by the word identification tasks. After the children had been in the training program for 15 weeks the language action tasks assumed a position of less prominence. On many days, they were not presented at all (particularly on test days, when the list of words became quite long); however, these tasks were often used as rewards for a good performance.

The Word Lists

Each child worked from a slightly different word list, and none of the lists was identical to that used by the hearing subjects. The lists were constructed primarily according to the individual child's ability to articulate different sounds. Also, difficult words were introduced from time to time in an attempt to see how long it would take the subject to master these, whether they had a deteriorating effect on the other words the child had mastered, whether their introduction facilitated the child's ability to generalize to new words, and whether more practice was required for these words or for words presented at the beginning of the program.

During most of the training, the trainers followed a performance formula for introducing new words. The formula was based on a 70% to 80% first trial performance. If a child's performance level fell below 70%, the trainer dropped words in the vocabulary and firmed the remaining words. When the first trial performance exceeded 80%, the trainer introduced new words and integrated these with the others in the child's vocabulary.

Reinforcers

Positive reinforcers were used with all subjects on sentence identification tasks. The reinforcement schedule varied according to the task presented and to an individual child's behavior. Initially, each child received 1 point for every correct response. After earning 10 points, he received a penny or a nickel. If a child developed a pattern of guessing, the schedule was changed so that the child had to make a set number of consecutive correct responses before earning a nickel or a penny. At the end of each training period, the child was given an opportunity to purchase items that had been placed in the "store," or he was allowed to keep the money.

Initially, no points or money were awarded for face to face work. Later, contingencies were introduced so that the child was reinforced for performing acceptably on words or phrases that had been practiced in face to face work. For example:

Trainer: Get ready. (pause) Touch the glass.

Subject: Touch. . .the. . .glass.

Trainer: Good.

The trainer then awarded 2 points to the

child and said face to face, "Two points. You said *glass*. So I gave you a point for good talking."

Results with Deaf Subjects and Discussion

Subjects were tested weekly on words in isolation that were presented in random order: The performance of the deaf subjects was similar to that of the hearing subjects, although perhaps slightly slower during the early stages of training.

Subject 1. Subject 1 was the most experienced deaf subject, with 48 weeks of practice. His performance is summarized in Figure 2. The top of each bar indicates the number of words in his vocabulary. The shaded part of each bar indicates the number of words correctly responded to on the first trial of each week's test.

As the figure indicates, the rate of subject 1's mastery accelerated as a function of continued practice. By the 36th week he had mastered only 1.94 words per week on the average. From the 36th week through the 48th week, however, he averaged 4.75 new words mastered a week. The rate of vocabulary growth paralleled identification performance. At the end of the 36th week, the subject had a tactual vocabulary of 81 words, which is larger than the hearing subjects' vocabularies. By the 48th week, however, subject 1's tactual vocabulary had nearly doubled, to 152 words. In 12 weeks, 71 words were added to his vocabulary. During these 12 weeks his word mastery rose from 70 to 127, an increase of 57 words. (Subject 1 had required about 33 weeks to master his first 57 words.)

Subject 1's performance is even more impressive when the number of trials involved in the word mastery is considered. He required 14 weeks of practice to master the first 27 words that were introduced. These were the only words in his tactual vocabulary; therefore, the practice time was devoted exclusively to these words. He required approximately 14,000 trials to master these words. From week 31 through 36 (a 5 week period) 27 words were introduced. Subject 1 required approximately 1,400 exposures to master these words. Another 27 words were introduced between the 45th and the 48th week. These words required less than 300 exposures. The rate at which subject 1 was able to identify new words increased about 46 times during the period reported.

The following is a sample of subject 1's performance on mastering 5 new words presented during the 34th week of instruction. The words were *eat, go, jump, give,* and *put*. The 5 words were presented in random order until the child achieved two consecutive perfect runs. Then the words were randomly integrated with 16 familiar words and again presented until the child achieved two perfect runs on the 5 new words. Four trials were needed on both occasions to achieve the two consecutive perfect runs.

Subject 2. Figure 3 summarizes the performance of subject 2 on first trial correct identification for his 26 weeks of participa-

tion in the experiment. The heavy vertical lines on the figure mark the period during which the subject did not wear his hearing aid (weeks 9 through 17). During the remaining weeks (1 through 8 and 18 through 26) subject 2 used both his hearing aid and the vocoder during the training sessions.

Subject 2 progressed quite rapidly during the first 8 weeks of training. When he was prohibited from using his aid, he virtually had to start over. His rate of progress without the aid, however, seemed reasonable. By the end of the 16th week, his vocabulary consisted of 24 words, only 4 less than subject 1's vocabulary at this time.

With the reintroduction of his hearing aid, subject 2 again progressed rapidly, particularly during weeks 23 and 24. Twenty-nine words were added to his vocabulary during these weeks, while his performance consistently remained at or above 70%.

The extent to which the subject relied on information received through his hearing aid is not easy to determine. What seems to have happened during the training was that the subject became more proficient at "hearing" the training words through his aid. When tested during the 8th week he performed at about 65% accuracy in response to training words when he used *only* his hearing aid (not using the vocoder and not looking at the trainer). His performance with only the vocoder was about 40% accuracy on the same words. His performance when both the vocoder and aid were used was about 94%. We were quite surprised, however, to find that the subject's performance on common words not in the vocabulary was only about 20% accurate when the subject used the hearing aid only. The conditions were the same as those used to test the training words. Apparently, the subject learned to use his hearing aid with far more precision than he had in the past. Perhaps the repetition and focus of the training taught the child to attend to information to which he had not previously attended.

Subject 2 was dropped from the experiment after the 26th week, at which time he was able to perform acceptably with a vocabulary of 95 words. The primary reason for dropping him was that the training sessions were conflicting with other activities in which the subject wanted to participate.

Subejct 3. Figure 4 shows the performance of subject 3 on first trial accuracy. At the end of the 12th week his word list consisted of *elephant, cow, monkey, glass, chair, shoe, book, table, tape recorder, Rodney, paper, light, sister, M & M* and *ashtray*. The performance of this subject was slower than that of the others. During a 2 week period, he was not available for training and during most of the experimental period (12 weeks) he was experiencing a number of personal problems. We make no assumptions about the extent to which these affected his performance, except that they resulted in frequent absences.

Subject 3's rate of progress during the first 4 weeks was as rapid as that of subject 2 and surpassed that of subject 1. Subject 3's performance deteriorated somewhat following a 2 week absence from the training;

however, his performance was not substantially behind that of subject 1 at the end of the 12th week (at which time subject 3 withdrew from the experiment).

Subject 4. As Figure 5 indicates, subject 4 progressed less rapidly than the other deaf subjects. During the 16th week of training subject 4 had trouble adjusting to new firming procedures. At that time, the number of words in his vocabulary was reduced from 29 to 22. Eight weeks passed before the number of words in his tactual vocabulary exceeded 30. What seemed to be lacking from his performance was the acceleration apparent with subjects 1 and 2, particularly after the 30th week of instruction.

Subject 4 averaged only 1.25 words mastered per week through the 37th week (compared with nearly 2 words per week for subject 1). There was some increase in subject 4's mastery rate near the end of the reported period. From the 27th week through the 37th week, subject 4 averaged 1.7 new words mastered per week. This figure is substantially behind that of subject 1.

Possibly, subject 4 required more practice before his rate of mastery would begin to accelerate. Possibly, his absences accounted for his poor performance. (He averaged slightly more than one absence a week from the 30th through the 37th week.) According to his trainers, he learned quickly but had trouble remembering the words. In the 29th week, he required six run throughs or 30 trials to master five new words.

Conclusions

The following observations have been made in our experiment with the vocoder:

1. Deaf subjects can be taught to hear fine speech discriminations through the tactual mode, even discriminations as fine as those involved in "fly . . . sly" or "teef . . . teeth."

2. The performance of subjects is positively correlated with practice and seems to be clearly a function of training.

3. The quest for the appropriate tactual display of speech, therefore, must be conducted *within the training context*. The adequacy of a display is evident only after sufficient training has been provided.

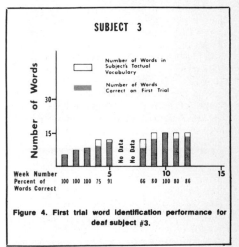

Figure 4. First trial word identification performance for deaf subject #3.

4. Hundreds of corrected repetitions are required for either a deaf or hearing subject to learn simple tactual discriminations.

5. Initially deaf subjects learn more slowly than hearing subjects; however, their rate seems to match that of hearing subjects once an initial set of perhaps 30 to 40 words is reliably mastered.

6. The rate at which a subject is able to learn new words increases with the number of words the subject has mastered (a relationship that cannot be maintained indefinitely but which is apparent during perhaps the first year of instruction and probably will hold for a longer period).

7. It was observed that deaf subjects as well as hearing subjects are able to attend to prosodic features of speech including stress and pitch when speech is presented tactually.

8. Perception of sentences is apparently no more difficult for the hearing subjects than perception of isolated sounds or individual words.

The tactual experiment provides a unique glimpse into the amount and type of practice needed for a person to learn to use a new sensory modality. The performance of these deaf children is encouraging. With more sophisticated and portable hardware, we believe that a deaf infant could learn to "hear" using tactual input in exactly the same way a hearing child learns to hear.

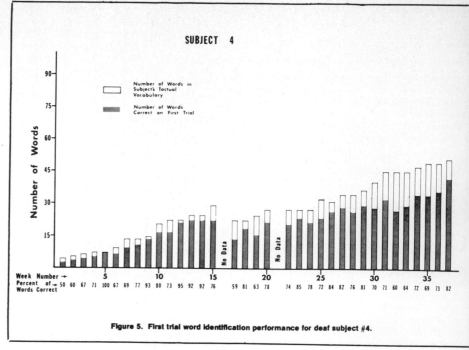

Figure 5. First trial word identification performance for deaf subject #4.

References

Flanagan, J. L. *Speech analysis, synthesis and perception.* New York: Academic Press, 1965.

Gault, R. H., & Crane, G. W. Tactual patterns from certain vowel qualities instrumentally communicated from a speaker to a subject's fingers. *Journal of General Psychology,* 1928, *1,* 353-359.

Guelke, R. W., & Huyssen, R. M. J. Development of apparatus for the analysis of sound by the sense of touch. *Journal of the Acoustical Society of America,* 1959, *31,* 799-809.

Heinz, J. M., & Stevens, K. N. On the properties of voiceless fricative consonants. *Journal of the Acoustical Society of America,* 1961, *33,* 589-596.

Hughes, G. W., & Halle, M. Spectral properties of fricative consonants. *Journal of the Acoustical Society of America,* 1956, *28,* 303-310.

Kringlebotn, M. Experiments with some visual and vibrotactile aids for the deaf. *American Annals of the Deaf,* 1968, *113,* 311-317.

Pickett, J. M., & Pickett, B. H. Communication of speech sounds by a tactual vocoder. *Journal of Speech and Hearing Research,* 1963, *6,* 207-222.

Wiener, N., Wiesner, David, E. E., Jr., & Levine, L. Operation "Felix." *Quarterly Progress Reports,* Research Laboratory of Electronics, Massachusetts Institute of Technology, Cambridge, 1949-1951.

Use of a Computer-Based System of Speech Training Aids for Deaf Persons

Arthur Boothroyd, Ph.D., Patricia Archambault,
Robb E. Adams, and Robert D. Storm

The authors are all affiliated with the Clarke School for the Deaf, Northampton, Massachusetts. Dr. Boothroyd is Director of Research and Clinical Services; Ms. Archambault is Coordinator of the Speech Program; Mr. Adams is a teacher in Middle School; and Mr. Storm is a teacher in Upper School. During the duration of this project, Mr. Adams and Mr. Storm held half-time appointments as research-teachers in the Research Department.

A computer based system of speech analysis and display, developed specifically as a speech training aid for the deaf, is described. It has been used in a two-year evaluative study in the speech program at the Clarke School for the Deaf. Work with the system has consisted of remedial tutoring, self-instruction, and formal research studies. Students involved in this work have shown gains in isolated speech skills and in the incorporation of these skills into rehearsed speech material. Gains were also noted in unrehearsed and spontaneous speech, though to a significantly lesser extent. It is felt that a system such as this has great potential for diagnosis, remediation, and self-instruction. It is, however, only a tool, and its effectiveness will depend on the quality of the program in which it is employed and also on the skill and training of its users.

A. Introduction

The digital computer is one of the more significant inventions of recent decades. It has already affected our lives, and its ultimate impact on society will probably be as dramatic as that of the internal combustion engine. One factor which will accelerate this impact is the reduction of both size and cost brought about by improvements in component manufacture. It is now possible to consider computer applications which would have been unthinkable only a few years ago. This report is concerned with one such application in the field of education—speech instruction for deaf children.

During the two-year period from September 1972 to August 1974, a computer-based system of speech training aids was in daily use in the speech program at the Clarke School for the Deaf. The system was designed and developed at Bolt Beranek & Newman (BBN), Inc., of Cambridge, Massachusetts, under an Office of Education Contract (#0-71-4670). The contract not only provided for the initial construction of the system, but also required its evaluation and further development within the context of an on-going speech program. The co-principal investigators were Dr. Raymond S. Nickerson and Dr. Kenneth N. Stevens of BBN. It was their belief that an effective way to develop a worthwhile system would be to place a working, but not necessarily optimized, device into the hands of teachers and to continue its development through a process of interaction (Nickerson & Stevens, 1973; Boothroyd, 1974).

Thus, the goals of the two-year study described in this report were twofold: 1) to evaluate the potential role of a general purpose system of speech analysis and display in speech training; and 2) to provide direction for the development of a more ideal system.

B. Background and Rationale

It is via the sense of hearing that we first learn to control our speech organs and ultimately learn to talk. Deprived of a normal hearing mechanism, the deaf child, if he is to acquire speech, must have other means of perceiving speech models and receiving feedback. These can be grouped under three headings: descriptive, natural, and processed.

The teacher provides the child with a descriptive input when she* tells him what to do with his speech organs or points to a phonetic symbol to indicate an error. Natural models and feedback refer to the child's reception of unprocessed information directly from the speech signal. For this, he may use his eyes, his hands, or his defective ears. The use of residual hearing leads to the most natural approach, though it does require amplification.

Techniques of speech processing, in which the form of the stimulus is changed, may also use all three sensory modalities. The literature on this topic is too extensive to survey fully here. Instead, the reader is referred to *American Annals of the Deaf,* Vol. 113, No. 2 (1968); *Sensory Training Aids for the Hearing Impaired,* edited by H. Levitt and P.W. Nye and published by the National Academy of Engineering (1971); and *Speech Communication Ability and Profound Deafness,* edited by G. Fant and published by the A.G. Bell Association for the Deaf (1972). All three are the reports of proceedings of conferences on this topic.

Despite considerable research on speech processing aids for the deaf during the past 50 years, the results have been rather disappointing. Only the hearing aid has found general application in educational programming for deaf children. With a few isolated exceptions, the speech processing devices have fallen into disuse following initial trial.

With so many speech processing devices available and so little apparent success, one might reasonably ask, "Why try again—what can a computer do which hasn't already been done?" We have three reasons for believing that a computer-based system introduces an essentially new dimension.

a) By its very nature, the computer has the potential to perform complicated transformations of the speech stimulus, thus making it possible to develop inputs which are matched to the capacities and needs of the sensory modality being used.

b) Computers are inherently simple to use. Once programming has been accomplished, the most complicated series of actions can be initiated by the pressing of a single button.

---

*For ease of reading, we shall refer to the teacher as "she" and the child as "he."

c) It is usually easier to modify a computer program than to modify a machine. If, therefore, a teacher decides she would like to try some modification to a speech training aid, it is more likely that her request will be met if it requires a programming change than if it requires that the equipment be rebuilt.

In summary, the development of speech processing devices as training aids for the deaf has a long and rather disappointing history. It was felt by those who designed the system to be described that the advantages offered by the

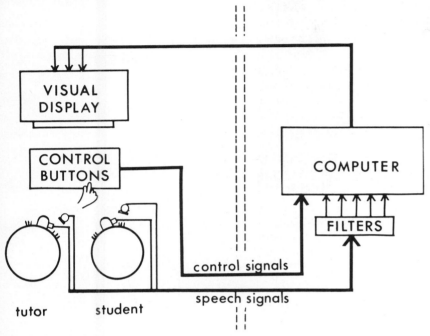

Figure 1.

Block diagram of computer-based system of speech training aids. Speech signals from microphones and vibration detectors are analyzed by the computer, and the results are used to generate pictures on the display. Control is accomplished from a button box in front of the display.

computer in terms of power, human engineering, and flexibility were sufficiently great to merit its attempted application in this field.

C. The Evaluation Program

1. The System.

A block diagram of the computer-based system is shown in Figure 1. Speech signals are picked up by a microphone and also by an accelerometer (vibration detector) which is attached either to the nose or to the larynx (see Figure 2). After preliminary analysis by a bank of filters, the speech signals are measured and stored in the computer memory. This information is then used to generate patterns on an oscilloscope screen. It should be stressed that these are "real time" patterns; they appear on the screen as the speech is being generated. There are provisions for two inputs (usually a teacher's and a student's), and control of the system is accomplished from a button panel situated in front of the oscilloscope screen (see Figure 3).

During the two years of this project, four programs have been available. One provides for the display of various parameters, as functions of time. The parameters are loudness, pitch, voicing, nasality, tongue position in vowels, aspiration, and certain combinations of these. Parameter selection is made from a "menu" which can also be displayed on the screen. Displays can be stored, compared, and/or replayed. Moreover, horizontal and vertical criterion lines can be positioned on the screen either for measurement or as performance targets (see Figure 4).

2. RESEARCH, DIAGNOSIS, AND ASSESSMENT

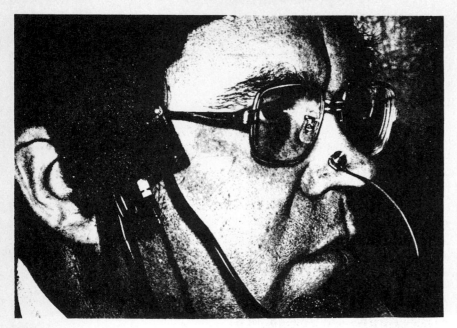

Figure 2.
A small accelerometer (vibration detector) is used to provide information for the computer. It can be placed on the nose to detect nasal vibration or on the larynx to pick up vocal cord vibration. For one subject, the accelerometer was placed under the chin to detect forced voicing during obstruent consonants. Attachment is by means of double sided adhesive tape.

The second program produces a "vertical spectrum" of the speech signal. This is a shape derived from the speech signal in which the width shows the amount of energy at a given frequency, low frequencies being at the bottom and high frequencies at the top (see Figure 5).

The remaining two programs provide simpler and perhaps more motivating displays. In one, the student modifies certain features of a cartoon face

Figure 3.
General view of the system in use. Teacher and student can observe the displays on the screen and control the system by means of the button panel. The computer and associated hardware are in an adjacent room.

(see Figure 6); in the other he can play a game. The object of the game is to transfer balls into a basket on the right-hand side of the screen. Two "obstacles" must be negotiated by appropriate control of vocal pitch (see Figure 7). It should be stressed that these four programs in no way represent the limit of the system. Nor are they considered ideal. They represent a starting point and indeed were modified as this work progressed.*

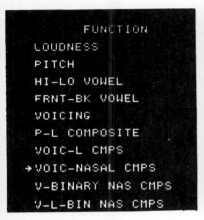
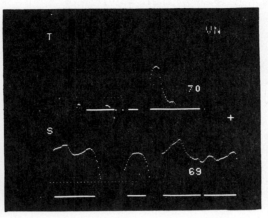

Figure 4.
In the "time plot" program, the parameter to be displayed is selected from a "menu" (shown at left). In the example illustrated, both voicing and nasality are displayed as functions of time. The solid horizontal line reveals voicing, and the line over it shows the amount of nasal vibration. The utterance displayed here is "today or tomorrow." The teacher's tracing (T) reveals only one nasal consonant, but the student's tracing (S) shows nasalization throughout. This is a common feature of the speech of deaf children. The velum is not visible, and it is difficult for the deaf to learn how to control it properly. This example also shows the abnormal time patterns usually present in the speech of the deaf.

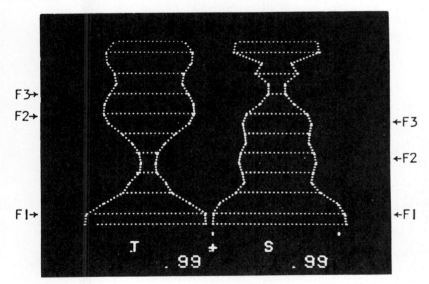

Figure 5.
An instantaneous display of a speech spectrum. The width of the shape corresponds with the amount of energy present in the speech, low frequencies being at the bottom and high frequencies at the top. The example shown here is of the sustained vowel /i/. In the teacher's model at left, the second formant is very high, but the student fails to imitate this and produces a vowel which sounds more like /ǝ:/. The horizontal lines are used to indicate the presence of voicing.

---

*For a more complete description of the system and currently available software, the reader is referred to other publications and reports by Nickerson and Stevens, 1973, and Nickerson, Kalikow, and Stevens, 1974 (see references).

2. RESEARCH, DIAGNOSIS, AND ASSESSMENT

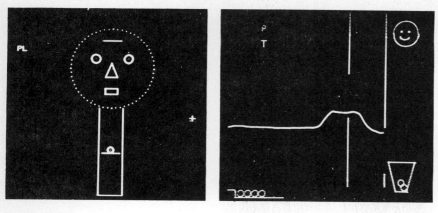

Figure 6. (left)
A cartoon face display designed for motivation of younger children. The size of the mouth is controlled by the loudness of the speech and the height of the Adam's apple by pitch. This particular display also contains an /s/ indicator and can easily be modified to reveal nasal vibration.

Figure 7. (right)
The basketball game. The student attempts to transfer balls from the left-hand side of the screen into a basket at the right. To do so, he must pass through two "holes" in the walls, the height and width of which are adjustable by the teacher. Once voicing starts, the ball moves across the screen from left to right at a constant speed. The student must use the pitch of his voice to control the height of the ball and thereby negotiates the obstacles. Success is rewarded by the "happy face." The game concept can obviously be applied to a variety of speech parameters and provides considerable motivation.

Figure 8. Better ear hearing level distribution of 42 experimental subjects.

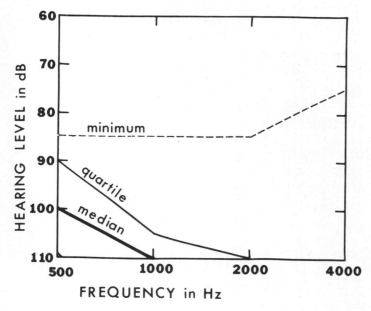

2. Remedial Tutoring

a) Subjects

Students were selected for participation in this program either on the basis of a request from their speech teachers or from the coordinator of the speech program (P.A.), or because of their suitability for some short-term research study. Each student received 20 minutes of instruction per day for multiples of seven weeks. Tutors were trained teachers of the deaf employed specifically for this project (R.A. and R.S.). During the two years covered by the project, 42 students participated. Their ages ranged from 8 years to 18 years, the median age being 11. There were 18 boys and 24 girls. The total number of tutoring sessions (excluding sessions spent on evaluation and tape recording) ranged from 11 to 96, with a median of 28. Thus, the typical child received a total of some 9 hours' tutoring with the system although a few received over 20 hours. Figure 8 shows a composite audiogram of the 42 students. It will be seen that, with a few exceptions, the students were profoundly deaf (ANSI three-frequency average in excess of 90 dB) and that many had little, if any, residual hearing.

During the first year of the project, there was a tendency to select students with very bad speech whose problems had long resisted remediation. In the second year, an attempt was made to select a more representative sample of the students at the Clarke School.

b) Training

Before training, both subjective and objective evaluations of speech were made. The objective measures were in the areas of pitch, timing, and velar control. Subjective evaluations also included articulation and voice quality. On the basis of these and other observations, areas requiring remedial attention were defined. These were discussed with the student's speech teacher, and remedial objectives were worked out. Sometimes these objectives were rather vague (for example, "improve velar control," or "lower average pitch"). Sometimes they were more specific (for example, "reduce duration of unstressed syllables," or "produce a pitch fall at the end of a sentence"). It should be stressed that the delineation of problems, the preparation of tutorial objectives, and the monitoring of progress were responsibilities shared by the authors of this paper and the co-principal investigators for the project as a whole.

At the beginning of training and at seven-week intervals during training, a speech sample was recorded from each student. This contained 33 isolated words representing a broad distribution of phonemic categories, a set of phrases and sentences containing the same words, some special phrases requiring specific skills in velar control and intonation, a sample of spontaneous speech generated by having the student talk about a humorous picture sequence, and six prepared sentences taken from a pool of 600. With the exception of the 600 prepared sentences which were developed previously by Magner (1972), this speech sample was developed for the purpose of this project and will be the subject of a separate report. Its aim was to permit a variety of speech measures to be made, even though the exact nature of those measures might not be defined until after training. Material from this speech sample was never used during training. When it was desired to have a measure of improvement in rehearsed speech, a special speech sample, suitable for a given student's program, was also recorded.

While the details of the tutorial program obviously varied from student to student, the same general format was followed with all students. This consisted of four phases: vocal gymnastics, rehearsed speech, internalization, and carry-over. These will be discussed separately.

Phase I: Vocal Gymnastics

The expression "vocal gymnastics" was coined to describe all activities which did not involve meaningful language. Under this heading fall such activities as sustaining a vowel at a given fundamental frequency, producing rhythm patterns with nonsense syllables, and alternating nasal and non-nasal vowels. The basketball display lent itself naturally to this type of activity when pitch control was being developed.

Phase II: Rehearsed Speech

In this phase, the student would incorporate his newly perfected skills into real speech. This material was generally prepared by the tutor on the basis of the student's particular program.

Phase III: Internalization

The purpose of this phase was to wean the student away from the visual display. There is clearly little to be gained by teaching a student skills which require the continuous presence of visual feedback. He must learn to control these skills by auditory, tactile, kinesthetic, or proprioceptive feedback, or he must practice the motor patterns to the point where they become automatic.

Two methods were used to facilitate internalization. One was to ask the student to alternate good and bad productions of test utterances. It was hoped that in this way he would become more aware of the contrast between them. The other was to require self-evaluations in the absence of visual feedback. For this work a "delayed" display mode was used. The student would generate his utterance and the machine would store but not display it. The student was then required to indicate on a special form whether the utterance did or did not meet the criterion which had been established. Having made this decision, he would then push a button to reveal the display and re-evaluate its adequacy. This procedure not only provided a record of the student's success, but also showed to what extent he was aware of his errors before seeing the visual display.

Phase IV: Carry-Over

Even though a student may have acquired a new skill, rehearsed it in familiar phrases, and learned to evaluate his utterances without visual feedback, there remains the critical question of carry-over. Does the student apply his new skill in unrehearsed material, in spontaneous communicative speech and, most important, outside the context of the tutoring room?

Obviously, one of the goals of Phase III was to facilitate carry-over, but additional procedures were used to this end. For example, students in the later stages of tutoring were presented with samples of unfamiliar material to read, or were engaged in free conversation, without being able to see the visual display. If the tutor detected an error, he would freeze the display and point this out to the student.

Interaction with classroom teachers was essential for a variety of reasons, but it was particularly relevant to carry-over. By keeping teachers informed of the student's progress and providing opportunities for observation of tutoring, it was possible to have more people remind the student to apply his new skills outside the tutoring room. Such interaction also provided feedback to the tutors which might affect the conduct of the student's program.

c) Results of One-to-One Tutoring

Table 1 shows the numbers of students who worked on specific types of speech problems. It was found that the system and programs were most suitable for work on certain suprasegmental features of speech. The displays provided clear and unambiguous information on timing, pitch, and control of the velum.

Work on voice quality met with limited success. The problem of hypernasality could be dealt with using the nasality display, and certain other aspects of "deaf" voice could be revealed in the context of open vowels. But other problems such as harshness, breathiness, raised pharyngeal resonance, and falsetto voice were not amenable to instruction with the displays available.

Under the heading of articulation, those problems which related to poor control of the velum could be dealt with. So also could the articulation of vowels, diphthongs, and fricatives in isolation. Again, however, it was the reaction of the tutors that the possibilities in this area were limited. It should

Area of Tutorial Emphasis	General Specific	Timing Rate and Rhythm	Pitch Average	Intona-tion	Voice Quality Larynx Function	Hyper-nasality	Articulation Nasals	Others*	Totals
Number of Students	First priority	16	1	10	2	11	1**	1	42
	Second priority	9	1	7	1	2	0	1	21
	Third priority	1	1	1	1	0	0	1	5
Totals		26	3	18	4	13	1	3	
		26	21		17		4		

*Vowels, diphthongs and /s/.

**This student learned to articulate /ŋ/.

Table 1 This table shows the speech problems dealt with in one-to-one tutoring and the number of students who worked on each type of problem. Of the 42 students, 21 concentrated on only one problem. Sixteen worked on two problems and 5 worked on three problems. For a given student priorities were assigned to problems on the basis of the proportion of time spent on each. It will be seen that the problems receiving most attention were timing, intonation, and hypernasality.

be stressed that these limitations are not necessarily inherent in the system, but relate only to the programs which have so far been evaluated.

There is no space in this report to give complete quantitative data on all 42 students. Instead, we give below the results of tutors' ratings. These ratings were based on subjective evaluations of the students' progress and any quantitative data which were available. Each student was rated by his tutor on four dimensions:

A — improvement of vocal gymnastic skills
B — incorporation of these skills into rehearsed speech
C — carry-over to unrehearsed speech (formally presented)
D — carry-over to spontaneous speech

Ratings were made on a five-point scale as follows:

0 — no improvement noted
1 — a small improvement noted, but of questionable significance
2 — a moderate and significant improvement noted
3 — considerable improvement noted, but student failed to meet all criteria or showed inconsistent performance
4 — student showed considerable improvement and learned to meet criteria consistently, and with ease.

Rating Dimension	Tutor Ratings No progress ↔ Considerable progress 0	1	2	3	4	Mean Rating
A — Vocal Gymnastics	0	3	11	16	12	2.9
B — Rehearsed Speech	1	5	16	13	7	2.5
C — Unrehearsed Speech	2	18	13	7	2	1.7
D — Spontaneous Speech	9	16	11	5	1	1.4
Totals	12	42	51	41	22	2.1
	Number of Students					

Table 2 Distribution of tutors' subjective ratings of progress for 42 students on four rating dimensions. Ratings on dimensions C and D (both measures of carry-over) were significantly poorer than those on dimensions A and B. (Differences significant at the 1% level, based on χ^2 approximation to the Kolmogorov-Smirnov test, 2 d.f.)

2. RESEARCH, DIAGNOSIS, AND ASSESSMENT

It should be noted that these ratings were based on the goals set for tutoring. Thus, two students who received the same rating were not necessarily accomplishing tasks of the same difficulty.

Table 2 shows the ratings of the 42 students on each of the four dimensions for the speech area of primary emphasis. A comparison of ratings on the four dimensions shows that the dimensions of vocal gymnastics and rehearsed speech were rated significantly higher than the two dimensions related to carry-over. This is in keeping with our observations that the learning of gymnastic skills and their incorporation into rehearsed speech could generally be accomplished with little difficulty in a seven-week period. The generalization of these skills to unrehearsed and spontaneous speech required a much longer period of tutoring and even then was accomplished by only a small number of students.

Significant differences were demonstrated between the ratings for students participating in the first and second years of this project. It will be recalled that the students in the first year tended to be selected from a pool of "difficult" cases, whereas a more representative sample was chosen for the second year. Also, much more attention was given to internalization and carry-over in the second year; and it was only on the dimension of carry-over to spontaneous speech that the difference between the ratings for the two years reached the 5% level of significance. A further factor of relevance to this observation is the increased experience of the tutors during the second year of the project.

A comparison of the students on the basis of speech problems revealed few differences between the pitch, nasality, and timing groups. The pitch group was, however, rated significantly lower on the dimension of carry-over to spontaneous speech. It was also found that girls were rated significantly higher than boys on the dimension of vocal gymnastics (differences significant at the 5% level). No significant effects were found due to etiology, age, or hearing loss.

In summary, we found that the system, as evaluated, lent itself to work on suprasegmental rather than articulatory features. Moreover, it was relatively easy for students to use the displays for the acquisition of vocal gymnastic skills and the improvement of rehearsed speech. While students responded well to various internalization activities, less than half of them showed significant generalization to unrehearsed or spontaneous speech.

3. Unsupervised Drill

One potential benefit of instrumental speech training aids is an increase in teacher efficiency. If a portion of a student's program can be devoted to unsupervised drill, then the effective case load of a remedial speech teacher, or for that matter a classroom speech teacher, can be increased. With this in mind, it was decided to investigate the potential of the computer based speech training aid system for unsupervised drill.

At the time of writing, 6 students in the age range of 13 to 17 years had been involved in self-instruction. They were assigned hours, outside the regular school day, when they could practice material prepared for them. A given student would have two or three such sessions a week, the duration varying from 25 minutes to over an hour, depending on his interest and motivation. The total number of sessions for a given student ranged from 13 to 65, with an average of 34.

To illustrate the nature of this work, it is perhaps easiest to describe a typical self-instruction session.

> The student enters the outer room which contains the computer, and switches on the machine. If necessary, he loads his program from a digital tape recorder, using a program which is resident in the machine's memory. He then starts his program and enters an inner room containing the headsets, control box, and

screen. He puts on his headset and attaches the accelerometer. His assigned material has been left by his tutor. It contains photographs of correct utterances together with instructions. He practices this material, recording his successes and failures on a special evaluation sheet. He will be given some criterion, such as 10 correct successes, for moving from one step to the next. At the end of his session, he may make comments on his evaluation sheet—perhaps informing his tutor of his problems. He then signs his name on a user chart, switches off the machine, and leaves. He will meet with his tutor later in the week for a review of progress and problems.

The students reacted well to unsupervised drill. They quickly learned how to start up the system and load programs from digital tape. They were enthusiastic and worked hard at their assigned tasks. As might be expected, it was found that students working alone generated two or three times as much speech in a given period of time as did students working with a tutor.

Two problems were encountered in this work. One was the difficulty of preparing sufficiently extensive and carefully graded exercises. The other was the tendency for the student to develop bad speech habits unrelated to the specific skill involved in the drill. A live tutor would immediately spot the error and attempt to correct it. The computer system provided no feedback about features not involved in the exercises.

Despite these problems, it was apparent that the concept of unsupervised drill has much to recommend it and may provide an effective means of increasing teacher efficiency.

4. Formal Research Studies

A number of formal research studies were carried out within the context of the program described earlier. Small groups of children working on the same problem were given specially designed tests before, during, and after training. The aim was to obtain group data on each of the following: 1) physical measures of speech, 2) subjective evaluations by listeners, and 3) intelligibility.

Studies of this type were carried out in the areas of rhythm, intonation, and velar control. In each case, it became necessary to collect data from normally hearing subjects in order to determine the extent to which the physical measures deviated from normal. The results of these studies will be reported separately (Nickerson, *et al.,* 1974; Stevens, *et al.,* 1974; Boothroyd, *et al.,* 1974).

In general, these studies served to confirm the observations made earlier, namely, that students did learn to reduce the faults in rehearsed speech and (to a lesser extent) in unrehearsed speech. In addition, we were able to confirm that some of the improvements were audible to listeners faced with a paired comparison task. With a few exceptions, we were not able to demonstrate improvements of intelligibility. At this stage we cannot say whether there were no changes of intelligibility or whether our techniques of measurement were too crude to detect them. We should stress, however, that it is unreasonable to expect significant improvements of intelligibility from a short-term tutoring program. It may be a long time before the assimilation of new skills is detectable through intelligibility measures.

5. Work with Younger Children

All the work reported in the foregoing was concerned with speech remediation rather than speech development. Preliminary work with two younger children (aged 4 and 6) revealed no difficulties of interaction or comprehension. The children enjoyed working with the system and quickly learned how to control the displays. We see no reason why such a system should not find a role in developmental speech work, but the problems of designing suitable exercises and avoiding the establishment of undesirable speech habits will be more serious than those encountered in remedial work.

D. Discussion

It must be stressed that the data reported in this paper do not represent the results of controlled experiments. It was not our intention to compare instrumental with noninstrumental techniques of remedial speech training. Nor did we set out to try to prove one method of speech instruction superior to another. The primary purpose of this work was to gain experience with an innovative system of speech training aids and to provide direction for future development.

This experience has convinced us of the great potential of a general purpose system of speech analysis and display within the context of an active and on-going speech program. We do, however, have three caveats. One relates to teacher training, the second to expectations for this type of system, and the third to residual hearing.

The power and versatility of a system such as this places great demands on the tutor. In particular, a knowledge of acoustic phonetics and physiology is required beyond that acquired in a typical teacher training program. If greater use is to be made of this or other speech training aids, considerable attention must be paid to the question of teacher preparation.

Our second caveat relates as much to what speech training aids should not be expected to accomplish as it does to what they should. Speech processing aids of the type described here can have a direct impact on only one aspect of behavior—namely, imitative speech. They are designed to permit a tutor to provide unambiguous models and to allow the student to assess the adequacy of his attempts at imitation. These are activities on which a hearing person spends little time after the first three or four years of life, but which a deaf student must engage in for 12 or more years if he is to acquire functional speech. Imitative speech is, however, only one of the behaviors in which the deaf child must engage. Moreover, it is not the most significant in terms either of total time or of ultimate development. Cognitive development, language acquisition, and interpersonal communication are much more important to him. While imitative speech behavior may contribute to these areas, it does so indirectly. The point to be made is that the application of speech processing aids for the deaf must be seen in perspective. Such devices must not be viewed as potential short-cuts in the difficult process of educating deaf children.

Finally, we should emphasize that in our search for alternatives to hearing, we must not overlook hearing itself. It has been amply demonstrated that even small amounts of residual hearing can be used for the perception of speech models and the development of speech skills. While we work to develop something which is clearly superior, we must not ignore our responsibility to pursue the maximum use of the auditory channel in those children with sufficient residual hearing.

E. Conclusions and Future Directions

1. The computer-based system was found to be an effective tool within the context of a remedial speech program.
2. With an average of 9 hours of tutoring, most students made marked and obvious gains in the areas of vocal gymnastics and rehearsed speech material.
3. Carry-over to unrehearsed speech and spontaneous speech was observed, but to a much lesser extent.
4. Students were able to use the system for unsupervised drill, thus permitting a teacher to serve more children.
5. The system was particularly useful as a means of providing diagnostic information on students' speech.
6. It is our belief that effective application of a tool such as this requires both an effective speech program and adequate teacher preparation.

7. We further feel that more work is needed if such a system is to find general application in education of the deaf. This should involve: a) wider evaluation in a variety of educational settings with different types of students; b) refinement of displays to provide more effective feature extraction and more information on segmental features; c) development of quantitative diagnostic procedures to facilitate program planning and the evaluation of progress; and d) evolution of modified teaching strategies, especially in the areas of speech development.

REFERENCES

Boothroyd, A. Teacher/researcher interaction: A model and an example. *Proceedings of the 46th Meeting of the Convention of American Instructors of the Deaf.* Washington, D.C.: U.S. Government Printing Office, 1974. Pp. 122-129.

Boothroyd, A., Nickerson, R.S., & Stevens, K.N. Temporal patterns in the speech of the deaf: A study in remedial training. Submitted to *Journal of Speech and Hearing Research,* 1974. Available in report form [S.A.R.P. # 15] from the Clarke School for the Deaf.

Fant, G. (Ed.) *Speech communication ability and profound deafness.* Washington, D.C.: The Alexander Graham Bell Association for the Deaf, 1972.

Levitt, H., & Nye, P.W. (Eds.) *Sensory training aids for the hearing impaired.* Washington, D.C.: National Academy of Engineering, 1972.

Magner, M. *Speech intelligibility test for deaf children.* Northampton, Mass.: Clarke School for the Deaf, 1972.

Nickerson, R.S., Kalikow, D., & Stevens, K.N. A computer-based system of speech training aids for the deaf. Submitted to *American Annals of the Deaf,* 1974.

Nickerson, R.S., & Stevens, K.N. Teaching speech to the deaf: Can a computer help? *I.E.E.E. Transactions in Audio and Electroacoustics,* 1973, **21**(5), 445-455.

Nickerson, R.S., Stevens, K.N., Boothroyd, A., & Rollins, A. Some observations on timing in the speech of the deaf and hearing speakers. Submitted to *Journal of Speech and Hearing Research,* 1974.

Stevens, K.N., Nickerson, R.S., Boothroyd, A., & Rollins, A. Assessment of nasality in the speech of deaf children. Submitted to *Journal of Speech and Hearing Research,* 1974.

FOCUS...

Manual Sign Language Numeration

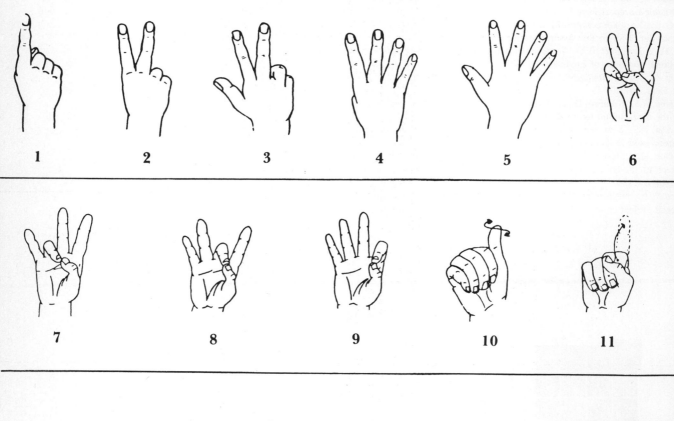

1   2   3   4   5   6

7   8   9   10   11

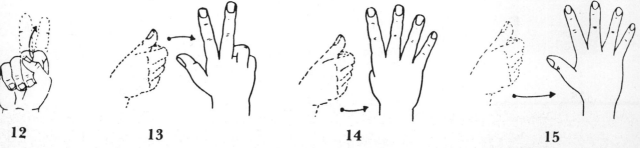

12   13   14   15

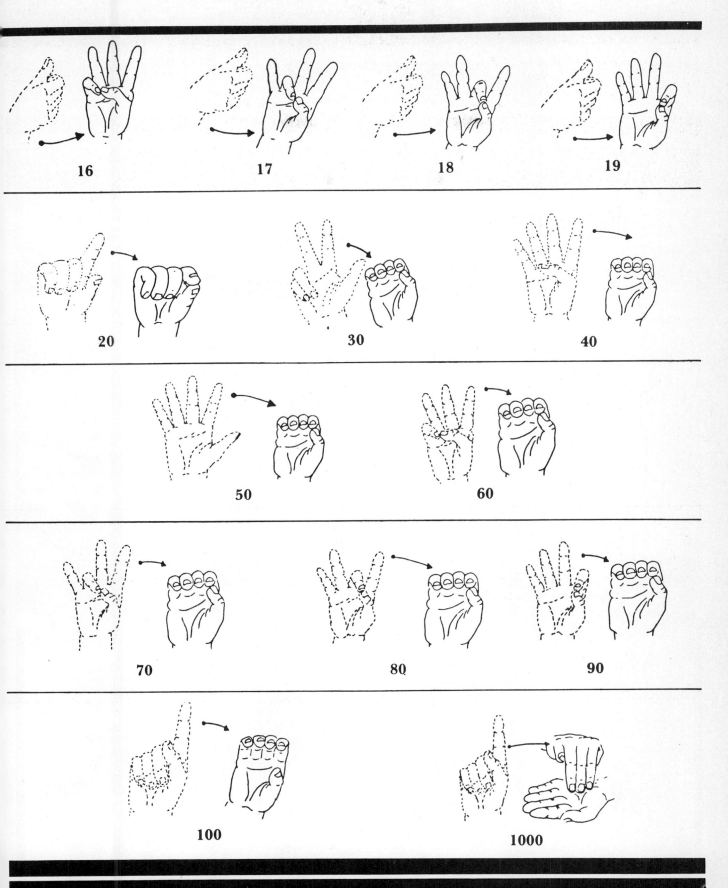

16

17

18

19

20

30

40

50

60

70

80

90

100

1000

Special Learning Corporation
42 Boston Post Rd. Guilford, Connecticut 06437

Linguistic Development

A developing child with intact sensory processes learns language spontaneously and brings with him to the educational setting, at age 5, a vocabulary of approximately five thousand words, a knowledge of the structure of language, and the necessary speech to express his ideas, interests, and needs. This early language development is presupposed by instructional programs in regular schools. By contrast, a deaf child entering a school program usually does not know his name or perhaps even the fact that he has a name. Despite the possibility that he may have had many other types of experiences, the verbal language which comes naturally to the hearing child is not known to him. Therefore, a specially designed program must be employed which will introduce him to language, in both the receptive and expressive forms. As language proficiency develops, he will learn the same subject matter as normal children, but he will learn in a different manner and at a different pace. This is one factor that makes it unrealistic to expect a deaf child to benefit from placement in a regular classroom, until a point that effective language has been acquired.

Prior to the acquisition of language, which is the foundation of learning in all academic areas, the deaf child will not have gained the concepts of self, family, or environment, which have been naturally acquired by a child with normal hearing.

Since the first five years of a child's life are the critical period for language acquisition, language training should begin as soon as possible with the deaf child. As he begins to discover that language exists and that through language there is an efficient way of expressing his needs, the deaf child will adjust to sound amplification, develop the attentiveness necessary for the learning process, and hopefully gain security in the learning environment.

Characteristics of the Speech Of Deaf Persons

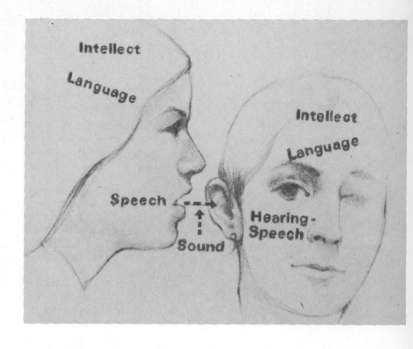

Raymond S. Nickerson, Ph.D.

The fact that profound prelingual deafness prevents the normal acquisition of speech is well known. In spite of the pioneering work of such men as L'Epee, Heinicke, Gallaudet, and Bell, and the concerted efforts of many skilled teachers, attempts to overcome this problem through intensive speech training have met with only limited success.

In recent years considerable attention has been given to the possible use of electronic devices to facilitate speech training by providing visual or tactual representations of speech sounds to compensate for the auditory feedback that the deaf child lacks (Pickett, 1971; Pronovost, 1967). With the advent of the high-speed digital computer and sophisticated signal processing and display-generation techniques it is now possible to develop a great variety of training displays designed to convey information about many aspects of speech (Nickerson & Stevens, 1973). Before this technology can be used with maximal effectiveness, however, more information is needed about the characteristics of the speech of deaf persons and, in particular, about how the objective parameters of speech relate to its perceptual properties.

The purpose of this article is to summarize some of the research findings on the speech characteristics of deaf persons and the consequent effects on speech communication. It is recognized at the outset that no two individuals, whether they have hearing or not, produce speech that is exactly the same; consequently, any description of the speech of a group of people is bound to fail in some respects to describe the speech of any given member of the group. Nonetheless, studies have shown that, on the average, the speech of individuals with a profound hearing loss that dates either from birth or shortly thereafter tends to differ in some quite specific ways from the speech of people with normal hearing. This paper focuses on these differences.

The discussion is organized around five topics: timing and rhythm, pitch and intonation, velar control, articulation, and voice quality. No claim is made for the superiority of this organization over others that might be used; however, some structuring is necessary, and this method has proven to be convenient. This organization is not intended to suggest that the various types of problems that are identified are considered to be independent. The fact is that no matter how the various deficiencies are categorized, very little can be said about any given category without implicating others.

"Characteristics of the Speech of Deaf Persons," Raymond S. Nickerson, Ph.D., *The Volta Review,* Vol. 77 No. 6. ©1975 The Alexander Graham Bell Association for the Deaf, Inc.

I. Timing and Rhythm

Poor timing has been considered by several investigators to be a major cause of the generally poor intelligibility of the speech of the deaf (Bell, 1916; Hood, 1966; Hudgins & Numbers, 1942; John & Howarth, 1965; Houde, 1973; Nober, 1967; Stratton, 1973). Precise specification of timing deficiencies is not possible simply because not enough is yet known about the temporal characteristics of normal speech. Research results do, however, suggest ways in which the speech of deaf persons may differ, in the aggregate, from that of hearing speakers with respect to temporal aspects. Many of these findings have been reviewed in greater detail by Nickerson, Stevens, Boothroyd, and Rollins (1974).

Deaf persons tend to speak at a much slower rate than do hearing persons (Boone, 1966; Colton & Cooker, 1968; Hood, 1966; John & Howarth, 1965; Martony, 1966; Mason & Bright, 1937; Nickerson, Stevens, Boothroyd, & Rollins, 1974; Voelker, 1938). It has been estimated that hearing speakers emit speech at the average rate of about 3.3 syllables (Pickett, 1968) or 10 to 12 phonemes (Miller, 1962) per second, although speech can deviate considerably in either direction from these norms and still be highly intelligible (Abrams, Goffard, Kryter, Miller, Sanford, & Sanford, 1944). Deaf speakers tend to speak more slowly than even the slowest hearing speakers, however; and when deaf and hearing speakers have been studied under similar conditions, the measured rates of syllable or word emission have often differed by a factor of two, three, or more (Hood, 1966; Mason & Bright, 1937; Voelker, 1938).

Deaf speakers fail to make the difference between the durations of stressed and unstressed syllables sufficiently large (Angelocci, 1962; Nickerson, et al., 1974). Although they prolong the durations of both stressed and unstressed syllables, the increase tends to be proportionally greater for the unstressed sounds. Hearing speakers lengthen stressed syllables and syllables in word-final and sentence-final positions (Parmenter & Trevino, 1935; Fry, 1958; Klatt, 1974; Lindblom & Rapp, 1973). A stressed syllable in final position is likely to be three to five times as long as a preceding unstressed syllable; for deaf speakers the ratio is typically much smaller than this. It is almost as though the deaf speaker produces only stressed syllables; and, in fact, some investigators have suggested that this problem is in part a result of training that puts great emphasis on the articulation of individual speech sounds in isolation or in isolated consonant-vowel syllables (Boone, 1966; John & Howarth, 1965).

Deaf speakers tend to insert more pauses, and pauses of longer duration, in running speech than do hearing speakers (Hood, 1966; Hudgins, 1946; John & Howarth, 1965; Nickerson, et al., 1974). These pauses often are inserted at inappropriate places, such as within phrases (Nickerson, et al., 1974).

Closely related to the problem of excessive and inappropriately placed pauses is that of poor rhythm. When listeners are asked to rate the adequacy of the rhythm or syllable grouping of the speech of deaf speakers, the ratings are below those for hearing speakers (Hood, 1966; Hudgins, 1946). The importance of speech rhythm for intelligibility has been demonstrated by Hudgins and Numbers (1942).

Both the problem of pauses and that of poor rhythm are related to, or perhaps result at least in part from, inadequate breath control during speech production (DiCarlo, 1964; Hudgins, 1934, 1936, 1937, 1946; Rawlings, 1935, 1936; Scuri, 1935). Apparently, deaf speakers expel much more breath while speaking than do hearing speakers (Hudgins, 1934, 1937, 1946; Rawlings, 1935, 1936), and consequently they are likely to interrupt the speech flow more frequently in order to permit the intake of air. Apparently, too, deaf speakers tend to use more breath while speaking

3. LINGUISTIC DEVELOPMENT

than when not speaking; whereas hearing speakers use about the same amount in both cases (Scuri, 1935). Scuri's data suggest that deaf persons sometimes seem to lack the ability to close the glottis completely, which could help account not only for the excessive expenditure of breath as a factor in producing poor timing and rhythm, but also for the quality problem of breathy voice.

Some timing problems that have been noted by investigators of the speech of the deaf are associated with the production of certain types of speech sounds. Fricative consonants, for example, may have an inordinately long duration (Angelocci, 1962; Calvert, 1961, 1962), as may the closure periods of plosive consonants (Angelocci, 1962; Calvert, 1962).

articulatory movements

Finally, speech sounds that require the precise coordination of the timing of different articulatory movements or the rapid transition from one articulatory position to another may be a problem. The timing of voice onset relative to release for a voiceless stop consonant (Angelocci, 1962), and that of the onset of nasalization for a nasal consonant (Stevens, Nickerson, Boothroyd, & Rollins, 1974) are cases in point, as is the timing of the movements required to produce consonant blends or diphthongs, or that of the transitions represented by the junctions between fricative or nasal consonants and vowels (Martony, 1966).

Although timing deficiencies are widely considered to be important causes\of the lack of speech intelligibility, there is no well-developed theory of timing from which performance objectives and evaluation criteria can be inferred. While gross timing deficiencies may be easily recognized, it is difficult to say with assurance precisely how the timing of a given utterance should be modified to make it right. Until an adequate theory of timing is developed, attempts to rectify timing deficiencies will, of necessity, be somewhat *ad hoc*.

Some progress toward a theory of speech timing is being made (Klatt, 1974; Lindblom & Rapp, 1973; Martin, 1972; see Nickerson, Stevens, Boothroyd, & Rollins, 1974, for a brief summary). It is important, however, to distinguish between a theory that is descriptive of the speech of persons with normal hearing and one that will provide the basis for establishing training goals for individuals with profound hearing deficits. Normative timing patterns derived from statistical studies of speech do not necessarily constitute reasonable targets toward which all deaf children should be encouraged to strive. What is needed is a much better understanding of how intelligibility and quality of speech depend on various temporal features. This can come only from extensive studies of the speech of the deaf *and* of the hearing that are designed to answer precisely this question.

II. Pitch and Intonation

The fundamental frequency (F0), often loosely called the *pitch,* of voiced speech sounds varies considerably in the speech of a given speaker; and the average, or characteristic, F0 varies over speakers. Average F0 decreases with increasing age until adulthood for both males and females, as shown in Figure 1. The average drop for females is roughly 75 Hz (from about 275-300 Hz to about 200-225 Hz) during the time from prepubescence to adulthood. For males the drop over the same period is likely to be about 150 Hz (from about 275-300 Hz to about 100-150 Hz), about 100 Hz of which may occur abruptly as a result of the adolescent voice break (Curry, 1940; Fairbanks, 1940). Several studies of voices of males between 20 and 30 years of age have placed the average F0 for this group between 119 and 132 Hz (Hanley, 1951; Hollien & Shipp, 1972; Philhour, 1948; Pronovost,

1942). There is some evidence that the F0 may again increase by as much as 30 or 40 Hz with advancing age, at least in the case of males (Hollien & Shipp, 1972; Mysak, 1959). Of course, for any given age, average individual F0s span a considerable range, but about 90% would be expected to be within plus or minus 30-40 Hz of the population norms (Fairbanks, 1940; Fairbanks, Wiley, & Lassman, 1959; Hollien & Paul, 1969). These ranges of average F0 for female and male speakers are shown in Figures 1a and 1b, respectively.

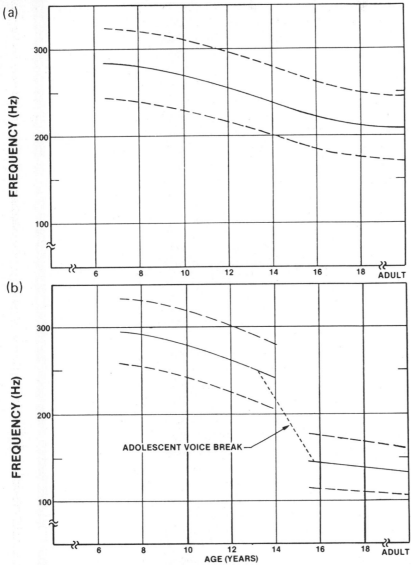

Figure 1   Mean fundamental frequency of deaf and hearing speakers.

The solid line shows mean fundamental frequency used by normally-hearing female speakers (a) and male speakers (b) at different ages. Mean frequencies of 90% of the speakers are expected to lie within the range indicated by dashed lines. The adolescent voice break (in 1b) can occur at different ages for different individuals.
(Figure courtesy of Kenneth Stevens. Data from Fairbanks; 1940; Fairbanks, Herbert & Hammond, 1949; Fairbanks, Wiley, & Lassman, 1949; Hollien & Paul, 1969.)

The fundamental frequency varies in the speech of an average speaker over a range of 1 to 1½ octaves (Fairbanks, 1940). This variation is used to indicate stressed and unstressed vowels, to add emphasis to what is being said, and to carry information about the structure and meaning of a sentence. Stressed syllables are usually spoken with higher pitch than are unstressed syllables, although it may be more accurate to say that stressed syllables are accompanied by pitch *change,* either within the stressed vowel or in an adjacent vowel. The way in which pitch, amplitude, and duration interact to establish stress is still not fully understood.

Linguistic and semantic information is carried by pitch in several ways. A falling pitch is used, for example, to signal the end of the final stressed vowel in a declarative sentence. At a major syntactic break within a sentence, such a fall is followed by a rise in pitch to indicate that the sentence is to continue. For certain types of questions, a pitch rise occurs in the final stressed syllable. Sentences that are ambiguous when printed (e.g., "Does he speak French or German?", "She gave her dog food.") can be spoken in an unambiguous way partly because of the intonation pattern that is imposed on the words. Also, messages beyond the words—sometimes subtle, sometimes poignant—can be conveyed by the way the utterance is inflected.

The difficulties that the deaf speaker has with pitch are of two general types: inappropriate average pitch and improper intonation. Intonation problems may in turn be divided into two major types: monotone voice and excessive or erratic pitch variation.

Several investigators have noted that deaf speakers are apt to have a relatively high average pitch or to speak in falsetto voice (Angelocci, Kopp, & Holbrook, 1964; Boone, 1966; Engelberg, 1962; Martony, 1968). There is some evidence that this problem is greater for teen-agers than for pre-adolescents and that it is particularly troublesome for adolescent boys (Boone, 1966). The results of the study by Angelocci, Kopp, and Holbrook (1964) suggest not only that the fundamental frequencies of deaf speakers are higher than those of hearing speakers, on the average, but also that the average F0 for different speakers spans a wider range.

insufficient pitch change

Deaf speakers often tend to vary the voice pitch much less than do hearing speakers, and the resulting speech has been described as flat or monotone (Calvert, 1962; Hood, 1966; Martony, 1968). A particular problem is that of inappropriate or insufficient pitch change at the end of a sentence (Sorenson, 1974). A terminal pitch rise—such as that occurring at the end of some questions—may be even more difficult for a deaf child to produce than a terminal fall (Phillips, Remillard, Bass, & Pronovost, 1968). Deaf speakers who tend to produce each syllable with equal duration may also generate a similar pitch contour on each syllable. Such speakers may fail to indicate variations in stress either by changing the syllable durations or by modifying the pitch contours on the syllables. Thus, for example, a common error would be to fail both to shorten an unstressed syllable and to lower the pitch on such a syllable.

Pitch problems vary considerably from speaker to speaker. Whereas insufficient pitch variation has been noted as a problem for some speakers, excessive variation has been reported for others (Martony, 1968). Such variations are not simply normal variations that have been somewhat exaggerated but, rather, pitch breaks and erratic changes that do not serve the purpose of intonation.

It has been suggested that some of the unusual pitch variations that occur in the speech of deaf persons may result from attempts by the speaker to increase the amount of proprioceptive feedback that he receives from the activity of producing speech. Martony (1968) and Willemain and Lee (1971) have observed that deaf speakers sometimes tend to begin a breath group with an abnormally high pitch and then to lower the pitch to a more normal level. Willemain and Lee also noted that the average pitch of deaf speakers sometimes increases with the difficulty of the utterance. Inasmuch as the production of high pitch requires increased vocal effort (such as increased tension in the cricothyroid muscle and increased subglottal air pressure), they hypothesized that deaf speakers generate high-pitched tones as a way of providing kinesthetic cues concerning the onset and progress of voicing. A similar conjecture was put forth by Angelocci, Kopp, and Holbrook (1964) who found that F0 varied more from vowel to vowel when the vowels were produced by some deaf speakers than when produced by hearing speakers, while the reverse relationship held for first- and second-formant frequencies. These investigators attributed this type of abnormal pitch variation to efforts by the deaf speakers to differentiate vowels by varying the F0 and amplitude rather than the frequency and amplitude of the formants. "In physiological terms, he is achieving vowel differentiation by excessive laryngeal variations with only minimal articulatory variations" (p. 169).

use of muscles

Some of the pitch variation from vowel to vowel may be the consequence of improper use of the muscles or use of inappropriate muscles or muscle groups in controlling the vowel articulations. These inappropriate muscle contractions may result in inadvertent tensing or slackening of the vocal cords, resulting in excessive variations in pitch.

Pitch has been described as a particularly difficult property of speech for deaf children to learn to control (Boothroyd, 1970). One possible reason for the difficulty is that deaf children may lack a conceptual appreciation of what pitch is (Anderson, 1960; Martony, 1968). Hearing people describe it in terms of a high-low dimension; but the description is somewhat arbitrary, and may not be meaningful to an individual who has not had an opportunity to learn by hearing what "high" and "low" refer to in the auditory domain. A lack of intuitive grasp of the concept may help explain why deaf children often attempt to raise their pitch by increasing their vocal intensity (Phillips, Remillard, Bass, & Pronovost, 1968).

III. Velar Control

The velum or soft palate functions as a gate between the oral and nasal cavities. It is lowered to open the passage to the nasal pharynx when a sound such as one of the nasal consonants is made, which requires that the air be emitted through the nose. It is raised, thus sealing off the passage, for non-nasal sounds and, in particular, for those requiring the build-up of pressure in the mouth (obstruent consonants). Improper control of the velum has long been recognized as a source of difficulty in the speech of the deaf (Brehm, 1922; Hudgins, 1934). If the velum is raised when it should be lowered, the speech may be described as hyponasal; if it is lowered when it should be raised, hypernasality is the result. Miller (1968) has speculated that the type of hearing loss may be a causative factor in some nasalization problems. Hyponasality, he suggests, may be more prevalent among people with conductive loss than among those with sensorineural loss because nasal sounds may appear excessively loud to the former, due to the transmittability of nasal resonances via bone conduction. Individuals with sensorineural loss, on the other hand, may welcome the additional cues provided by the nasal resonances and therefore tend to nasalize sounds that should not be nasalized.

Nasality has been described as a "quality" problem because improper velar control can give the speech a characteristic sound. In addition to affecting quality, however, poor control of the velum can also lead to articulatory problems. There are three nasal consonants /m, n, ng/ which, in combination, account for about 11%-12% of the occurrences of speech sounds in English (Denes, 1963; Dewey, 1923). A primary difference between the articulatory gestures involved in the production of these nasal consonants and those that are used to produce the three stop consonants /b, d, g/ is that the velum is lowered for the nasals and raised for the stops. If the velum is raised when it should be lowered, or lowered when it should be raised, confusions between pairs of these sounds may occur. Such substitutions are found in the speech of deaf persons (Stevens, Nickerson, Boothroyd, & Rollins, 1974).

Learning velar control is difficult for a deaf child for two reasons: (1) raising and lowering the velum is not a visible gesture and is therefore not detectable by lipreading; (2) the activity of the velum produces very little proprioceptive feedback. Normally-hearing persons are relatively un-aware of the activity of this part of the articulatory apparatus and may be unable, without practice, to manipulate it intentionally, say while making a steady vowel sound. Obviously, the movement of the velum must be timed accurately when producing words with abutting nasal and stop consonants if the appropriate sounds are to be produced and the resulting speech is to be fluent. Deaf speakers often have considerable difficulty producing such clusters (Stevens, Nickerson, Boothroyd & Rollins, 1974).

influencing factors

Improper velar control is difficult to judge subjectively, in part because the distinctive perceptual features of nasalization have not been clearly defined and in part because the perception of nasality may be affected by factors in addition to the activity of the velum. A deliberate constriction of the nasal pathways, for example, can modify the resonant characteristics of nasal consonants and adjacent vowels, thus producing a type of nasal speech which does not necessarily involve improper velar control. Also, some researchers have suggested that the perception of nasality may be in-fluenced by such factors as malarticulation, pitch variation, and speech tempo (Colton & Cooker, 1968). For these reasons, objective measures that correlate with velar activity are of considerable interest to investigators of speech. Acoustic properties of nasal sounds that have been investigated include shifted and split first formant (Fujimura, 1960; House, 1961) and enhanced amplitude of the lowest harmonics (Delattre, 1955). Attempts to detect nasalization directly have included the measurement of the flow of air through the nose (Lubker & Moll, 1965; Quigley, Shiere, Webster, & Cobb, 1964), measurement of the acoustic energy radiated from the nostrils (Fletcher, 1970; Shelton, Knox, Arndt, & Elbert, 1967), and measurement of the vibration on the surface of the nose (Holbrook & Crawford, 1970; Stevens, Kalikow, & Willemain, 1974).

Procedures have not yet been developed for quantitatively assessing the severity of nasalization problems. Indeed, normative data are lacking that would provide the necessary baseline measures in terms of which deviance could be judged. Moreover, what may be more important—at least for intelligibility—than the overall nasality of an individual's speech, is the dif-ference in the degree of nasalization of sounds that should be nasalized and those that should not be, and the adequacy of the velar adjustments that are required in order to produce nasal consonants in the context of other sounds. Stevens, Nickerson, Boothroyd, and Rollins (1974) have defined for this purpose an index based on detection of vibration by an accelerometer attached to the surface of the speaker's nose. The index is intended to indicate how well the speaker differentiates nasal consonants and non-nasal vowels in running speech. It is defined as the difference between the average amplitude of the accelerometer signal (in decibels) for nasal consonants and the amplitude for vowels that should be produced without nasalization. Measurements obtained from normally-hearing speakers produced values of this index in the range 10-20 dB. Values close to zero would suggest a failure to differentiate nasal from non-nasal sounds. Such failure could result from either excessive hyper- or hypo-nasality.

IV. Articulation

Articulatory problems of a variety of types have been identified. Failure to develop certain sounds, failure to differentiate between others, substitution of one sound for another, use of the neutral schwa /ə/ (as in *a*bout) as a general-purpose vowel, and other distortions of pronunciation of various sorts are all articulatory difficulties that are encountered in the speech of deaf persons. Unfortunately, the information that exists about these problems is fragmentary and not easily integrated into a consistent whole. No large-sample study has been conducted for the express purpose of cataloging the various articulatory problems that are found in the speech of the deaf, or of determining either the prevalence of individual problems or their relative importance vis-a-vis intelligibility and speech quality. Several investigators have reported specific articulatory difficulties that they have observed among particular groups of deaf children, and it is these reports that will be summarized here. It will be apparent that an intensive study of a large enough sample of the speech of the deaf to provide some reliable prevalence data, and a concerted attempt to relate articulatory deficiencies to intelligibility and quality measures, could increase greatly our understanding of these problems.

The failure to produce appropriate vowel sounds has been noted as a problem by several investigators (Angelocci, Kopp, & Holbrook, 1964; Boone, 1966; Hudgins & Numbers, 1942). The problem may take the form of a failure to differentiate one vowel sound from another or of the production of diphthongs in place of vowels. Typically, vowel errors tend to involve spectrally similar sounds (Smith, 1973).

Inasmuch as the formant frequencies—especially F2—provide much information that is needed to distinguish among different voiced speech sounds, one might guess that the speech of the deaf would tend to show some deficiencies in this respect. Some such deficiencies have been noted. Boone (1966), for example, found that the second-formant frequency tended to be lower for deaf than for hearing children, a fact which he attributed to the tongue being held too far back toward the pharyngeal wall. This observation is consistent with Mangan's (1961) identification of faulty front vowel production as one of the major contributors to the errors that listeners sometimes make in transcribing PB words read by deaf speakers.

Angelocci, Kopp, and Holbrook (1964) have also focused on formant frequencies in a comparison of the speech of another sample of deaf and hearing children. In this case, the range of mean values of F1 was much smaller for the deaf than for the hearing children, and the difference between F0 and F1 was smaller for the former group. The range of the means of F2 was also smaller for the deaf children than for those with normal hearing, and the dependence of the frequency and amplitude of F3 on which vowel was being spoken seemed to differ considerably for the two groups. As has already been noted in the discussion of pitch and intonation, F0—in contrast to F1 and F2—varied more with vowels for the deaf than for the hearing speakers.

Angelocci, et al. present several coordinate plots of F2 against F1, showing the scatter of these coordinates for each vowel for both deaf and hearing speakers. What is clear from the plots is that the degree of overlap among the areas representing different vowels is much greater in the case of the speech samples obtained from the deaf. For the hearing speakers, the easiest and most difficult vowels to identify were, respectively, /i/ (98%) and /æ/ (48%); /æ/ was frequently misidentified as /ɛ/. The best

3. LINGUISTIC DEVELOPMENT

and worst vowels produced by the deaf speakers were, respectively, /u/ (46%) and /ð/ (21%).

Several investigators have claimed that as a rule deaf speakers produce consonant sounds more clearly than vowel sounds (Huntington, Harris, Shankweiler, & Sholes, 1968; Joiner, 1922; Jones, 1967; for a counter example, see Nober, 1967). Nevertheless, many difficulties associated with consonant sounds have been noted. Stewart (1969) identifies the production of fricatives and affricates as one difficulty and points out that /s/ and its voiced cognate /z/ are often omitted altogether, particularly from the final syllable position. Other investigators have also identified /s/ as a special difficulty (Borrild, 1968; Brehm, 1922; Nober, 1967), as well as the failure to distinguish between /s/ and /š/ (shoe). This is perhaps not surprising inasmuch as most of the energy of the /s/ sound is concentrated at the high end of the frequency range, where the hearing deficit of many hearing impaired individuals—particularly those with sensorineural loss—tends to be most severe. (Apparently, even people with close-to-normal hearing for low frequencies may have difficulty producing good sibilants if they have severe hearing loss above about 1 kHz [Miller, 1968] or speech difficulties not related to hearing [Irwin, 1966].) Also, the articulatory gestures involved in producing /s/ and /š/ are relatively invisible.

voiced and voiceless consonants

Failure to distinguish between voiced and voiceless consonants is another problem (Calvert, 1961, 1962; Mangan, 1961; Smith, 1973). One form of this problem is the "surdsonant error" (Calvert, 1962, 1964; Mangan, 1961) in which intended voiced plosives are perceived as voiceless plosives, or the reverse. Calvert (1962) measured the durations of closure and release periods of consonants and found that when a plosive was intended to be unvoiced (e.g., /p, t/) and was heard as voiced (e.g., /b, d/), the duration of the release period was about the same as that of the voiced consonant when produced by a hearing speaker. Similarly, when a voiced consonant was intended and its unvoiced cognate was perceived, the measured duration of the release period was appropriate to the perceived form.

Another form of the voice-voiceless problem is continuous phonation, a defect which, according to Millin (1971), is observed in a "sizeable segment" of the hearing impaired population and contributes significantly to reducing the intelligibility of their speech. Millin notes that continuous phonation is not necessarily perceived immediately; listeners are more likely to be aware of severe misarticulation of phonemes that results from it than of the continuous phonation itself.

omitted consonants

Another articulatory difficulty that has been observed is the omission of arresting and releasing consonants (Hudgins & Numbers, 1942). In particular, Stewart (1969) has noted both the introduction of intrusive stop elements into the pronunciation of fricatives and the omission of stop elements when they should be there. The pronunciation of *sheep* as *cheap* is an example of the first type of problem, and the pronunciation of *chair* as *share* is an example of the second. He notes that intrusive stop elements can give the speech a somewhat clipped quality if they occur frequently enough.

There is some evidence from electromyographic data that the articulatory behavior of deaf speakers is more nearly like that of hearing speakers with respect to lip movements than with respect to tongue movements (Huntington, Harris, Shankweiler, & Sholes, 1968), and, consequently, labial consonants produced by deaf persons tend to be more intelligible than lingual consonants and vowels. This could be due either to the greater visibility of lip movements or to the possibly greater inherent complexity of tongue gestures; however, Huntington, et al. concluded against attributing the difference to the greater difficulty of tongue movements on the grounds that a similar greater intelligibility of labial sounds was not found for hearing individuals who had speech difficulties stemming from central nervous system disorders. The importance of the relative visibility of articulatory gestures in determining the ease with which deaf persons learn to produce specific sounds is further suggested by the Guttman, Levitt, and Bellefleur finding (1970) of a positive correlation between the quality of a speaker's articulation and his lipreading ability. In the same vein, Levitt (1974) has pointed out that the speech production errors that were documented by Smith (1973) show patterns of confusions among phonemes that are similar to those found by Erber (1974) in studies of lipreading.

Perhaps the most compelling evidence concerning the importance of visibility as a determinant of articulatory competence has been reported by Nober (1967). He found that when consonants, classified in terms of place of articulation, were rank ordered in accordance with the relative frequency with which they were correctly articulated by the 46 deaf children in his study, the resulting order (from best to worst: bilabial, labiodental, glottal, linguadental, linguaalveolar, linguapalatal, linguavelar) was very similar to the order that would represent relative visibility. (Nober also reported the following order for articulatory competence in terms of manner of articulation, again from best to worst: glides, stops, nasals and fricatives.) Visibility is not the only factor, however; several studies of consonant articulation problems arising from causes other than hearing loss (retardation, cleft palate) have shown similar trends with respect to the rank ordering of consonants in terms of how problematic they appear to be. Such consistency, Nober notes, is suggestive of the importance of maturational factors and of differences in the inherent difficulty of articulating and of discriminating different phonemes.

combination of speech sounds

It is important in discussing articulatory problems to distinguish between the ability to produce appropriate individual speech sounds in isolation and the ability to combine those sounds in such a way as to produce fluent speech. Deaf children often have the former ability, but not the latter (Borrild, 1968; Jones 1967). Difficulties in executing smooth transitions between speech sounds such as consonant-vowel transitions (Jones, 1967) and malarticulation of compound and abutting consonants (Hudgins & Numbers, 1942) are examples of articulation problems that probably affect fluency detrimentally. These difficulties may also help to account for the finding that consonants occurring in initial sound position tend to be articulated better than those occurring in medial position, which in turn tend to be better than those in final position (Nober, 1967). Durational aberrations in transitional sounds (Jones, 1967) would be especially detrimental to smoothly flowing speech, as would many of the timing deficiencies discussed in section I.

A few investigators have attempted to determine how the spontaneous development of speech sounds differs between deaf and hearing children. Some have suggested that during the first year of life, deaf and hearing children do not differ greatly in their spontaneous vocalizing and babbling (Carr, 1953). However, recent findings have provided evidence of differences in babbling of deaf and normally-hearing infants as early as 22 weeks (Murai, 1961; Mavilya, 1970 [cited in Menyuk, 1972]). In general, the relatively easier sounds appear to be the more prevalent, e.g., middle as opposed to extreme front and back vowels, and voiced labial consonants as opposed to unvoiced and lingual consonants (Heider, Heider, & Sykes, 1941; Neas, 1953 [cited in Carr, 1964]). However, there is some evidence that most of the sounds that occur in standard English can be found in the spontaneous vocalizations of deaf children (Sykes, 1940; Carr, 1953; Fort, 1955 [cited in Carr, 1964]). According to Carr (1953), children's speech shows a greater frequency of vowel sounds than of consonant sounds (see also Neas, 1953) and of front vowels than of back vowels; also, at least in the case of deaf children, front consonants occur more frequently than back consonants. In addition, voiced consonants are more prevalent than their unvoiced cognates. Carr points out that the differences between the speech sounds of deaf and hearing children become more apparent with increasing age, suggesting that the spontaneous development of sounds by deaf children does not continue much beyond one year. She suggests that the higher frequency of front consonants among deaf children may be attributed to the greater visibility, and, hence, imitatability of the articulatory gestures involved. It is believed that the articulatory maturation of children with normal hearing is complete by about the eighth year (Templin, 1957).

V. Voice Quality

There seems to be general agreement that deaf speakers have a distinctive voice quality (Bodycomb, 1946; Boone, 1966; Calvert, 1962); however, what exactly is meant by voice quality is not entirely clear. More specifically, the question arises as to whether it is more appropriate to think of the speech of deaf persons as having a distinctive voice quality, or as having a variety of qualitative properties which characterize the speech of different individuals to different degrees. Unfortunately, data which relate perceived quality to the acoustic properties of speech are sparse, almost to the point of being nonexistent.

The term "quality" is sometimes used in contrast with "intelligibility," the idea being that the quality and intelligibility of speech may vary somewhat independently. Sometimes the term also appears to be used to connote steady-state as opposed to dynamic properties of speech. In this sense, hypernasality and hyponasality might be considered qualitative properties of speech, whereas rhythm and timing aspects probably would not. Another example of a steady-state characteristic that could contribute to qualitative distinctiveness is breathiness (Hudgins, 1937; Peterson, 1946; Scuri, 1935, reviewed by Hudgins, 1936), a characteristic that Hudgins attributed, in large measure, to inappropriate positioning of the vocal cords and poor control of breathing during speech. In particular, too large a glottal opening may be produced by failure to close properly the vocal folds: "the result is a large expenditure of air and a voice of poor quality" (Hudgins, 1937, p. 345).

This list of problems relating to speech quality could be extended considerably. Calvert (1962), in fact, was able to find 52 different adjectives that had been used in the literature as descriptors of deaf persons' speech. When 15 teachers of the deaf were asked to select from these 52 words those that they considered to be the most accurate, the words most often chosen were "tense," "flat," "breathy," "harsh," and "throaty."

Calvert (1962) also attempted to determine empirically whether, in fact, the speech of deaf persons is distinguishable on the basis of quality from that of people with normal hearing. He had teachers of the deaf attempt to determine by listening whether recorded speech sounds (vowels and diphthongs in isolation, nonsense syllables, words, and sentences) had been produced by profoundly deaf speakers, speakers imitating deaf speakers, speakers simulating harsh and breathy voice, or normally-hearing speakers. Isolated vowels, from which onset and termination characteristics had been clipped, could not be distinguished as to source; however, the sources of the sentences were identified with 70% accuracy. Calvert concluded that deaf voice quality is identified not only on the basis of relative intensity of the fundamental frequency and the harmonics, but also by the dynamic factors of speech such as the transition gestures that change one articulatory position into another.

loudness of speech

Although it is questionable whether inappropriate loudness or volume of speech is best thought of as a quality deviation, it is perhaps as reasonable to mention it here as under any of the other organizational categories in this review. The problem as noted by several investigators (Carhart, 1970; Martony, 1968; Miller, 1968) may take several forms: voicing may be too soft or too loud, or the volume may vary erratically. Miller (1968) points out that the way in which the volume of a speaker's voice is affected by hearing loss may depend on the nature of the impairment. An individual with a sensorineural loss may tend to speak in an abnormally loud voice because he does not receive feedback via bone conduction, whereas an individual with a conductive loss may tend to speak very softly because his own voice, which he may hear via bone conduction, may appear very loud as compared with the speech of persons with whom he is talking. Carhart (1970) advocates that deaf people be trained to talk at each of four or five general levels of loudness and to shift from one to the other—depending on kinesthetic cues and reactions from listeners—to judge the appropriateness of the level at which they are talking at any given time.

How important voice quality is for intelligibility has not really been determined. One can find a variety of views on this issue in the literature. Peterson (1946), for example, considers voice quality to be relatively unimportant as a determinant of intelligibility. Adams (1914), on the other hand, points out that while it may have little effect on intelligibility in a technical sense, it can play a very important role in determining whether what a deaf speaker is saying will in fact be understood by an unfamiliar listener. She states that people who are unfamiliar with deaf persons may find their speech so disagreeable when they first encounter it that they may not make the effort necessary to understand it, even if it is adequate for effective communication.

Interrelatedness of Problems

It has been convenient to discuss the problems encountered in the speech of the hearing impaired under several topics. It is important to note, however, that the problems that were considered under separate topics are not independent; in fact, they interrelate in many ways. For example, the importance of accurate timing at the phonetic level for correct articulation is apparent, as is the necessity for accurate velar control.

Calvert (1962) makes the point that the types of durational distortions that impair the intelligibility of the speech of the deaf (e.g., extension of unstressed vowels, fricatives and closure periods of plosive consonants) may also contribute to perceived speech quality. He notes that deaf speakers are more easily distinguished from speakers with normal hearing as the articulatory complexity of the utterance increases, and he concludes that distortions in phoneme durations may be significant determinants of what is commonly called "deaf voice." Hudgins (1934, 1936, 1937, 1946) has extensively documented the interrelationship between the problem of inappropriate control of breathing during speech and that of poor timing and rhythm.

Peterson (1946) speaks of the lack of pitch variation as one of the three major quality problems in the speech of deaf persons. (The other two that he identifies are breathiness and nasality.) Lack of pitch variation, or monotone speech, has been classified as a pitch control problem, but it clearly could be discussed under the topic of speech quality. Furthermore, the inappropriate laryngeal posture that seems to be a concomitant of breathy voice quality undoubtedly has an influence on the control of laryngeal muscles that produce changes in pitch and the distinction between voiced and voiceless consonants. Colton and Cooker (1968) have suggested that the perception of nasality may be influenced by such factors as articulatory errors, pitch variations, and slower-than-normal tempo.

While conceptually distinct, the problems of volume control and pitch control are probably closely related in practice. There is some indication that a deaf child has difficulty gaining separate control over volume and pitch; often he tends to increase vocal effort when trying to increase pitch (Phillips, Remillard, Bass, & Pronovost, 1968). That pitch, volume, and timing are intimately interdependent as determiners of stress patterns is well known, but exactly how they relate is not. In some cases a change of emphasis might be indicated by a change in any one of these properties. In other cases, however, changes probably occur together. A vowel that carries a falling pitch contour, for example, may be lengthened to accommodate this contour.

The list of factors that interrelate could be extended; indeed, one might argue persuasively that each of the problems that has been discussed here is related in some way to each of the others. But perhaps the point has been made. While an analytical approach is undoubtedly necessary in order to make tractable the task of studying deficient speech, a problem-by-problem approach to training may be bound to yield only limited success. Perhaps the most distinguishing characteristic of speech is its integrity, and it may be that training techniques will continue to produce disappointing results until methods are developed that will provide a child with an ever-present visual or tactual representation of his own and other people's speech that is as rich as the representation that the hearing person gets by ear. But exactly what information should be represented in such a display and how that information should be encoded are questions that have yet to be answered. Until they are answered, an analytic approach to training is probably the only path that is open.

Note: Preparation of this article was supported by a contract with the Media Services and Captioned Films Branch of the Bureau of Education for the Handicapped, Contract No. OEC-0-71-4670 (615). The author is grateful to the Clarke School for the Deaf for the use of its library facilities and to Dr. Kenneth Stevens for many substantive suggestions concerning the contents of the article.

REFERENCES

Abrams, M. H., Goffard, S. J., Kryter, K. D., Miller, G. A., Sanford, J., & Sanford, F. H. Speech in noise: A study of factors determining its intelligibility. Harvard University, Psychoacoustics Laboratory, 1944. OSRD No. 4023, PB 19805.

Adams, M. E. The intelligibility of the speech of the deaf. *American Annals of the Deaf,* 914, **59**, 451-460.

Anderson, F. An experimental pitch indicator for training deaf scholars. *Journal of the Acoustical Society of America,* 1960, **32**, 1065-1074.

ARTICULATION TRAINING THROUGH VISUAL SPEECH PATTERNS

Ian B. Thomas, Ph.D.

and Ronald C. Snell

The testing and evaluation of a machine which provides a real-time visual display of first versus second formant frequencies is described. In a pilot test, hearing subjects were trained to identify visual patterns corresponding to 20 monosyllabic English words enunciated by a male speaker. An average identification score of 97 percent was obtained by five subjects after a training period of less than one hour. Subsequently, three profoundly deaf male subjects attempted, during training periods of two or three hours, to match visual patterns corresponding to 16 c o r r e c t l y articulated monosyllabic English words. The intelligibility of the words spoken by the deaf subjects after training was found to be considerably higher than the intelligibility of the same words recorded prior to training.

I T HAS LONG BEEN HOPED THAT improved articulation among the profoundly deaf could be achieved through the use of devices which present significant speech information to one of the other senses in real-time. A visual display suggests itself as a convenient and easily implemented method for presenting this information. Indeed, the basic idea of a visual display of speech sounds is not at all new; numerous visual displays have been built and described in the literature (Steinberg and French, 1946; Potter, Kopp and Green, 1947; Stark, Cullen and Chase, 1968; Pickett and Constam, 1968; Pronovost et al., 1968; Cohen, 1968; House, Goldstein and Hughes, 1968; Risberg, 1968; Borrild, 1968; Kringlebotn, 1968; Phillips et al., 1968; Upton, 1968). In those cases where there has been sufficient time for a complete evaluation of these aids the results obtained have been equivocal. As a result, it has been argued that there may exist a basic incompatibility between the visual and auditory senses to the extent that the speech decoding processes may not be neurally accessible through the visual senses (Liberman et al., 1968). If this were so, then the outlook for visual aids would be grim indeed. However, when one considers the success of deaf individuals in lipreading and in the reading of textual material (whether the onset of deafness has occurred either prior to or subsequent to language acquisition) the outlook appears considerably brighter. If we are to be optimists, then we must assume that the information presented to deaf subjects by some of the existing displays is somehow "indigestible" to the visual sensory system.

After a thorough review of existing visual display devices it was felt that in most cases either too much or too little information had been provided to the deaf subject or that the information had been presented in a form which required considerable cognitive processing of the basic information displayed before a sound could be identified. In addition, it was felt that the patterns displayed should be able to be readily related to articulatory gestures. Considerations such as these led to the conclusion that the type of visual display which satisfied most of the criteria considered essential for a successful visual aid was a plot of first versus second formant frequencies (a so-called F1-F2 plot).

First versus second formant frequency plots are not new; they appeared in the literature as early as 1948 (Potter and Peterson, 1948). However, these and subsequently published F1-F2 plots were obtained indirectly from spectrograms and were not available in real-time. On the other hand, despite the ready availability of real-time first and second formant data from formant trackers for many years, we have been unable to find any instance in the literature of the application of real-time F1-F2 plots as prosthetic aids for the deaf. Of the existing visual display devices, the Gallaudet Visible Speech Trainer (Pickett and Constam, 1968) represents the closest approximation to a device for producing F1-F2 plots at

3. LINGUISTIC DEVELOPMENT

least for the vowel sounds. However, there are several important distinctions between its analysis techniques and those required for a true F1-F2 plot.

Let us briefly review the desirable features of an F1-F2 plot. Firstly, the frequencies of the first two formants have long been recognized as basic parameters in the perception and synthesis of speech in the sense that they contain a great deal of the information which enables the various speech sounds to be distinguished. Secondly, it is known that the position of the tongue hump along the vocal tract is monotonically related to the frequency of the second formant and that the height of the tongue hump is monotonically related to the frequency of the first formant (Miller, 1951). Because of this, there is a very simple isomorphism between the location of the vowels on an F1-F2 plot and the relative locations of the vowels on the vowel triangles and trapezoids familiar to linguists, phoneticians, and teachers of the deaf. In short, the location of a sound on an F1-F2 plot is intimately related to the articulatory configuration required to produce that sound. Thirdly, the F1-F2 plot provides this information in an extremely simple way; the relationship between the formants is indicated by the position of an illuminated spot on a plane. It is surely a much simpler perceptual task to observe the location of a spot on a plane than to determine the relative locations of spectral peaks or bands as is necessary in some of the other displays previously mentioned. Finally, the F1-F2 plot provides an objective and readily perceived estimate of the "proximity" of a sound produced to a desired sound. In view of all the desirable features associated with an F1-F2 plot it was decided to design and construct a machine to provide such a display. The machine was also designed to provide an indication of the type of excitation present in the incoming speech (i.e., voicing, friction, or both). Technical details of the machine's operation have been discussed elsewhere (Thomas, 1968a). Since it is the purpose of this paper to

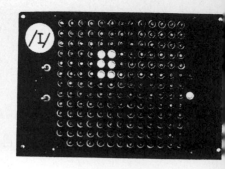
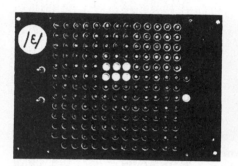
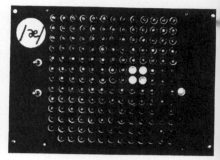

Figure 1

present results obtained by using the machine, no description of its operation will be given here.

The visual output of the machine appears on a 12 x 12 array of neon glow lamps as shown in Fig. 1. The vertical axis of the display corresponds to a quantization of the entire second formant frequency range into 12 smaller frequency ranges each represented by one light. Likewise, the first formant frequency is displayed on the horizontal axis. The two additional sets of 12 lights below and to the left of the main array form, in effect, first and second formant axes for the main array. Two switches on the display panel enable the user to "project" the pattern in the F1-F2 plot onto either or both of these axes. This feature has been found useful in displaying the behavior of individual formants in words and phrases. Finally, the two lights on the right of the main array indicate voicing (bottom) and noise excitation (top). During use of the machine a clear plastic writing surface is installed over the face of the display panel. The trajectories corresponding to correctly articulated words can be drawn on this surface by a china marking pencil.

PILOT TEST OF WORD RECOGNITION

The object of this test was to determine if, after training, subjects could discriminate between the words of a given list solely from the display patterns representing these words on the machine. While we do not believe that this machine has any great value as a substitute for lipreading in the *reception* of speech, we were nevertheless interested in seeing if normal hearing subjects could perceive and remember the differences between patterns corresponding to a selected set of words.

Accordingly, 20 monosyllabic English words were selected primarily on the basis of their vowel or glide content. These words were as follows: heed, hid, head, had, bah, bought, hoed, hood, who'd, hud, heard, we, you, I, why boy, how, eight, hoe, your. A tape recording was prepared using these words in the following way. The list was recorded, the first time, by reading the words consecutively, repeating each word four times in succession; then, a second time, reading the words only once each in the order shown. Then a test list was recorded; the speaker read the list in random order, repeating each word twice (for example:—"Heed, Heed"—"Boy, Boy"—). The word pairs were spaced at five-second intervals. The speaker was an adult male who spoke a standard American English dialect.

The training period and test constituted a single encounter with the machine which lasted approximately 45 minutes. During the training period the subject was first told the overall objective of the test and the machine operation was demonstrated. Next, the training tape was played through the audio system (audio amplifier and speaker) and through the machine in parallel so that the subject could simultaneously listen to the words and watch the patterns corresponding to the words appear in the visual display. The subject was supplied with a copy of the list of test words. The training tape was played as many times as a subject felt necessary. If the subject desired, the tape was stopped and words would be replayed.

During the recognition test, the audio system was disconnected and the test tape containing the scrambled list of words was played into the machine. The subject was asked to write down the words which he felt corresponded to the patterns seen on the visual display. If the subject so desired, the tape was stopped after a given word and it alone would be repeated. Five adult male subjects took part in the test; they were either students or members of the faculty at the University and had had no previous experience with the visual display device prior to the test.

The subjects in this test achieved an average recognition score of 97 percent for the words used. It is evident from this score that the subjects were very well able to recognize the words solely from the display patterns representing these words on the machine. Analysis of the results revealed that, of the few errors made, most were due to confusion between words having very similar display patterns (and therefore, very similar articulatory gestures in their enunciation).

The accuracy with which patterns could be classified was greatly encouraging from two points of view. Firstly, it demonstrated very directly that recognition of an initially verbal signal is possible from a visual display, at least for a limited set of words, after a relatively short training period (less than one hour for a total of 20 words). Secondly, it provided the justification for proceeding on to an attempt to improve the articulation of profoundly deaf subjects by having them try to match patterns corresponding to correctly articulated words.

ARTICULATION TRAINING TEST

The object of this test was to determine if, over a short training interval, profoundly deaf subjects could increase the intelligibility of their speech by attempting to match patterns corresponding to correctly articulated words on the visual display. Before having any contact with the visual display device, each subject was asked to recite the following list of 16 words as clearly and as well as he could, reading the words consecutively, repeating each word twice in succession: heed, hid, head, had, bah, bought, boat, cool, I, why, we, you, boy, how, eight, your. A tape recording was made of this recitation; these recorded words were used later as reference for measuring the increase in intelligibility for each deaf subject after he had worked with the machine.

The visual display was then demonstrated to the subject. He was shown in what manner the machine displays vowels, glides, and words. The significance of the voicing and friction indicators was explained and demonstrated. The subject was then seated in front of the display panel and one of the authors (Ronald Snell), using his own voice, demonstrated a word from the above list. The pattern of the word as pronounced by this speaker was then drawn on the plexiglass display screen with a china marking pencil. The subject was instructed to try to match this pattern as closely as possible in both location and timing. The speaker remained available to demonstrate the timing of

the pattern as often as the subject desired. The subjects were told that the closer they could approximate the indicated pattern, the more "acceptable" would be their pronunciation of the particular word.

No specific time limit was set for working on each word, but each training session was limited to one hour. After two training sessions (i.e., a total of two hours) for one of the subjects and after three training sessions (i.e., a total of three hours) for each of the other two subjects, it was felt that sufficient improvement in articulation had been achieved for obtaining a measurable difference in the intelligibility of the words from the list. Accordingly, at this time a final tape of the same word list was made using the identical recording apparatus as used previously. The subject was told to read the list using the machine to judge, via the patterns marked on the display panel, if the word had been correctly articulated. The subject was told to repeat the word until he considered that the associated pattern was as close to the "goal" pattern as he could make it, then to go on to the next word until the list was completed. All of these attempts were recorded. The last two utterances of the group of attempts at a given pattern were retained and used in the preparation of the final tape for the evaluation of increase in intelligibility.

Three profoundly deaf males were used as subjects; particulars are shown below:

Subject X:
1. 23 years old
2. Profoundly deaf (> 80 db hearing loss, ISO)
3. Educational background:
   a. Privately tutored from 20 months to five years old at home.
   b. 12 years at a residential school for the deaf, 1953-1965, graduated 1965.
   c. 4 years in high school, 1965-1969, graduated June 1969.

Subject Y:
1. 19 years old
2. Profoundly deaf (> 80 db hearing loss, ISO)
3. Educational background:
   a. 12 years at a residential school for the deaf, 1953-1965, grad-

71

3. LINGUISTIC DEVELOPMENT

uated 1965.
  b. 4 years in high school, 1965-1969, graduated June 1969.

Subject Z:
1. 22 years old
2. Profoundly deaf (> 80 db hearing loss, ISO)
3. Educational background:
   a. 12 years at a residential school for the deaf, 1951-1963, graduated 1963.
   b. 4 years in high school, graduated 1967.
   c. 2 years at University of Massachusetts, presently a sophomore.

The words recorded before and after training were now used in an intelligibility test to determine if the intelligibility of the speech of these subjects had increased. An intelligibility test tape was compiled from the tapes made before and after training. The word pairs from these tapes were re-recorded in a random order on the intelligibility test tape forming a recorded sequence of 96 word pairs. A period of five seconds was introduced between word pairs (i.e., "Boy, Boy" —five-second delay—"Heed, Heed" —etc.). The following introduction was recorded at the beginning of this tape:

"You are about to hear a list of single syllable English words recorded by deaf males. You will hear a word repeated twice followed by five seconds of silence. Please write down the word you hear. If you don't understand a word, please guess, as this will help with the correlation of the results. Please listen carefully."

Ten subjects (nine males, one female) took part in the intelligibility test. All subjects were students or faculty at the University, having no known hearing deficiencies, and no previous extensive contact with deaf persons.

The subjects were seated at a table and were supplied with paper and pencil. The intelligibility tape was played to them through headphones. They had no knowledge of the structure of the word list or of the experiment previous to the test other than what they heard in the introductory message on the tape. They were simply asked to write down the words they heard.

RESULTS

The results of the intelligibility tests are shown in Tables I and II.

TABLE I

Scores for Intelligibility Test: scores indicate the number of correct vowel identifications out of a possible 16 words.

LISTENER	Subject X* Number Before	Subject X* Correct After	Subject Y* Number Before	Subject Y* Correct After	Subject Z** Number Before	Subject Z** Correct After
A	6	10	4	14	8	12
B	7	11	10	13	10	14
C	4	9	7	9	8	10
D	9	14	10	12	8	11
E	4	8	3	10	9	11
F	3	9	5	12	3	8
G	5	9	5	9	5	10
H	7	7	5	10	5	11
I	3	7	4	9	6	10
J	7	12	7	12	8	11

*Three Training Sessions   **Two Training Sessions

The scores shown in Table I indicate the number of *vowels and glides* correctly recognized in the stimulus words recorded before and after training. Table II shows the number of *words* correctly recognized by each of the listeners for the three deaf subjects. It will be seen that in almost all cases there is a consistent and substantial increase in the intelligibility scores for the words recorded after training. Analysis of the test results revealed that the greater part of the overall increase could be attributed to improved recognition of the stimulus words containing glides. This is very likely due to the fact that, during training, the deaf subjects utilized extrapolation of their initially limited glide patterns as a useful and relatively rapid means of approaching the correct pronunciation of the vowels at the extremes of articulation, particularly /i/ and /u/. As a result, the subjects devoted perhaps an inordinate share of the total available time to working on the words containing glides.

It was observed that the area of the F1-F2 plot occupied by the total vowel system of each deaf subject prior to training was very small compared with the normal area occupied by the vowel system of a normal speaker. Typically the "vowel system" of each of the deaf subjects before training was clustered around a point between the vowels /ae/ and /a/; most glide movements were along an approximately constant second formant line drawn through this location. This fact was confirmed by examining spectrograms of the words containing glides recorded before training had begun. After training, the glide patterns of the deaf subjects approximated more closely those of normal speakers. In particular, they exhibited considerably more movement of the second formant. The increased intelligibility of words possessing more "normal" movements of the second formant frequency is consistent with the results of experiments which have demonstrated the great significance of this formant in speech intelligibility (Thomas, 1968b).

It will be observed in both Tables I and II that there is a wide range in the scores of individual listeners for all test words. This implies that some listeners were consistently able to recognize the words spoken by the deaf subjects much more readily than others. It is nevertheless true that there was an *increase* in the scores obtained for the words spoken after training in almost every case. One-tailed t tests were performed to determine the statistical significance of these increases. For each deaf subject aver-

TABLE II

Scores for Intelligibility Test: scores indicate the number of correct absolute word identifications out of a possible 16 words.

	Subject X*		Subject Y*		Subject Z**	
	Number	Correct	Number	Correct	Number	Correct
LISTENER	Before	After	Before	After	Before	After
A	1	7	4	10	6	9
B	5	8	8	10	9	10
C	1	6	3	7	5	7
D	9	13	8	11	7	10
E	4	3	2	8	5	10
F	2	6	4	9	3	7
G	3	6	3	5	3	8
H	4	5	3	5	4	7
I	2	4	3	6	4	7
J	5	11	3	9	6	9

* Three Training Sessions   ** Two Training Sessions

age increases in both vowel/glide and absolute word recognition attained by the listeners were found to be significant beyond the 0.0005 level except for word recognition for subject X; in this case the average increase is significant beyond the 0.01 level.

CONCLUSIONS

The results of the statistical tests applied to the data indicate that we are well justified in claiming that the intelligibility of the words spoken by the deaf subjects was higher after training than it was before training. Can this increase be attributed wholly or partially to the visual display device? We believe the answer is a qualified "yes." We say "qualified" because we cannot be sure that our subjects, who in the past have received extensive therapy, did not improve in their articulation simply because their attention was drawn forcibly again to the correct articulation of words. This, then, is our major reservation about the significance of the results of these tests.

The subjects in these tests received no therapy whatsoever in the traditional sense either during the training sessions or during the periods between training sessions. This was insisted upon since we wished to establish the value of the machine alone as a teaching aid. It is reasonable to assume, however, that with a combination of normal therapy and training on the machine, subjects could achieve greater gains in intelligibility more rapidly. Since the machine provides an objective real-time evaluation of the vocal productions of a subject and since it can be used by the subject alone, it can relieve the therapist of much of the drudgery of the normal therapy session. It is felt that the presence of a therapist would be invaluable in helping the subject to achieve acceptable articulation of speech sounds more quickly and consistently. However, once the instructions have been given, the therapist can withdraw and allow the subject to practice alone on the machine.

There are many unanswered questions: for example, how long are the effects of such training sustained? Future research is being planned to determine the effectiveness of the combination of therapist plus visual display device. For the moment, however, the tentative establishment of the usefulness of the visual aid described is considered to be a significant step along the way to more rapid and complete rehabilitation of the profoundly deaf.

ACKNOWLEDGEMENTS

We wish to extend our thanks to Dr. Arthur Boothroyd of the Clarke School for the Deaf, Northampton, and to Dr. Kenneth Gough of the Communication Disorders Section of the Department of Speech at the University of Massachusetts for their valuable comments and suggestions.

In addition, we gratefully acknowledge the financial support provided for this work by the National Institutes of Health under Grant NB-08306-01 and by the National Aeronautics and Space Administration under Contract NAS-12-606.

REFERENCES

BORRILD, K., "Experience with the Design and Use of Technical Aids for the Training of Deaf and Hard of Hearing Children," Am. Ann. Deaf, 113, 168-177 (1968).

COHEN, M. L., "The ADL Sustained Phoneme Analyzer," Am. Ann. Deaf, 113, 247-252 (1968).

HOUSE, A. S., GOLDSTEIN, D. P. AND HUGHES, G. W., "Perception of Visual Transforms of Speech Stimuli: "Learning Simple Syllables," Am. Ann. Deaf, 113, 215-221 (1968).

KRINGLEBOTN, M., "Experiments with Some Visual and Vibrotactile Aids for the Deaf," Am. Ann. Deaf, 113, 311-317 (1968).

LIBERMAN, A. M., COOPER, F. S., SHANKWEILER, D. P. and STUDDERT-KENNEDY, M., "Why are Speech Spectrograms Hard to Read?" Am. Ann. Deaf, 113, 127-133 (1968).

MILLER, G. A., Language and Communication, McGraw-Hill, New York, p. 39 (1951).

PHILLIPS, N. D., REMILLARD, W., BASS, S., PRONOVOST, W., "Teaching of Intonation to the Deaf by Visual Pattern Matching," Am. Ann. Deaf, 113, 239-246 (1968).

PICKETT, J. M. AND CONSTAM, A., "A Visual Speech Trainer with Simplified Indication of Vowel Spectrum," Am Ann. Deaf, 113, 253-258 (1968).

PICKETT, J. M., "Recent Research on Speech-Analyzing Aids for the Deaf," IEEE, Transactions on Audio and Electroacoustics, AU-16, 227-234 (1968).

POTTER, R. G. AND PETERSON, G. E., "The Perception of Vowels and Their Movements," J. Acoust. Soc. Am., 20, 528-535 (1948).

POTTER, R. G., KOPP, G. A., GREEN, H. C., Visible Speech, New York, Van Nostrand, 1947.

PRONOVOST, W., YENKIN, L., ANDERSON, D. C., AND LERNER, R., "The Voice Visualizer." Am. Ann. Deaf, 113, 230-238 (1968).

RISBERG, A., "Visual Aids for Speech Correction," Am. Ann. Deaf, 113, 178-194 (1968).

STARK, R. E., CULLEN, J. K., AND CHASE, R. A., "Preliminary Work with the New Bell Telephone Visible Speech Translator." Am. Ann. Deaf, 113, 205-214 (1968).

STEINBERG, J. C., AND FRENCH, N. R., "The Portrayal of Visible Speech," J. Acoust. Soc. Am., 18, 4-18 (1946).

THOMAS, I. B., "Real Time Visual Display of Speech Parameters," Proc. N.E.C., 24, 382-387 (1968a).

THOMAS, I. B., "The Influence of First and Second Formants on the Intelligibility of Clipped Speech," J. Audio Engin. Soc., 16, 182-185 (1968b).

UPTON, H. W., "Wearable Eyeglass Speechreading Aid," Am. Ann. Deaf, 113, 222-229 (1968)

SPEECH | in the Preschool for the Deaf

ELEANOR VORCE

SPEECH is primarily a means of communication, of translating thoughts and ideas into spoken words. As a means of establishing the habit of talking for communication, the early speech program is bound to the child's total program and should be correlated with every activity that takes place in or out of the school or the home.

If deaf children are to be able to express themselves spontaneously and naturally in rhythmical and intelligible phrases and sentences, we must be sure that the habit is established early in their lives. To some degree an adequate expressive vocabulary and fluent, natural speech can be accomplished by the time these children are ready to enter the lower school grades. Certainly the foundation has been laid and the child's use of speech and his feeling for it have been established by this time.

If speech is communication, the primary emphasis must first be placed on the spoken language of the ideas to be communicated, and the necessary speech skills should be an outgrowth of this expression rather than a pregrowth to it. In this frame of reference it would seem unwise to teach the young deaf child conscious use of speech skills and techniques or the acquisition of a prescribed list of speech patterns if he has not first caught the "speech idea" and does not have the desire to express himself verbally.

As with normally hearing children, the beginnings of real speech occur long before the first word is spoken, for impression invariably precedes expression. With the normally hearing child, this usually happens during the time that his muscles and nerves are maturing—before he becomes a mobile and independent individual. His experiences are limited and his world is circumscribed by what can come to him. His world is a "talking" world, and as a result of hearing countless repetitions of spoken words he learns to understand much of what is said to him. The deaf child who is about to learn to talk is usually much older—his nerves and muscles have already developed; he is an extremely mobile creature who can control certain facets of his environment rather than be controlled by them. As a consequence of his physical maturity and longer period of existence, he brings to this "threshold of talking" a completely different background of experiences and interests. He has already undoubtedly found some means of self-expression and communication (usually nonverbal); he has begun to see relationships and to build concepts of the world about him; he is interested in exploring and doing. To him the world is not normally a "talking" one—but if he is to learn to understand and to use speech as his natural means of expression, his environment must be made speech and language centered.

It is for us, the adults about him, to consciously create this "talking environment" and to interest and involve him in it in such a way that he will not only begin to understand through speechreading, but will eventually try to imitate what he sees and to use his voice to express his own desires and thoughts. And all of this must be done as informally and naturally as possible. Once the child has learned to watch the face for expression and explanation, the talk should be centered about his activities and, whenever possible, should occur at the time he is involved in the activity. This should be connected with as many and as varied daily experiences as is possible for "the greater the number of a child's experiences, and the broader the child's environment the richer his vocabulary should be."[2]

It should go without saying that the climate of the nursery or preschool or the home—the feeling that the children have toward adults and toward one another—is of utmost importance in interesting them in looking to the face, in learning to form ideas and concepts through speechreading, and later in creating a desire to talk. Only when the environment nourishes and expects speech will it become truly functional.

The beginnings of purposive vocalizations follow close upon the heels of understanding for most young deaf children. If the impressions built through speechreading are vital to the child's experiences and feelings, he will usually try to imitate—to shape his lips in imitation of what he has seen, and to use his voice with communicative purpose. When there is some indication that the child is trying to transmit to others the impressions which he has up to now been receiving, he is ready for help in the active production of speech. Again, we feel that this should be as informal as possible—and whenever opportunity permits, it should occur in connection with a situation in which the child is interested and involved. If the resulting speech is to be spontaneous and expressive, it must be "individual" centered rather than "course of study" centered. A child should be permitted and helped to say anything that the situation calls for, whether or not he has previously developed the proper skills to say the words correctly. He must learn through experience that some form of vocal response is expected from him.

Students of speech have reported that the first words of the normally hearing child are egocentric and tinged with emotion. Remembering that the experiences and interests the deaf child brings to his speech learning are vastly different from those of the hearing baby, we were curious to know if the feelings and ideas to which the deaf children wish to give expression, and for which they will need to be given the language and speech are different from those reported for hearing children. For the past three years the teachers in training at the Lexington School have observed and recorded the communications of our nursery children during play. They were asked to put into words as best they could the ideas the children were expressing through gesture, dramatization, vocalization, or even by an occasional sign. The results of these investigations to date have been most interesting.

By all odds, the most frequently repeated words and phrases were these:

"Speech in Preschool for the Deaf," Eleanor Vorce. ©1970 The Alexander Graham Bell Association for the Deaf, Inc.

Look at me! Let me see! Stop! That's mine! Help me! ——is broken. —— fell. ——is bad. I don't like——. No! Where is——? What's that? May I have——? Little naming was reported —coat, sweater, bathroom, milk, hearing aid, downstairs, upstairs, home, hospital, outside and lunch being the nouns most often reported. As used by the children in these particular situations these words functioned as sentences or phrases in expressing a whole idea as: "hospital" meaning, "I went to the hospital this morning," or "outside," meaning, "It's time to go outside and play." Sleep, eat, and fell seemed to be the most popular verbs, and cold, good, bad, sick and funny the most common adjectives. This is quite unlike the traditional speech vocabulary for the young deaf child, though these are evidently the words the children would have been using if they had had sufficient speech to do so. Though not conclusive evidence, the recurrence of vocabulary over a period of three years would seem to indicate that the language needed to help the maturing deaf child communicate as he would wish involves words which fall into the following categories: words of egocentricity; words which express rather strong emotions; words which express negative feelings; words of inquiry or question; words which explain activities.

What of the speech the children use at play? Regardless of the number of words that had been taught in the tutoring room, the first words used spontaneously by our present group of three-year-olds, according to their tutors and nursery teacher, were broke, fall, milk, bye-bye and home. In the spontaneous words spoken most frequently in the playroom they listed hot, cold, warm, cry, baby, bathroom, wash, home, stop, bye-bye, up, finished, more, hello, dirty, fish, and thank you. In both cases (the first words spoken spontaneously and the speech used most frequently) there is again an indication that children are using words which express whole thoughts, which are concerned with their own activities and daily life, and words which are highly tinged with emotion. There is no evidence here that children first use the words which are easy to say. If we are teaching speech for expression of thought and emotion, these studies would indicate that the early speech vocabulary should grow from careful observation of the child and his desires rather than from the visibility of certain sounds or the ease with which a sound or a combination of sounds may be made. Perhaps our early vocabularies should contain more adjectives, expressions, and nouns that

are connected with children's emotional experiences. We believe that this speech should be taught initially through simple imitation of these whole words needed for communication through the combined use of the tactile, visual, auditory and kinesthetic senses and that only later—when the child has the habit of verbal communication and uses established speech patterns—should he be made conscious of techniques and skills or of correction.

Throughout his pre-verbal existence, the normally hearing baby vocalizes, babbles, experiments and listens to himself make sounds which he later associates with meanings. While he is doing this, although he is completely unaware of the process, he is developing muscular skills which will later help him to produce speech. As he plays with sounds he produces all the consonants and vowels of his native language. McCarthy[4] tells us that at no time in his spontaneous spoken language can a child use a sound that he has not previously babbled in speech play. If this is true, it has serious implications for the speech of the deaf child who has not heard the speech sounds of others, who has not heard himself experiment and play with sound and who probably stopped babbling and vocalizing at an early age. He has been deprived of these experiences which give muscular practice for so many of the fine adjustments needed to form the sounds of speech. Even with maximum use of residual hearing and with tactile, visual and auditory senses being brought into play, the constant repetition of whole words is seldom sufficient to build all the skills needed for good speech in the child whose hearing is severely impaired. Again, it is for us, the teachers and adults in his life, to contrive a variety of interesting activities which will build these same muscular speech skills—using different stimuli to approximate the informal and almost unconscious process by which the hearing child acquires them. Until he has well established speech habits and is socially, intellectually and physically mature enough to understand and cooperate in building and using these skills, we must find games and activities which will help the deaf child to develop better breath control, to modulate the pitch and intensity of his voice to some degree, to gain some ability to imitate number and stress of syllables in a breath group, to gain flexibility and control of his tongue, to enunciate as many of the consonants and vowels as is possible, and these in as many combinations as is possible. The ingenuity

and careful planning of an experienced teacher is needed, for the more skills that can be developed unconsciously as far as the child is concerned, the better the resulting speech and the more spontaneous and fluent it will be. As the child matures there should be a growing awareness of the skills involved. What was once taught through a blowing game, an activity in eurythemics or a game of imitation can be approached more directly as "Make your voice pretty." "I didn't hear your 's'." "That's a nasal sound." These same processes should not have conscious application at the time the child is learning speech as communication, however. Skills must not be neglected—not even at the beginning—but the child need not connect the pleasant activity in which he is involved with any mechanical aspect of speech.

Perhaps the greatest problem with which we are confronted in this approach to speech is that of the degree of perfection which may be expected in spontaneous speech. To be sure, early imitations and vocalizations may be mere approximations of the total pattern—perhaps not even intelligible to the casual listener—but they need not remain so as the child matures and is guided to a better understanding of the speech process. We suspect that more perfect sounds and perhaps even "better" beginning speech can be acquired in a carefully controlled vocabulary of simple words than in the more unpredictable vocabulary of truly expressive speech. It is easier to practice the combined sounds in easy words such as bow, baby, arm, thumb, shoe, than to try to say cry, fell down, milk, rhythm, no more—any of which the child is more likely to need to express an idea. For the older preschool child it is easier to be content with "Mary is home" for news than to question the reason for her absence, to think beyond the obvious. This will invariably bring about such tongue twisters as "Maybe her stomach hurts" or "I think she broke her leg" or "Maybe the doctor gave her a shot." But is the perfection of a limited speech vocabulary worth the restrictions of mental development? On the other hand, is it inevitable that the speech suffer to an irreparable degree and that slovenly and incorrect habits be firmly established? We do not believe so. Each year we come closer to the solution of this very important problem, for we are not willing to sacrifice the mental growth and development, the formation of broad concepts, the understanding and use of language, the spontaniety of expression for the

3. LINGUISTIC DEVELOPMENT

perfection of a restricted teacher-controlled vocabulary. Neither do we wish our children to have understanding and use of a wide oral vocabulary which is unintelligible to the listener. Actually, neither extreme need exist. The solution lies in a well-planned program in the hands of teachers who understand general developmental problems, but who are sensitive to the needs of individual children; who understand the language development necessary to broaden the children's horizons, but who also understand the inherent speech problems—the necessity for building and using the best speech possible; teachers whose ears are tuned to each individual child's capabilities and who are wise and capable enough to expect and receive from each child the best he can give. We need good teachers for beginning speech. Language and thought must not be sacrificed for speech—and speech need not be sacrificed for language and thought.

Recognition of this dual nature of speech—one aspect concerned with the expression of ideas and the other with the development of speech skills neces-

sary to convey these ideas—and planning for the development of each should not lead to the neglect of either. What appears as extremely casual and incidental teaching should be well planned by the teacher and casual only to the child. From a beginning which emphasizes understanding and expression of whole words accompanied by the development of skills through vocal play, to the conscious application of these skills in spontaneous spoken language (both during special speech periods and in the conversational speech which occurs throughout the day) is the speech program of the Lexington preschool. Though the children continue to acquire new language and vocabulary in the context of situations and as whole words or expressions, by the time they are ready to enter lower school they have considerable understanding of the way in which speech is produced. Through color cues (or from the words themselves) they understand and can control the manner in which a sound is produced—breath, voice or nasal; they are able to phrase several words in a breath group; they have gained considerable

conscious control of the tongue; and they have begun an informal understanding of specific sounds. The resulting speech is not perfect—but it is spontaneous and natural; the children have begun to express themselves in sentences or phrases with words that are descriptive of their individual feelings; their voices are generally rather free and unstrained; the connected language is quite rhythmical; most words are pronounced intelligibly; almost all the consonants and vowels can be consciously enunciated. The children are now ready for further refinement and correction of speech through more formal methods.

[1] Beasley, Jane, *Slow to Talk*. New York: Bureau of Publications, Teachers College, Columbia University, 1956.

[2] Berry, Mildred and Eisenson, Jon, *Speech Disorders, Principles and Practices of Therapy*. New York: Appleton-Century-Crofts, Inc., 1956.

[3] Ewing, Irene and Ewing, A. W. G., *Speech and the Deaf Child*. Washington, D. C.: The Volta Bureau, 1954.

[4] McCarthy, D., "Language Development in Children," *Manual of Child Psychology*, 2nd edition L. Carmichael, ed. New York: John Wiley and Sons, 1954.

[5] New, M. and O'Connor, C. D., *Lexington School Outline for Speech*, New York: Lexington School for the Deaf, 1954.

The Phonological Systems of Deaf Children

Barbara Dodd

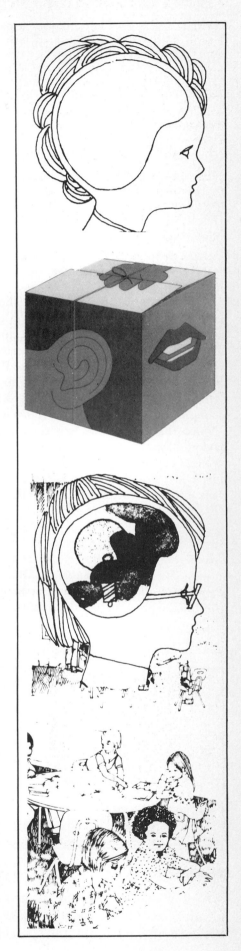

The phonology of the deaf is usually described in terms of its deviation from normal phonological systems. Lenneberg (1967) found differences in prelinguistic utterances between normal and deaf children after six months of age. Silverman (1963) surveyed the literature and concluded that deaf speech was characterized by arhythmia, excessive nasality, neutral and prolonged vowels, superfluous syllables between abutting pairs, few pitch changes, lack of distinction between voiced and voiceless pairs, malarticulation, and the omission of consonant clusters, consonants, diphthongs, and vowels.

A different approach to the phonology of the deaf has been suggested by West and Weber (1973) in their presentation of a linguistic analysis of the phonological system of a hard-of-hearing four-year-old child with 58-dB air-conduction loss in the better ear. Analysis to determine what her speech did express revealed that the child's phonology contained rudimentary patterns of linguistic development such as the elongation of vowels to designate final consonants and the use of phonemic contrast. Oller and Kelly (1974) studied a hard-of-hearing child who suffered an average 60-dB loss in both ears and found that she produced errors similar to those of young hearing children.

If signs of a structured phonological system can be found in a young partially hearing child, it may be possible that the profoundly congenitally deaf also acquire some consistent phonological behavior. The purpose of the first experiment was to test this possibility. The second experiment was designed to assess the predictive value of any rules derived from the first study and to investigate the effect of two different inputs, reading and lipreading, on these rules.

EXPERIMENT 1 METHOD

Subjects

Ten profoundly congenitally deaf children acted as subjects. Eight of the subjects had a mean pure-tone average loss for the better ear for frequency range 0.5, 1, and 2 kHz of 102.2 sound pressure in dB, SD 11.09 dB, re ISO norms. Two of the subjects had mean thresholds which exceeded 120 dB. Known causes of their deafness were found in school medical records and included maternal rubella, thalidomide poisoning, sickle-cell anemia, and

3. LINGUISTIC DEVELOPMENT

familial deafness. The subjects' mean chronological age was 11 years zero months, range nine years five months to 12 years four months. There were six males and four females. All subjects attended a junior school for the deaf in inner London. School policy encouraged the use of spoken language in the classroom, and children were encouraged to learn to lip-read.

Procedure

Forty-five colored pictures of familiar objects and animals on 4″ x 4″ flash cards were presented to each subject in random order. The children were asked to name the pictures. The procedure was repeated to gain two examples of articulation for each name. Testing was carried out in a quiet room in the school building. The procedure was tape-recorded on a Uher Royal Stereophonic tape recorder.

Transcription of Utterances

Two speech pathologists made phonetic transcriptions of all recorded utterances made by each subject. The transcriptions were concerned only with consonants and the semivowels /j/ and /w/; vowels were not considered. Appendix A contains phonetic transcription of those deviant utterances which were acceptable for analysis because they were produced consistently by a subject on both naming trials and also transcribed identically by both speech pathologists. Correct productions are not listed in Appendix A, and only one example of each deviant form is given though many replications occurred.

Since the aim of the experiment was to find consistent phonological behavior, it was necessary to disregard those utterances which gave rise to differences between the two transcriptions, and also to those utterances not produced identically by each subject on both the naming trials. However, less than 15% of the utterances had to be disregarded for these reasons.

RESULTS

Repertoire of Phonological Units. Phones which were not produced by subjects are shown in Table 1. All other of the 24 English consonant phones were used either appropriately or inappropriately by the subjects. All subjects exhibited more than half the complete phone repertoire of English.

TABLE 1. English consonant phones not produced by subjects.

Subject	Number of Phonemes Not Used	ŋ	θ	ð	j	tʃ	dʒ	ʃ	ʒ	h	s	z	t	d	k	g
1	2		θ	ð												
2	3		θ	ð	j											
3	1	ŋ														
4	5	ŋ	θ	ð		tʃ	dʒ									
5	4	ŋ	θ	ð	j											
6	5		θ	ð	j	tʃ	dʒ									
7	9	ŋ			j	tʃ	dʒ	ʃ	ʒ	h	s	z				
8	11	ŋ			j	tʃ	dʒ	ʃ	ʒ	h			t	d	k	g
9	1	ŋ														
10	4	ŋ	θ	ð	j											
Mean 4.5	Totals	7	6	6	6	4	4	2	2	2	1	1	1	1	1	1

Phonological Rules

A set of phonological rules was derived for each subject which accounted for all errors made by that subject. Those rules held in common by two or more of the subjects are shown in Table 2. There were 13 examples where one subject produced an error type consistently that no other subject made; these are not included in the table. Table 2 shows the number of subjects producing errors on listed phonological features, those features being organized in terms of the functions: cluster reduction, consonant harmony, and simplification of the sound system.[1] Table 2 also shows the number of subjects using each phonological rule.

The table does not fully describe phonological systems used. The purpose of the analysis was to describe phonological rules commonly held by the group of subjects. It should be noted that some subjects occasionally used different

TABLE 2. Phonological rules.

Rule Function and Phonological Configuration	Number of Subjects in Error on Phonological Configuration	Example	Phonological Rules All Rules Optional	Number of Subjects Using Each Rule
Cluster Reduction				
Nasal plus consonant	10	[hæd] *hand*	Nasal deletes before consonant	8
		[ɒrɪn] *orange*	Consonant deletes after nasal	2
		[fɪːə] *finger*	Total deletion of consonant cluster	6
/s/ plus consonant	10	[pun] *spoon*	/s/ deletes preconsonantally	10
		[poʊs] *post*	/t, k/ delete after /s/ finally and medially	4
		[bɪːɪt] *biscuit*	Total deletion of consonant cluster	8
/k, t, g/ plus /l, r, w/	9	[lɒk] *clock*	/k, g/ delete before /l, r, w/	9
		[gas] *glass*	/l/ deletes after /k, g/	2
/l/ plus consonant	8	[soʊdə] *soldier*	/l/ deletes before /d, k/	8
		[mə] *milk*	Total deletion of consonant cluster	8
/b, p, f, t, d/ plus /l, r/	8	[bɪdʒ] *bridge*	/r, l/ delete after /b, p, t, d/	8
		[rəɪn] *train*	/d, t, f/ delete before /r, l/	4
Consonant Harmony				
/t/ Before Syllabic /l/	8	[kekal] *kettle*	Velarization of /t/ before syllabic /l/	8
Systemic Simplification				
Nasals	10	[deɪl] *nail*	/n/ is substituted for by [d] initially	7
		[baʊs] *mouse*	/m/ is substituted for by [b]	10
		[treɪ] *train*	/n/ deletes finally	10
		[skɪpɪn] *skipping*	/ŋ/ is substituted for by [n]	8
/h/ Initially	7	[ænd] *hand*	/h/ deletes initially	7
Nonsonorant consonants	10	[fɪ] *fish*	/ʃ, dʒ, tʃ/ deletes finally	8
		[dæm] *jam*	/dʒ, tʃ, θ, ð, ʃ/ are substituted for by [d]	7
		[fɪs] *fish*	/ʃ, dʒ, tʃ/ are substituted for by [s] and [z]	4
		[brɪʒ] *bridge*	/dʒ/ is substituted for by [ʒ]	6

---

[1] For discussion of the functions see Smith (1973).

TABLE 2. Phonological rules. *(Continued)*

Rule Function and Phonological Configuration	Number of Subjects in Error on Phonological Configuration	Example	Phonological Rules All Rules Optional	Number of Subjects Using Each Rule
/g, k/	9	[dɜl] *girl*	/g, k/ are substituted for by [d, t]	7
		[klɒ] *clock*	/g, k/ delete finally	7
		[ɜl] *girl*	/g, k/ deletes initially	2
/l/	4	[gɜ] *girl*	/l/ deletes finally	2
/s/ after /n/	9	[pantəl] *pencil*	/s/ is substituted for by [t] after /n/	9
/s/ and /z/	9	[maʊt] *mouse*	/s/ and /z/ are substituted for by [t, d]	3
		[haʊ] *house*	/s, z/ delete finally	7
		[ʒɛbrə] *zebra*	/z/ is substituted for by [ʒ]	2
/r/	3	[tweɪn] *train*	/r/ is substituted for by [w]	3
/t/ /d/	5	[bɪskɪ] *biscuit*	/t/ deletes finally	5
/f/ /v/	6	[plaʊ:ə] *flower*	/f, v/ are substituted for by [p, b]	4
		[li] *leaf*	/f/ deletes finally	2
syllabic /l/	4	[pənsu] *pencil*	syllabic /l/ vocalizes to [u]	4

rules in dealing with a particular consonant cluster; for example, one subject reduced nasal plus consonant clusters by deleting the nasal in *hand* [hæd], but the nonnasal consonant in *orange* [ɒrɪn]. In this sense the rules were optional.

Morpheme Structure

There were two morpheme structure conditions that deaf subjects imposed. All 10 subjects reduced multisyllable words by deleting unstressed, initial syllables ([nanʌ] for *banana*, [matoʊ] for *tomato*); six of the subjects interpolated vowels, or consonants to obtain *CVCV* forms ([fɒlaʊlɔ] for *flower*, [hæməl] for *hammer*).

DISCUSSION

The results demonstrate that hearing is not essential for the acquisition of an extensive phone repertoire or for the development of an at least partially rule-governed phonological system. While the results do not represent a total description of either the phone repertoires of the subjects or their phonological systems, they do show that the deaf subjects used some phonological rules consistently, both individually, and as a group.

Only two subjects exhibited any real paucity of phones, one having acquired 13, and the other 15 of the possible 24 English consonant phones. The other eight subjects' repertoires were almost complete, and those sounds missing are often acquired late by hearing children (Reese and Lipsitt, 1970). Another similarity between the phonology of the deaf and young hearing children is that all the rules used by the deaf subjects also appear in the rule systems of hearing children at some time (Dodd, 1974).

There are two major hypotheses which could explain the consistent rule-governed nature of the deaf subjects' phonological systems. The deaf could be internalizing an incomplete acoustic trace through speech teaching using residual hearing (Fry, 1966) and mapping their vocal output from this information in much the same way as normal children. This explanation would predict less homogeneity in the error pattern than has been found in this experiment. There appears to be no pattern in the phone repertoires which would indicate that those phones produced, or not produced, belonged to particular frequency bands.

A more likely explanation is that the deaf children were internalizing a lip-read trace for words and using this visual input as the primary source of information from which to map their vocal output. One indication that this may be the process deaf subjects were using was their treatment of /k/ and /g/. These sounds are difficult to lip-read being produced by raising the back of the tongue to touch the soft palate. They may be deleted in clusters and in final position simply because they are difficult to see in those environments. This may also explain the absence of /ŋ/ from seven of the subjects' phone repertoires.

In order to validate the findings of this experiment and to investigate the role of lipreading as an input to phonological systems another experiment was carried out to test the hypotheses:

1. That rules frequently used by the deaf subjects in Experiment 1 are predictive of other deaf childrens' phonological systems.
2. That different types of input, such as reading the written word and lipreading, will affect phonological output, because those sounds which are difficult to lip-read will be produced differently according to input.

EXPERIMENT 2 METHOD

Subjects

Eight profoundly, prelinguistically deaf children, and two severely deaf children acted as subjects. The mean pure-tone average loss for the better ear for frequency range 0.5, 1, and 2 kHz for seven of the profoundly deaf subjects was 96.25 dB, SD 15.2, re ISO norms: the other profoundly deaf subject had a mean threshold that exceeded 120 dB. The two severely deaf subjects had a mean pure-tone loss of 65.83 dB. Those causes of the subjects' deafness that were known were obtained from school medical records and included maternal rubella, meningitis at 10 months, and familial deafness. The subjects' mean chronological age was 14 years 11 months; range 12 years nine months to 16 years 11 months. Older subjects were necessary for this experiment because subjects had to be able to read well. All subjects attended a senior school for the deaf in inner London. School policy encouraged the use of spoken language, and children were expected to be able to lip-read.

Procedure

Thirty-six nonsense words were designed to test nine of the rules used consistently by seven or more children in Experiment 1. The rules are listed in Table 3, and the nonsense words are in Appendix B. The nonsense words

3. LINGUISTIC DEVELOPMENT

TABLE 3. Phonological errors made on nonsense words.

		Reading			Lipreading		
Rule	Number of Examples	Rule	Correct	Other Errors	Rule	Correct	Other Errors
1. nasals delete before consonants	40	22	8	10	20	9	11
2. /s/ deletes preconsonantally	30	25	2	3	21	3	6
3. /k, g/ delete before /l, r, w/	50	8	13	29	19	15	16
4. /l, r/ delete after /p, b/	40	18	18	4	22	18	0
5. /n/ is substituted for by [d] initially	20	4	9	7	5	7	8
6. /m/ is substituted for by [b]	70	41	26	3	42	25	3
7. /k, g/ are substituted for by [t, d]	60	7	41	12	3	30	27
8. /k, g/ delete finally	70	29	25	16	51	9	10
9. /n/ deletes finally	30	7	16	7	16	8	6

consisted of 18 *CVC* words, 10 *CCVC* words, three *CVCC* words, two *CVCVC* words, one *CVCCVCC* word, one *CVCCV* word, one *CVCCVC* word. Five subjects were asked to read the words aloud from printed cards and then to reproduce the same word after lipreading the examiner's production. The other five subjects were asked to lip-read first and reproduce the words and then to read them aloud from the printed cards. Subjects were told that the words were nonsense words. The procedure was tape-recorded on a Uher Royal Stereophonic tape recorder, and testing was carried out in a quiet room in the school building.

Transcription of Utterances

Two speech pathologists made phonetic transcriptions of all the recorded utterances made by each subject. The transcriptions were concerned only with consonants and consonant-vowels; vowels were not considered. Since the design of this experiment necessitated that data be obtained for all stimuli, any inconsistencies which occurred between the two transcriptions had to be resolved by listening to the appropriate utterances again. However, it was not possible to make a reliable transcription of eight of the utterances, and for statistical purposes these utterances were classed as "other errors." "Other errors" also include errors made in the production of phonological configurations which were not in accordance with the phonological rules tested.

RESULTS

Predictive Value of Rules

Table 3 lists the nine rules tested and shows the expected frequency of rule usage, actual frequency of rule usage, correct productions, and "other errors" for reading and lipreading conditions.

Table 4 shows the results of related *t* tests comparing rule use against the

TABLE 4. Related *t* ratios for rule usage versus other errors.

	Reading		Lipreading	
Rule	t	Significance	t	Significance
1. nasals delete before consonants	2.25	< 0.05	2.39	< 0.05
2. /s/ deletes preconsonantally	3.99	< 0.01	2.50	< 0.05
3. /k, g/ delete before /l, r, w/	3.84	< 0.01	0.45	< 0.05
4. /l, r/ delete after /p, b/	2.26	< 0.05	6.14	< 0.001
5. /n/ is substituted for by [d] initially	0.82	N.S.	0.76	N.S.
6. /m/ is substituted for by [b]	5.12	< 0.001	4.61	< 0.001
7. /k, g/ are substituted for by [t, d]	0.83	N.S.	3.68	< 0.01
8. /k, g/ delete finally	2.33	< 0.05	5.94	< 0.001
9. /n/ deletes finally	Means Equal	N.S.	2.02	N.S.

production of "other errors" on reading and lipreading conditions, data which are shown in Table 3. In all cases a significant difference indicates the rule was used more often than other errors. In the case of the consonant clusters /kl, kr, kw, gl, gr/ in the reading condition, subjects used the rule "/l, r, w/ delete after /k, g/." When this rule usage was tested against the production of other errors it was found to be significant ($t = 2.34$, $p < 0.05$).

In the lipreading condition six of the nine rules have predictive value; that is, they were used more frequently as a method of reducing consonant clusters and simplifying the system of phonological units than any other error type. These rules were:

> nasals delete before consonants
> /s/ deletes preconsonantally
> /l, r/ delete after /p, b/
> /m/ is substituted for by [b]
> /k, g/ are substituted for by [t, d]
> /k, g/ delete finally

Neither of the rules dealing with /n/ were validated (although there was a trend for subjects to delete /n/ finally). The clusters /kl, kr, kw, gl, gr/ were not simplified in any consistent manner.

In the reading condition five of the nine rules were found to have predictive value, and one of the rules (/k, g/ delete before /l, r, w/) was replaced by another rule which stated the opposite (/l, r, w/ delete after /k, g/). These six rules were:

> nasals delete before consonants
> /s/ deletes preconsonantally
> /l, r/ delete after /p, b/
> /m/ is substituted for by [b]
> /k, g/ delete finally
> /l, r, w/ delete after /k, g/

Again the rules dealing with /n/ were not validated and there was no consistent manner in which subjects dealt with /k, g/ initially. The other major error types produced by subjects are shown in Table 5.

Difference scores were obtained by substracting lipreading scores (for rule usage, correct production, and other errors) from corresponding reading scores shown as group data in Table 3, for each subject on all nine rules tested. These difference scores were then tested against zero, using a related t test. If subjects were using the same phonological rules for both reading and lipreading then none of the ts should be significant. The results are shown in Table 6.

Subjects performed significantly differently in response to the two conditions on the following phonological features (see Table 3 and 6).

1. /k, g/ plus /l, r, w/. When lipreading subjects used the rule /k, g/ delete before /l, r, w/ more frequently than when they were reading (note that in fact when reading subjects used the rule /l, r, w/ delete after /k, g/); and when reading subjects produced more other error types than when lipreading.
2. /k, g/ initially. When lipreading subjects made more errors on /k, g/ initially than they did when reading.
3. /g, k/ delete finally. When lipreading subjects used the rule /k, g/ delete finally more often than they did when reading. Subjects made fewer errors when reading /k, g/ finally, than they did when lipreading.
4. /n/ finally. When lipreading subjects used the rule /n/ deletes finally more often than they did when reading, and when reading they more often correctly produced /n/ finally than when they were lipreading.

In all other phonological features tested subjects' performance did not differ according to the type of input, that is, reading or lipreading.

3. LINGUISTIC DEVELOPMENT

DISCUSSION

Predictive Value of Rules

Six of the nine phonological rules derived from the spontaneous speech of young totally deaf children, and tested on a group of older deaf children using nonsense words with lipreading as an input were found to have predictive value. There are three possible explanations as to why some rules could not be validated.

TABLE 5. Other error types used.

Phonological Configuration	Error Types*	Frequency of Error Types Reading	Lipreading
nasal plus consonant	total deletion of cluster	1	7
	consonant deletes after nasal	7	1
	others†	1	0
/s/ preconsonantally	consonant deletes after /s/ finally	2	3
	total deletion of cluster	0	3
/k, g/ plus /l, r, w/	/l, r, w/ delete after /k, g/	22	13
	total deletion of clusters	3	1
	others	1	0
/p, b/ plus /l, r/	/p, b/ delete before /l, r/	2	0
	others	1	0
/n/ initially	/n/ deletes	3	3
	/n/ is substituted for by [k]	0	4
	others	3	1
/m/ everywhere	/m/ deletes	0	2
	others	3	1
/k, g/ initially	/k, g/ are substituted for by [b]	0	6
	/k, g/ are substituted for by [h]	0	6
	others	5	4
/k, g/ finally	/k, g/ are substituted for by [t, d]	9	6
	/k, g/ are substituted for by [n]	3	0
	/k, g/ are substituted for by [b]	4	0
	others	0	3
/n/ finally	/n/ is substituted for by [p]	3	0
	/n/ is substituted for by [s]	0	3
	others	4	3

*The other error types, although not conforming to the rules set up were consistent in the sense that they were produced by more than one subject, and nine of them were consistent with errors shown in Table 3.

†Error types included under "others" were examples of errors produced once by one subject; they represented 23% of other errors for the reading condition and 15% of other errors for the lipreading condition.

TABLE 6. Related *t* ratios for reading—lipreading versus 0 for rules.

Rule	Rule Usage t	Significance	Correct t	Significance	Other Errors t	Significance
1. Nasals delete before consonants	0.80	N.S.	0.29	N.S.	0.26	N.S.
2. /s/ deletes preconsonantally	1.18	N.S.	1.00	N.S.	0.90	N.S.
3. /k, g/ deletes before /l, r, w/	3.16	< 0.025	0	N.S.	2.75	< 0.05
4. /l, r/ delete after /p, b/	1.00	N.S.	0	N.S.	1.81	N.S.
5. /n/ is substituted for by [d] initially	0.36	N.S.	0.69	N.S.	0.29	N.S.
6. /m/ is substituted for by [b]	0.18	N.S.	0.18	N.S.	0	N.S.
7. /k, g/ are substituted for by [t, d]	1.18	N.S.	1.49	N.S.	3.00	< 0.025
8. /k, g/ delete finally	3.84	< 0.01	2.52	< 0.05	1.62	N.S.
9. /n/ deletes finally	2.59	< 0.025	2.75	< 0.05	0.32	N.S.

1. The rules may have been imprecisely formulated. For example the rule /n/ is substituted for by [d] initially perhaps should have had added to it, "if not deleted."
2. The older subjects may have developed past the consistent use of certain rules, having acquired reading skills. For example younger subjects rarely included /k, g/ in clusters, but the older subjects did so inconsistently.

3. The nonsense words may have been badly designed, being mainly one-syllable *CVC* words, they may have been too simple to elicit errors, for example, the high number of correct productions of /k, g/ initially.

Whatever the reason for some rules failing to have predictive value, the fact that most were predictive of another group of deaf children's phonological errors on nonsense words, that is words that could not have been taught, validates the finding that the deaf acquire an at least partially rule-governed phonological system.

Effect of Differing Inputs

The role of lipreading in the acquisition of structured phonological systems by the deaf is clarified by the results of the comparison of the different outputs gained by using reading and lipreading as inputs. Most of the phonological features were unaffected by the nature of the input (nasal plus consonant clusters, /s/ preconsonantally, /p, b/ plus /l, r/ consonant clusters, /n/ initially and /m/ everywhere) and this may be taken as an indication that phonological systems acquired by the deaf are relatively stable.

However, some phones which are difficult to lip-read were affected by a change of input. For example, when reading, subjects retained /k, g/ in /kl, kr, kw, gl, gr/ clusters and deleted /l, r, w/, as compared to no preferred rule in the lipreading condition and the deletion of /k, g/ by the younger children when producing the same clusters. Also, when reading, subjects made fewer errors on /k, g/ when it occurred finally; and produced either correct or rule-governed productions of /k, g/ initially, as compared to the lipreading condition.

Obviously subjects were gaining more information about /k, g/ when reading than when lipreading and were thus able to produce it correctly more often. As pointed out earlier, the place and manner of articulation of velars makes them difficult to lip-read, and this result is therefore unsurprising. However, the finding that the older deaf children's treatment of /k, g/ in the lipreading condition was similar to that of the young children in their spontaneous utterances is important because it may indicate that lipreading is a primary source of information which deaf children use for partially governing their phonological output.

If further research confirms the indications of the results presented, and deaf children are found to be gaining information about phonological systems through lipreading, and are using a phonological system similar to that of normal-hearing children, two implications concerning general phonological acquisition theory will have to be considered.

First, the role of vision may be playing a more important role in the acquisition of phonological systems in hearing children than is at present indicated in the literature. This suggestion has already been hinted at by von Raffler Engel (1965) who noted that her son observed her lip movements in the early stages of his phonological development and "combined auditory and visual attentiveness" in attempting to pronounce words.

Second, the processes governing phonological output may be to some extent independent of input modality. Morton (1970) proposed that once information is transferred to a long-term store, it is independent of input modality. Thus, whether the information is gained through either the visual or auditory modality, that information which is transferred to the cognitive system (or long-term store) should be identical. Morton proposed that the form of information stored is semantic, and does not necessarily include phonological representation.

The findings of the exploratory studies presented suggest that the phonological systems of the deaf are partially rule-governed, dependent to some

3. LINGUISTIC DEVELOPMENT

extent on lipreading as an input, but also able to include information provided by written representations of speech. Further research is needed to describe the nature and extent of the phonological systems used. Results from work in this field should prove to be relevant for developmental phonological theory, and also for the teaching of deaf children.

APPENDIX A

Spontaneous Deviant Utterances of Deaf Children Used in Experiment 1

[ænd]	hand	[souːə]	soldier	[treɪ]	train
[æd]	hand	[sɛk]	snake	[laɪ]	lion
[ʃak]	snake	[təweɪn]	train	[kɒk]	clock
[æs]	house	[dif]	leaf	[bɜʒ]	bridge
[baɪs]	mice	[las]	glass	[dʒ]	train
[lɒk]	clock	[ʒʌmp]	jump	[eɪp]	leaf
[brɪd]	bridge	[bɪsət]	biscuit	[la]	glass
[reɪn]	train	[ɛləfən]	elephant	[tɛʔəl]	kettle
[das]	glass	[tɛləvɪn]	television	[toudə]	soldier
[kɛkəl]	kettle	[ɒrin]	orange	[ʌbɜrʌ]	zebra
[sɪpɪn]	skipping	[patou]	tomato	[fæːə]	flower
[dʌmp]	jump	[danʌ]	banana	[hæn]	hand
[æbə]	hammer	[læːə]	flower	[ɜl]	girl
[pɛntəl]	pencil	[ʌmbəlʌ]	umbrella	[neɪk]	snake
[poutbæ]	postman	[ɛdə]	eggs	[au]	house
[ɔrɪd]	orange	[dɛθə]	nest	[lou]	clock
[fɛdə]	feather	[brɛʒ]	bridge	[dæp]	jam
[djɛlou]	yellow	[treɪ]	train	[lim]	leaf
[gɛdrɪd]	zebra	[hæbəl]	hammer	[gat]	glass
[dɛl]	nail	[soulsʌ]	soldier	[bɪkət]	biscuit
[fɪs]	fish	[dɛbrʌ]	zebra	[dədə]	feather
[flæwəd]	flower	[paubə]	flower	[sɛlou]	yellow
[win]	queen	[su]	show	[fɪ]	fish
[spu]	spoon	[pu]	spoon	[wi]	queen
[ʌbri]	umbrella	[ʌbəbə]	umbrella	[ʌbəlʌ]	umbrella
[hæd]	hand	[dʒ]	girl	[bɪɪ]	mice
[nɛt]	nest	[aut]	house	[poubi]	postman
[soudjə]	soldier	[hæ]	hand	[gɒ]	clock
[bə]	bridge	[dam]	jam	[weɪ]	train
[ləp]	leaf	[dæt]	glass	[tɪpi]	skipping
[dʌp]	jump	[bɪdi]	biscuits	[kæbəl]	hammer
[lɒwi]	lorry	[tɛlibən]	television	[bɛdə]	feather
[bakou]	tomato	[dɛə]	chair	[du]	shoe
[bə]	nail	[ɛlou]	yellow	[pɛntu]	pencil
[nɛ]	nest	[ɛ]	girl	[neɪ]	snake
[ɛ]	house	[læm]	jam	[æ]	train
[pous]	post	[ri]	drink	[ɪp]	skipping
[ɛːɛ]	elephant	[ɛlʌ]	television	[ʌnə]	onions
[souːə]	soldier	[u]	shoe	[jəl]	girl
[gʌp]	jump	[pətu]	pencil	[pɛðə]	feather
[hauʃ]	house	[makou]	tomato	[hæmən̩]	hammer
[ɔʃɪʃ]	onions	[dɪk]	queen	[tʃu]	show
[ˈkəl]	nail	[plæːən]	flower	[dədanʌ]	banana
[lɛlou]	yellow	[pɛdə]	feather	[tousdə]	soldier
[poumæn]	postman	[reɪp]	grape	[dʒæb]	jam
[bɪːɪt]	biscuit	[gɜ]	girl	[mə] ´	milk

APPENDIX B

Nonsense Words Used as Stimuli for the Deaf*

kwan	yin	gred	zan
kruv	nuk	glep	nid
klig	pref	spid	brup
geb	plaf	yemet	blep
zok	dumil	mak	huk
veg	hif	zug	jom

*Not phonetic transcription

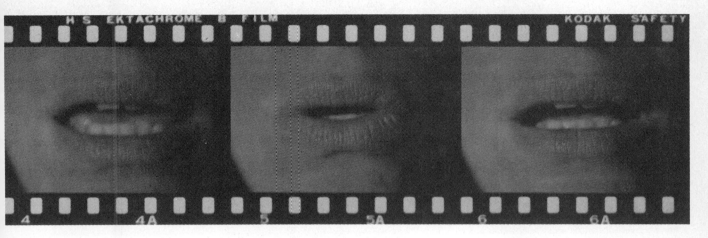

CAN....YOUR...EYES....
RE- PLACE...YOUR..EARS?

DAVID C GUILBERT

PEOPLE DIDN'T SEEM to be talking as loud as they used to. Our radio and TV didn't come through as clear as they had been. Even my cat's meow sounded muffled. Could it be my hearing was slipping?

"Yes," my ear doctor said as he read my test graphs. "About half the hearing in your left ear is gone. But we can help. First we can find a hearing aid for the weakened ear. Then I recommend that, as a hedge against possible future hearing losses, you take a course in lip-reading and train yourself to watch lips instead of eyes."

Accepting my hearing loss wasn't easy at first. With one good ear and half the other, I kept trying to convince myself that I wasn't having much trouble with ordinary conversation. Yet I did buy the hearing aid and, after patient practice, found it invaluable.

Gimmick or Godsend?

Then, as I talked with friends, I gradually made a determined effort to follow their lips. I wondered if anyone actually could learn to substitute seeing for hearing. Was lip-reading a gimmick—or a Godsend?

I started by asking various people what they knew about lip-reading. Some said they thought it was a delusion, worthless. A few, who told me they had attended such classes, found lip-reading either "difficult" or "impossible." An article by Bern Keating in *TV Guide*, quoting the principal of the Mississippi School for the Deaf, Hugh Prickett, said that lip-reading was 70% guesswork and 30% knowing what the other fellow was saying anyhow!

At the same time, I heard of fantastic successes—such as a young man who read lips so skillfully he almost passed an army physical exam until the doctor spoke behind him.

Increasingly, even though I still doubted its value, the idea of studying lip-reading challenged me. If others could read lips, so could I.

Cross-section of people

I enrolled in an evening class in lip-reading in a community college. Among the 11 students were a couple of alert, elderly women, a teacher of speech, a war veteran whose doctor had told him he'd lose all his hearing within three years, a utility service man, and a supermarket manager—all, like me, with some degree of hearing losses.

Our instructor talked without making a sound. She had unlimited patience and an immense supply of smiling encouragement.

In each session, a list of scientifically selected key words on a blackboard gave us a clue to the sentences we were expected to read from our teacher's lips or those of fellow students. Each person's mouth moved differently. Some lips danced, others hardly quivered. Many words looked exactly alike—for example: may, pay, bay.

More often than not, I understood little or nothing. Yet several of my classmates seemed to read those moving lips easily.

Then suddenly, my good right ear went totally deaf overnight. Instead of an ear and a half, I had only half an ear. My doctor recommended a more powerful hearing aid and recommended I keep at lip reading. When I fliply asked, "How about learning sign language?" he replied, "How many of your friends know sign language?"

Meanwhile, my lip-reading instructor urged me not to be discouraged. "Some learn more readily than others," she said. "You seem to be a perfectionist who wants to read every word. That's impossible. Many words aren't visible on the lips. Try to relax and get the general sense of the sentence."

Discouraged and frustrated

Frankly, I was discouraged. I was also frustrated and despairing.

Lip-reading was the most difficult

"Can...Your...Eyes...Re-Place...Your...Ears?" David C. Guilbert, *Retirement Living*, Vol. 17 No. 8, August 1977. ©1977 Retirement Living.

3. LINGUISTIC DEVELOPMENT

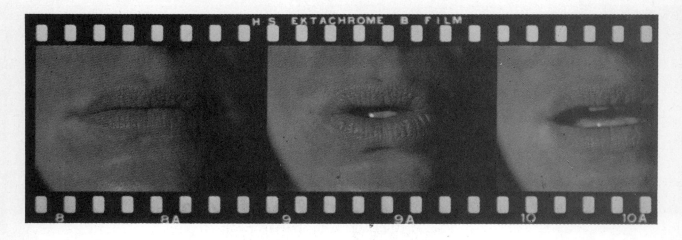

thing I'd ever tried to learn. I was worn out after concentrating so hard in the classes and after each day's 30-minute practice at home. I was ready to throw everything overboard. It seemed much easier to retreat into silence and let my friends, activities, and the rest of the world go by.

Then I forced myself to look at the alternatives. Was I really willing to give up, to cut myself off from everybody around me? I reread part of "Introduction to Speechreading," a booklet issued by the Sonotone Corporation, which said: "One of the problems of deafness is that it brings indifference. We cease to make an effort, and sink into a slough of unconcern.... We are almost persuaded that no one cares...and we are ready to abandon hope that anyone ever will..."

Most certainly, I could not accept a life like that. Here I was, retired from a successful career, in good health with what looked like many years of living still ahead. Lip-reading *must* offer a way to retain my interest in the future.

Hope or hopelessness?

I plunged into my studies again. I took private lessons. I offered myself as a guinea pig for training by graduate students in a college speech and hearing clinic.

I'm not sure exactly when the breakthrough occurred. But one day I went in for a hearing check-up which included a word comprehension test. The audiologist shut me in a sound-proof room and read a list of words to me through a window to see how many I could repeat accurately. I looked through a window at him as he read to me: "Say the word WATERFALL. Say the word PUMPKIN. Say..." I repeated almost every word until he took a card and covered his mouth—immediately I began to flounder.

At that point I realized I *had* learned enough lip-reading to subconsciously recognize many words. I *was* progressing.

I began to think more positively. I realized my classes had taught me several helpful tactics for the hard of hearing. Here are some I believe can help others to use whatever hearing and natural lip-reading ability they may have:

✔ *Get your back to the light.* When you're about to talk to somebody, place yourself so the light falls on the lips you're watching. You'll see them more easily. If you're in a group, move so the light is best on as many faces as possible.

✔ *Stay six feet away.* Keep away from the person who wants to yell in your ear. The best distance for lip-reading is six feet. This space lets you see not only lips but also other facial expressions and gestures, all of which help your understanding.

✔ *Don't hesitate to ask for help.* If you're having trouble understanding someone, ask the speaker to talk more slowly. This usually means the person will speak more clearly. If you're in a noisy place, and you need to carry on an important conversation, ask to move to a quieter spot.

Lip-reading instructor demonstrates lip position for long oo sound. Practicing before a mirror (below) is a good way to perfect your technique.

Most people are willing to oblige. On the other hand, if you are at a party where the noise is loud and the conversation is strictly chitchat, circulate from one small group to another greeting friends, and let it go at that.

Easier with familiarization

✔ *Broaden your interests.* Keep up with the news and local events. The better informed you are, the more readily you'll be able to pick up on a conversation by recognizing familiar words on the lips around you.

Even though I'm still far from being a "fluent" lip-reader, I can say that these helpful tips have benefited me greatly.

Looking back, I realize how much I profited by studying lip-reading to offset the dismaying effects of my hearing loss. Not only did lip-reading classes give me something to do each week, they also forced me to join others with similar problems and recognize I was not alone.

In these sessions I learned much about deafness—for example, that odd ear noises (whistles, swishes, thumps, and clicks) do not signal sinister diseases as some of us first suspect; also that hearing aids can usually be used most effectively with practice and experimentation.

Perhaps most serious of all, I learned that many of us foolishly put off facing up to our hearing loss. I've had people say to me, "Oh, I'm not deaf enough to study lip-reading, or I don't need an aid yet. I'll wait until I can't hear." From my experience, I feel delay is a terrible mistake.

If lip-reading is undertaken in the early stages of deafness, helpful habits can be acquired that make comprehension easier as deafness progresses.

Locating classes

Where can you find lip-reading classes? I suggest starting with the nearest community college or university, to see if it offers lip-reading among the adult education courses given for a small fee. In larger cities there are often lip-reading teachers in private practice. Large hospitals, particularly those connected with medical schools, sometimes have speech specialists who may give instruction, and the Veteran's Administration has a number of audiological centers.

Studying at home

Materials for studying lip-reading at home may be obtained from the Alexander Graham Bell Association for the Deaf, 3417 Volta Place N.W., Washington, DC, 20007, or the National Association of Hearing and Speech Agencies, 814 Thayer Avenue, Silver Springs, MD 20910. For small fees, both organizations distribute pamphlets on speech-reading, and may be able to refer you to classes and teachers near you.

Unfortunately, some people with normal hearing look on a hearing loss as a humorous nuisance. But I can assure you it's no joke. Friends, families, jobs, whole patterns of living are often at stake.

Yet a hearing loss is not the end of the world either. I'm reminded of the spunky, 80-year-old woman in one of my classes, who said, "I'm determined to learn to read lips. I'm not ready to be banished from the human race." Neither am I.

Computer-aided Speech Training for the Deaf

R. S. Nickerson, D. N. Kalikow, and K. N. Stevens

Bolt Beranek and Newman Inc., Cambridge, Massachusetts

An effort to develop a computer-based system of speech-training aids for the deaf is reported. The system is described, as are four different types of visual displays that have been programmed to date. The use of the system in a school for the deaf and an attempt to evaluate its effectiveness are described. The importance of close collaboration between researchers and teachers on efforts to develop innovative training aids is emphasized, as is the need to resolve some basic pedagogical issues.

This paper reports an effort to develop a computer-based system of speech-training aids for the deaf. The use of nonauditory displays of speech parameters to facilitate the teaching of speech to the deaf is not a new idea. In recent years, numerous instruments have been developed to produce a variety of visual and tactile patterns for use in training situations (Levitt, 1973; Pickett, 1968). Some of these displays depict certain speech parameters such as fundamental frequency and amplitude envelope as functions of time (Anderson, 1960; Boothroyd, 1972; Borrild, 1968; Martony, 1968). Others provide representations of the instantaneous spectrum shape (Risberg, 1968; Searson, 1965), or the presence or absence of certain speech features or specific sounds (Borrild, 1968; Martony, 1970; Pronovost, 1947).

The utilization of a computer as the heart of a system of such training aids is a relatively new idea. One reason for using a computer in this way is the flexibility that one gains thereby: not only does it become feasible to incorporate in one system many of the types of displays that have been implemented on specially designed devices in the past, but changes to displays that would require hardware modifications in special purpose devices can often be realized by program changes in a computer-based system. Another inducement for computer use is the fact that the computer's processing speed offers the potential for performing analyses on the speech signal that would be difficult, if not impossible, to accomplish in real time otherwise, and to display the results of these analyses in a very large variety of ways.

THE SYSTEM

The system is built around a minicomputer, the Digital Equipment Corporation PDP-8E. Speech information is obtained by means of a miniature accelerometer attached by double-stick tape either to the throat or the nose and a voice microphone. When the accelerometer (which weighs less than 2 g)

"Computer-Aided Speech Training for the Deaf," R.S. Nickerson, D.M. Kalikow, K.N. Stevens, *Journal of Speech and Hearing Research*, Vol. 41 No. 1, February 1976. ©1976 Journal of Speech and Hearing Research.

is attached to the throat, its output is fed to a circuit that measures pitch periods. When attached to the nose it measures the vibration on the nasal surface, which is used as an indication of the amount of acoustic coupling to the nasal cavity through the velopharyngeal port (Stevens, Kalikow, and Willemain, 1975). The output of the voice microphone is fed into a filter bank that determines the amplitude in each of 19 frequency bands within the range 100-6560 Hz. Data from the pitch extractor or nasalization circuit and the filter bank are sampled by the computer 100 times per second and used to generate a variety of visual displays. Control inputs from the user are given to the computer via a set of push buttons and knobs. Further details concerning the system are given in Nickerson and Stevens (1972, 1973).

DISPLAYS

Displays are generated by four independent programs, which we refer to as: (1) ball game, (2) vertical spectrum, (3) cartoon face, and (4) time plot. The fourth of these programs has been used most extensively and has evolved to the greatest extent.

Ball Game

The intent in developing the ball game program was to implement a display that would be motivating to a young child, and that would permit him to develop some speech-related skills in a gamelike situation. The game starts with several balls positioned in the lower left corner of the display. When the child starts voicing, a ball begins to move at a fixed rate toward the wall at the right of the display, its height being determined by the value of some parameter of the speaker's voice, for example, its pitch. The child's task is to make the ball go through the hole in the wall. If he succeeds, the ball drops in the basket that is positioned to the right of the wall, and a smiling face appears in the upper right corner of the display (see Figure 1a).[1] If the ball is either too high or too low to go through the hole, it bounces from the wall back to the starting position, and the child may try again. Both the height of the hole in the wall and its width are adjustable by the teacher. Such adjustments are made by turning appropriate control knobs.

In a more complicated version of the ball game display, a second wall may be added to the left of the first one (see Figure 1b). By adjusting the distance between the walls and positioning the holes at different heights, the teacher can define a task in which the child must make his pitch rise or fall by specific

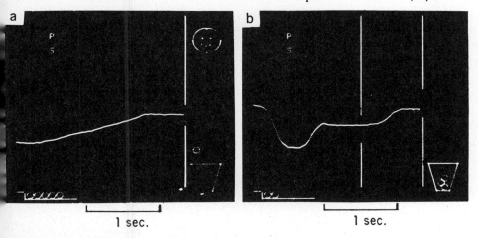

1 sec.   1 sec.

Figure 1. Ball game display. *a:* successful attempt with one-wall display. *b:* fourth success about to be achieved with two-wall display. The P and S at the upper left of each display indicate that the parameter that is being displayed is pitch and that the speaker who is producing the display is the student.

---

[1] All of the figures representing displays in this report were made by taking Polaroid snapshots of a "slave" oscilloscope that shows a duplicate, in miniature, of the display at the teacher-student station.

amounts within a certain time interval in order to be able to get the ball in the basket. The positions of the holes and their widths (in Hertz and fractions of an octave, respectively), and the distance of each wall from the starting position (in milliseconds) are displayed on demand.

Vertical Spectrum

The operation of the vertical-spectrum display is illustrated in Figure 2. Each shape in this figure is determined by the frequency spectrum of the sound from which the shape is generated. The width of the shape at a given height is proportional to the energy (on a logarithmic scale) within a specific frequency band. Voiced and voiceless sounds are distinguished by the presence and absence of the horizontal lines, respectively.

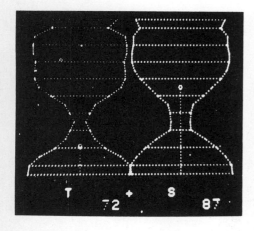

Figure 2. Vertical spectrum display. Left and right figures produced by male and female speakers, respectively, during utterance of the vowel /i/ in the word "be." The T and S below the shapes identify the teacher's and the student's displays, respectively.

The pitch of the speaker's voice is represented by the length of the "lollipop" rising from the center of the base. Note that in the example shown in Figure 2 the two shapes, both of which represent the vowel /i/, are quite similar in spite of the fact that the left one was produced by a male speaker with a fundamental frequency of about 100 Hz, and the right one by a female speaker with a fundamental frequency of about 210 Hz.

The right-hand shape in this display changes continuously as the student speaks, unless he is sustaining a steady sound. The shape on the left may be used as a standard that the student may be asked to match. In order to generate a standard, the teacher makes a sound and "freezes" the display by pressing a button when he has produced the desired shape. The student's (right-hand) display may also be frozen; and it may be transferred to the left side of the display where it can serve as a standard for future attempts at matching.

Whenever either of these displays is frozen, the computer retains a record of the speech that immediately preceded the freezing of the shape. The teacher can instruct the computer to replay either stored speech sample and to redisplay it as it is being replayed. The replay can itself be frozen at any given point and inspected frame by frame, if that is desired. The numbers below the shapes in Figure 2 indicate the replay in this case was frozen with the teacher's display on Frame 72 and the student's on Frame 87. The total number of frames in each sample is 100.

Cartoon Face

The cartoon face display is illustrated in Figure 3. The idea here was to develop a display in which several aspects of speech could be represented simultaneously in a single integrated scene. The presence of an Adam's apple on the throat signifies the presence of voicing, its height indicates the fundamental frequency of the voiced sound, loudness is represented by the size of the mouth, and the detection of an *s* or *z* is indicated by the appearance of the letter *s* or *z* in the cartoonist's balloon.

Time Plot

The time-plot program, which has been used most extensively to date, has the capability for displaying several aspects of speech as functions of time. Pressing a specific button causes a "menu," such as that shown in Figure 4, to appear on the display. An option may then be selected by pressing another button. The menu shown in Figure 4 represents the functions that are currently implemented in the time-plot program. It is not expected that all of these functions will be equally useful, or even that all of them will survive a period of testing. The list has already changed several times, and it is likely to undergo further changes as the program continues to evolve.

If the user selects the first option on the menu, speech amplitude, or what we loosely call loudness, is displayed as a function of time. This display tends

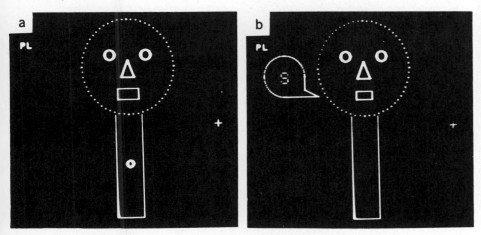

Figure 3. Cartoon face display. *a:* responding to a voiced sample of speech, showing the Adam's apple at a position related to the most recently sampled pitch, and the mouth opened proportionally to the loudness of the voice signal. *b:* the display during an unvoiced sample meeting the criterion for the *s*-detector. The PL indicates that the display is responding to pitch and loudness: the plus sign (+) indicates that the program is ready to accept more speech input.

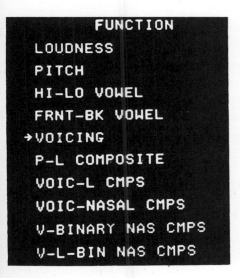

Figure 4. Time-plot program: function menu.

to indicate the fluctuations in intensity from one syllable to the next with minima during the consonantal intervals and maxima during the vowels.

Selection of the second menu option would result in a display of fundamental frequency, or pitch, as a function of time. The top tracing in Figure 5 shows this display for the utterance "It's a pencil," spoken with normal intonation; the bottom tracing represents the same utterance, but spoken in a monotone voice. Segments of the display for which no points are plotted represent either voiceless sounds or silent intervals. Figure 5 also illustrates the fact that the time-plot program provides for the possibility of representing two utterances on the display simultaneously. Typically, this feature is used for the purpose of providing the child with a pattern to match. The teacher makes an utterance and "freezes" the resulting tracing on the top half of the display. The child then attempts to make the same utterance and match the teacher's tracing with one of his own on the bottom half of the display.

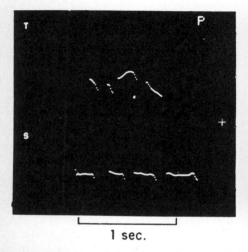

1 sec.　　　　　　1 sec.

Figure 5. Displays of fundamental frequency, or pitch, of the voiced segments of the utterance "It's a pencil," with appropriate intonation (top); with monotone voice (bottom). The T and S identify the teacher's and student's display areas, respectively.

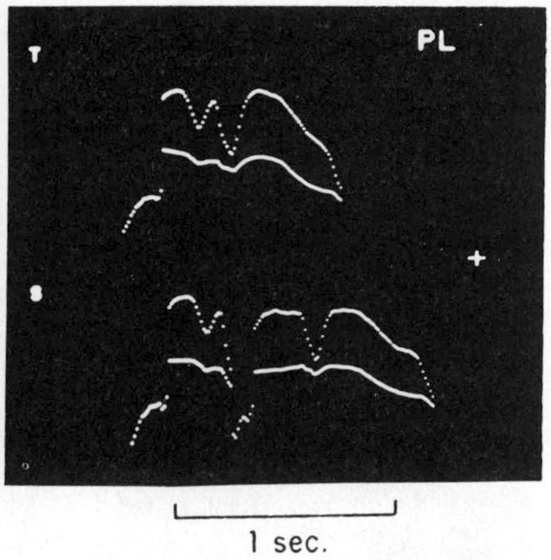

Figure 6. Pitch-loudness composite display for a male speaker's utterance of two sentences. Top: "She's a girl." Bottom: "She's a tall girl." See text.

The next two display options shown on the function menu, high-low and front-back, were developed originally for use in a system to aid in the teaching of correct pronunciation to learners of a second language (Kalikow and Swets, 1972). The high-low function is related to the frequency of the first formant, and the front-back function is similarly related to the frequency of the second formant. The first- and second-formant frequencies are known to be related to tongue height and to the front-back position of the tongue body, respectively (Peterson and Barney, 1952). Therefore, these displays are used to represent approximations of tongue position in both the high-low and front-back dimensions. While these functions are effective in displaying the high-low and front-back phonetic dimensions for individuals with normal, nonnasal vowel quality, the interpretation of the display is more ambiguous for deaf children with breathy voice quality or with excessive nasalization.

The voicing display shows a horizontal line whenever voicing is present, and nothing otherwise. This display can be used with suitable utterances to represent timing and rhythmic properties of speech. Typically, voicing is not shown by itself, but in combination with other parameters such as loudness or nasalization, as will be explained below.

Each of the time-function displays that has been described so far represents a single aspect of speech in isolation. The program provides the user also with several displays of combinations of features. Figure 6 is an example of a display that represents pitch and loudness in combination. The upper record represents the sentence "She's a girl"; the bottom one, "She's a tall girl." Two tracings are associated with each voiced segment of an utterance; the bottom tracing represents pitch and the top one loudness. The loudness function is plotted relative to the pitch tracing; each point being the sum of the pitch and loudness values at that point in time. Unvoiced sounds are represented by only a single tracing, which is the loudness function. Thus, in the lower record in Figure 6, one can distinguish two voiced and two unvoiced segments. The two unvoiced segments correspond to the fricative consonant /ʃ/ with which the utterance begins, and the voiceless /t/ at the beginning of the word "tall."

The display shown in Figure 7 is similar to that shown in Figure 6, except that here voicing instead of pitch is represented in combination with loudness. In this case, the phrase is "the teacher," spoken with a normal temporal pattern (top) and with a slower than normal tempo such as is often found in the speech of deaf children (bottom). Both of these displays (Figures 6 and 7) can be used to show patterns of timing and stress. They can also be used to assist the training of articulation. Missing or adventitious sounds, and in some cases

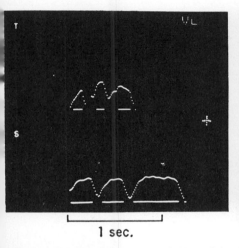

Figure 7. Voicing-loudness composite displays of the utterance "the teacher," spoken with normal timing (top) and with abnormally slow tempo (bottom).

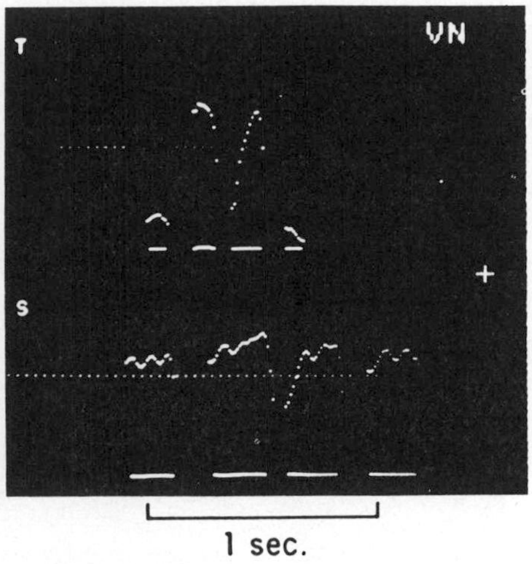

Figure 8. Voicing-nasalization composite display, for the utterance "You can drink it," spoken with proper velar control (top) and with all of the vowels nasalized (bottom). Concerning the horizontal dotted lines, see text.

speech-sound substitutions, often can be seen fairly clearly. Confusions between voiced and voiceless speech sounds may also be detected in this display.

The displays shown in Figure 8 combine representations of voicing and of nasalization. Whereas velar control has long been recognized to be a problem for many deaf speakers, not many attempts have been made to obtain objective measures of nasalization that could be used in real-time speech-training displays. The nasalization function illustrated in Figure 8 does distinguish between nasalized and nonnasalized sounds produced by speakers with normal hearing. The tracings shown in the figure represent the phrase "You can drink it." The top tracing shows how the display looks when only the nasal consonants and the preceding vowels are nasalized. In the utterance represented by the bottom tracing all of the vowels are nasalized. The solid lines below the nasalization functions represent voicing in these displays. The horizontal dotted lines in Figure 8 represent "criterion values" that can be adjusted by the teacher. In this example, the contours lie above the criterion line for nasalized vowels and below the line for nonnasalized vowels.

For some purposes one may wish to think of nasalization as a binary attribute. The final two display options shown on the menu in Figure 4 provide this possibility. Both of these displays represent voicing and nasalization in combination, each as a binary attribute. The last option, which is illustrated in Figure 9, represents loudness in addition to these other properties; a single horizontal line indicates voicing; double horizontal lines bracketing the voicing line indicate nasalization, and the curved tracing represents loudness. The

3. LINGUISTIC DEVELOPMENT

nasalization lines appear whenever the nasalization function exceeds the criterion that has been set by the user. Figure 9 represents the same utterance as does Figure 8 ("You can drink it"), and the criteria were set as indicated by the horizontal dotted lines on the latter figure. Thus, the bracketing horizontal lines shown in Figure 9 are associated with those segments of the speech for which the nasalization traces in Figure 8 rise above the criterion lines.

There is little doubt that the features represented in the various time-plot displays that have been described play important roles in the production and understanding of speech. There is a degree of arbitrariness, however, concerning the ways in which these features have been encoded in these displays. The use of time functions has a certain face validity inasmuch as speech is describable in terms of a set of time-varying properties. Moreover, representing time spatially means that the display has a "memory," which makes quite distinct some short-lived aspects of an utterance that might be difficult to detect in a display that represented properties of the speech only for the extent of their duration in real time. For example, the fleeting initial plosive in "testify" would be difficult to distinguish from the initial voiced consonant in "destitute" in a continuously changing real-time display with no memory, such as the spectral representation illustrated in Figure 2. The difference is easy to see, however, in the voicing-loudness time plots shown in Figure 10. A disadvantage in the use of time functions is the fact that many features cannot easily be represented simultaneously in an integrated fashion. Showing several time functions in parallel on the same display is a possibility; it is not clear, however, that the viewer can make effective use of such a display. Experimentation will undoubtedly be required not only to determine the relative utility of various types of information for speech training, but also to

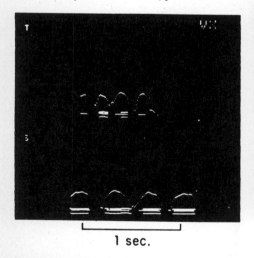

Figure 9. Voicing-loudness-binary nasalization composite display for the utterances represented in Figure 8. The nasalization criteria were set as indicated by the horizontal dotted lines in Figure 8.

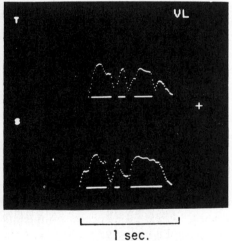

Figure 10. Voicing-loudness composite display for a male speaker's utterance of two three-syllable words. Top: "destitute"; bottom: "testify." Note breaks in the loudness function caused by total vocal-tract closure for the three medial occurrences of the /t/ in the two words.

evolve optimal ways of encoding that information for visual, or perhaps tactual, presentation.

Display-mode Options

Each of the function displays described in the preceding paragraphs can be operated in each of three modes. In graph mode, the display is generated from left to right as the speaker talks. The "now" position moves from left to right at a rate of about 9.3 cm per sec. When the display drops off the right-hand side of the screen, it "wraps around" and reappears on the left-hand side. This is the conventional mode of operation of standard oscilloscope displays. In flow mode, the "now" point is fixed at the right-hand side of the display and the past moves off to the left as the speech is produced. This is analogous to the operation of conventional strip-chart recorders. In delay mode, the function is not displayed while it is being generated, but only later, on demand. The display can be shown, for example, in order to confirm or invalidate the child's own evaluation of his effort to perform some task. This option is used to attempt to teach the child to rely on kinesthetic cues for judging his performance, and thereby to facilitate transfer of what he learns in the speech laboratory to everyday speech.

Additional Features. Two control knobs determine the heights of the two dotted horizontal lines across the face of the display (see Figure 8). One of these lines is associated with the teacher's display region (upper half of scope), and the other with the student's display region (lower half of scope). Each line is moved up and down by turning the associated control knob clockwise and counterclockwise, respectively, and can be made to disappear by turning the knob clockwise as far as it will go. The height of the lines may be determined at any time by pressing a button which causes a number to appear on each line designating the height of that line in terms of an arbitrary scale of 0–400. In the case of the pitch display, the number represents the fundamental frequency, in Hertz.

To use the lines as criteria, the teacher may adjust them to a position that represents the level of some parameter to which the student is to relate his speech. For example, if the student's problem is hypernasality, the teacher might adjust a line for use with the nasalization display and ask the student to attempt to keep the nasalization tracing below that line while producing speech sounds that should not be nasalized. Or, if the problem is falsetto voice, a similar procedure might be followed with the pitch display. The teacher may, of course, adjust a criterion to more and more demanding levels as the student acquires more skill at the task.

In addition to the horizontal lines the user can also display and adjust two vertical lines, either to set criteria for timing or to take duration measurements from a displayed trace.

USE AND EVALUATION OF THE SYSTEM

We want to stress that we do not view the system as a finished product. The project was begun with the assumption that an attempt to design a system of speech-training aids would probably fail and that a more promising approach would be to attempt to evolve one through use. Accordingly, the approach that was taken was to attempt to use the system as it was being developed, and then to utilize the insights gained by users to provide guidance concerning the directions that the modifications and extensions of its capabilities should take. The system was installed, therefore, at the Clarke School for the Deaf, Northampton, Massachusetts, as soon as it had been developed sufficiently to be used in a remedial speech-training program. To assure that the insights gained by the users did in fact guide the system's evolution, developers and users have been engaged in a continual dialogue concerning the desirability and feasibility of specific modifications and extensions, both in the training procedures that are used in conjunction with the system and in the characteristics of the system itself. The evaluative data have been collected more to provide an objective basis for eliminating displays and training procedures that are not effective and for improving those that show promise than to establish the effectiveness of the system per se.

About 40 students have been given speech training with the aid of the system, usually on a daily basis (20-minute sessions) for periods of 7–14 weeks. The system is used both in tutoring situations in which a teacher instructs a child and in unsupervised drill sessions in which a child works by himself. Tutorial sessions consist of various types of exercises graded in difficulty. The exercises that are used with a given child depend, of course, on what aspect of his speech is being emphasized. In general, however, they include both (1) "vocal gymnastics," in which the student practices such activities as sustaining certain vowel or consonant sounds, producing simple nonsense syllables or sequences of such syllables; and (2) production of meaningful utterances of various lengths, selected to contain the speech gestures of interest. Use of the system in self-instruction mode is attempted only by students who have had some experience in the tutorial sessions.

Although the system was developed primarily for use in speech training, it has also been applied to the diagnosis of speech deficiencies, the evaluation of training effects, and the collection of normative data regarding the characteristics of the speech of both deaf and hearing persons. The usefulness of the system for these applications stems from its ability to make quantitative measurements on various aspects of either live or recorded speech. Each of the display programs described has the capability of producing, on request, values of the speech parameters that are currently being displayed. An additional program has been written for the purpose of analyzing recorded speech.

The types of evaluative data that have been obtained include daily and weekly records maintained by the tutors concerning the objectives and accomplishments of the children during individual training sessions, subjective evaluations by each tutor of the overall progress of his students over the course of his training program, objective data on relevant acoustic characteristics of test utterances, listener judgments concerning specific speech features, and measures of intelligibility. Some of the resulting data have been presented elsewhere (Boothroyd, Nickerson, and Stevens, 1974; Boothroyd et al., 1975; Stevens et al., 1974). Briefly, they show that the training that has been done with the help of the system was effective in improving the students' speech in objectively measurable and perceptually detectable ways. Specifically, improvements were obtained in timing (including reduction in the durations of pauses, shortening of the durations of unstressed vowels, and increase in syllable production rate), in velar control, in pitch control (including lowering of pitch range, production of pitch fall at the end of an utterance, reduction in incidence of inadvertent pitch jumps), in voice quality, and in some articulatory skills. The amount of improvement obtained varied considerably from child to child and was greater for material that was used during training than for unrehearsed material and spontaneous speech. Measurable improvements in overall intelligibility of unrehearsed speech were not demonstrated for most students. We attribute the failure to obtain noticeable improvements in intelligibility in part to the relatively short period of time that was spent with each child, and in part to a lack of understanding of how specific speech features must be modified to realize such improvements. Ultimately, of course, the value of such a system will be judged in terms of its ability to help improve intelligibility and overall speech quality.

On balance, we consider the results encouraging and generally supportive of the idea that the computer represents a potentially powerful tool to apply to the difficult problem of teaching speech to the deaf. It seems clear, however, that how effective any speech-training aids will be in practice will depend very much on the specific ways in which they are used. Moreover, as technical developments provide increasingly sophisticated methods for the analysis of speech and the generation of displays, pedagogical uncertainties are likely to come more and more to the fore as the factors that really limit what one can expect to accomplish with speech-training aids. It also seems clear to us that the flexibility of a computer-based system provides opportunities for the type of exploration that is likely to be required to make progress on these types of problems.

The sort of close collaboration between researchers and teachers that we have attempted to maintain in this project is essential, we believe, if efforts to evolve effective training aids are to have a reasonable chance of success. Many writers have expressed the need for such collaboration (Borrild, 1968; Denes, 1968; Kopp, 1938). The strategy is a reasonable one, we feel, not only for the development of this particular system but for the development of any complex system that is to involve a close interaction between men and computers on problems for which approaches are not highly formalized and the solutions are not well understood. As David (1962) has pointed out, the great versatility of the computer represents both an opportunity and a challenge. The opportunity is for creativity and innovation; the challenge is to be discriminating and practical. A close interaction between a system's developers and its users is perhaps the only way to assure a balance of innovativeness and practicality from which something both new and useful may emerge.

ACKNOWLEDGMENT

K. N. Stevens is also affiliated with the Massachusetts Institute of Technology. Each of the following individuals has contributed significantly to the design, implementation, and use of the system described in this report: Robb Adams, Patricia Archambault, Arthur Boothroyd, Douglas Dodds, Ann Rollins, Robert Storm, and Thomas Willemain. This project was sponsored by the U.S. Office of Education Media Services and Captioned Films Branch of the Bureau of Education for the Handicapped, under Contract No. OEC-0-71-4670 (615). It is a pleasure to acknowledge the encouragement and helpful suggestions of Lois Elliott, who served as contract monitor during the initial stages of the project. Requests for reprints should be directed to Raymond S. Nickerson, Bolt Beranek and Newman Inc., 50 Moulton Street, Cambridge, Massachusetts 02138.

REFERENCES

ANDERSON, F., An experimental pitch indicator for training deaf scholars. *J. acoust. Soc. Am.,* **32,** 1065–1074 (1960).

BOOTHROYD, A., Sensory aids research project—Clarke School for the deaf. In G. Fant (Ed.), *Speech communication ability and profound deafness.* Washington, D.C.: A. G. Bell Association for the Deaf, 367–377 (1972).

BOOTHROYD, A., ARCHAMBAULT, P., ADAMS, R. E., and STORM, R. D., Use of a computer-based system of speech analysis and display in a remedial speech program for deaf children. *Volta Rev.,* **77,** 178–193 (1975).

BOOTHROYD, A., NICKERSON, R. S., and STEVENS, K. N., Temporal patterns in the speech of the

Communication Problems in Hearing Children of Deaf Parents

Naomi B. Schiff and Ira M. Ventry

The quality of a mother's speech to her child has traditionally been considered by speech pathologists, educators, and psychologists to have significant positive or negative implications for the child's speech and language development (Berry, 1969; Van Riper and Irwin, 1958; West, Ansberry, and Carr, 1957). Articulation errors and deviant phonatory and fluency patterns occurring in children and adults in the same family have often been interpreted as occurring on an imitation basis or as a consequence of inadequate speech and language models at home. However, no one has seriously raised the question as to why a large group of children from linguistically deprived environments (deaf

"Communication Problems in Hearing Children of Deaf Parents," Naomi B. Schiff, Ira M. Ventry, *Journal of Speech and Hearing Research*, Vol. 41 No. 3, August 1976. ©1976 Journal of Speech and Hearing Research.

families) have not been seen in prominent numbers in the speech clinics. This, despite the fact that one might expect a high prevalence of communicative disorders in this population.

A review of the literature has yielded only four studies concerning language or communication problems in these children. Two of these studies were case reports. One child came from a home in which manual communication was used (Todd, 1972), while the other came from a home where sign language was reportedly not used in communication with the child (Sachs and Johnson, 1972). Both of these children demonstrated syntactic or rule-learning deficits in their speech. Critchley (1967) studied three children and found one child who began school at five years of age with deviant articulation and some reading difficulty in the first grade. As the child matured, these problems disappeared. This child's spontaneous speech was also considered ungrammatical. A second child's verbal IQ scores were significantly lower than her nonverbal scores. No problem was noted in the remaining child. Brejle (1971) administered the Templin-Darley Tests of Articulation (Templin and Darley, 1969) and Peabody Picture Vocabulary Test (Dunn, 1959) to 56 subjects, 13 of whom were preschoolers. He found receptive vocabulary to be the same as that of the general population and articulation development to be better than that of the normal population.

There are a few published anecdotal reports which reveal contradictory observations of speech and language development in hearing children of deaf parents. Two observers report no speech and language problems in this population. Based on his experience with the deaf, Vernon (1974) concludes that hearing children of deaf parents do not have speech problems. Similarly, Lenneberg (1967) reported that he had observed several hearing children of deaf parents and concluded that "language onset is never delayed by this dramatically abnormal environment, even though the quality of vocalization of the preschool children tends to be different; children very soon become 'bilingual' in the sense that they use normal voice and speech for hearing adults and abnormal voice or 'deafisms' for the parents" (p. 137). On the other hand, Ervin-Tripp (1971) states, "We have observed two hearing children of deaf parents who heard a good deal of T.V. speech, but at three had not yet learned to understand or produce speech at all" (p. 195). Fant (1974), himself a hearing child of deaf parents, attributes his normal speech and language development to nearby hearing relatives. A slight deficiency in vocabulary disappeared before he reached the third grade.

In summary, there is very little information available concerning the communication problems of normal-hearing children of deaf parents. Most of these reports are either case reports of a few children or anecdotal reports. Only one study of a substantial number of children exists to date (Brejle, 1971), and the results of that study indicate normal articulation and vocabulary development. The purpose of this article is to report the results of these clinical evaluations in order to alert the professional community to the potential problems in this population.

EVALUATION PROCEDURES

Subjects

The only requirement for participation in this project was that both parents be deaf and that the child have normal hearing. This information was obtained from parental reports. No attempt was made to substantiate reports of the parents' deafness.

A total of 52 children from 34 families were evaluated. These children ranged in age from six months to 12 years. Subjects were referred from schools for the deaf, speech and hearing clinics, well-baby clinics, and the New York

3. LINGUISTIC DEVELOPMENT

Psychiatric Institute Project for the Deaf.[1] Families were asked to bring their children for evaluation at no expense to themselves, regardless of whether or not there appeared to be a problem. Therefore, it was not anticipated that the subjects referred would have a higher proportion of problems than the population they represented. However, this may not have been the case. It is likely that a program designed to evaluate and to provide therapy for hearing children of deaf parents would attract families suspecting communication difficulties. To our knowledge, however, only two families participated because problems were suspected.

Speech and Language

All children were assessed for their oral linguistic abilities relative to the normal population. The number of diagnostic sessions and specific procedures varied with the needs and age of each child and with the cooperation of the parents for follow-up evaluations. All evaluations were conducted either in the child's home or at the Teachers College Speech and Hearing Center. The evaluations were divided into two sessions: (1) an informal portion during which the examiner either conversed or played with the child and (2) a formal testing portion.

All children were primarily assessed for the following:

1. structure and function of the peripheral speech system
2. structure and meaning of utterances
   a. syntactic and morphological development
   b. cognitive notions expressed
   c. appropriateness of utterances relative to context
   d. organization and sequencing of material
3. phonemic development
4. stress and prosody patterns
5. vocabulary and word usage
6. vocal quality
7. comprehension of single words, phrases, sentences, and connected discourse
8. auditory discrimination

The time allotted to the informal portion varied with each child, but was not less than one-half hour with any child. For the younger children, the examiner had a variety of toys and the child was allowed to play with whatever he wished. The examiner followed the procedures for eliciting utterances as outlined by Bloom (1970, pp. 237–238), following the child's lead and talking in response to what the child did or said. For the older children conversation was directed around the child's interests (books, television, hobbies, daily activities).

All utterances obtained during the informal portion were recorded on a Sony cassette recorder TC90A. Most of the children were unaware they were being recorded. The tapes were analyzed for the structure and meaning of utterances relative to context, organization and sequencing of material, and speech characteristics.

The tests and scales listed below were routinely used in the formal evaluation:

1. A synthesis of the Anderson, Miles, and Matheny (1963) Communication Evaluation Chart, and Mecham (1971) and Doll (1966) developmental scales
2. Language and Learning Assessment for Training: Revised 1970 (Bangs, 1968)
3. Peabody Picture Vocabulary Test (PPVT) (Dunn, 1959)
4. Illinois Test of Psycholinguistic Abilities (ITPA) (Kirk, McCarthy, and Kirk, 1968)

---

[1]Subjects and their families were part of a research project conducted by New York Psychiatric Institute and were not being seen for psychiatric or psychological problems.

5. Templin-Darley Diagnostic and Screening Tests of Articulation (Templin and Darley, 1969)
6. Goldman-Fristoe-Woodcock Test of Auditory Discrimination (1970)
7. Wepman Test of Auditory Discrimination (Wepman, 1958)
8. Northwestern Syntax Screening Test (Lee, 1969)
9. Binet Designs (Terman and Merrill, 1973)
10. Goodenough "Draw a Man" Test (Harris, 1963)

Not all of the above tests were used with each child. Use depended upon the child's age, ability, and cooperation. Judgments about the child's speech and language ability were made by comparing the test results with the results of the informal evaluation. The speech and language findings were compared with other indexes of psychomotor development (developmental landmarks and visual-motor-perceptual development).

A general case history form was completed by the mother with the help of the examiner and hearing members of the family. The form was designed to obtain information concerning the history of the parents' deafness, their education, as well as the medical, neonatal, and developmental history of the child. Questions concerning the use of sign language and amount of interaction between the child and hearing adults, hearing children, and television were included.

Hearing

Despite the fact that the children participating in the project allegedly had normal hearing, audiological evaluations were conducted to confirm these assertions. The following audiometric techniques were applied, depending on the child's age and cooperation level.

1. conventional pure-tone audiometry
2. speech audiometry
3. conditioned orienting response (COR)
4. play audiometry
5. distraction audiometry
6. tympanometry

RESULTS AND CONCLUSIONS

Hearing

Six of the 52 children evaluated were found to have previously undiagnosed hearing losses requiring amplification. Three of these children were considered to have a moderate hearing loss, while the other three were considered to have a severe or profound hearing loss. All six children were under four years of age; one child was under one year. A seventh child appeared to have a mild-to-moderate hearing loss, but further testing to check the reliability of the results obtained was considered necessary before a definite statement could be made about the child's hearing status.

Speech and Language

Of the 52 children evaluated, 23 were considered to be developing speech and language normally. Two of these children were not living at home and only saw their parents on weekends. Most children appeared to be using two systems to communicate, one with hearing people and one with the deaf. That is, voice, articulation, and use of gesture and sign were often different depending on with whom the child was communicating.

Of the remaining 29 children, 23 appeared to have definite speech and language problems, and five were suspected of having difficulties. One very young child was not classified because evaluation was not considered feasible.

3. LINGUISTIC DEVELOPMENT

The five children with questionable difficulties were all under four years of age: All were judged to be functioning at age level in terms of mean length of utterance, but appeared to be limited in the semantic content of their speech, and according to communication indexes, scored slightly below age level on comprehension tasks. One of these children is being followed closely for a suspected mild-to-moderate hearing loss.

Of the 23 children who appeared to have definite speech and language problems, six had speech and language problems related to previously undetermined hearing loss, and six had factors other than the deafness of the parents contributing to the delay (psychomotor retardation, emotional disturbance, and brain damage). Eleven children (21% of the total sample) were considered to have speech or language problems with no other known contributory factors other than the deafness of their parents. (These children are referred to below as the problem group.) One child had only an articulation problem, two children had language problems, and eight children had both speech and language problems. Speech problems included defective articulation, deviant stress and intonation patterns, and fluency problems. The distribution of four categories of disorders among these 11 children is summarized in Table 1 and described below.

TABLE 1. Distribution of communication problems found in 11 children with no known contributory factors other than parents' deafness affecting speech and language. (+ indicates a problem.)

Subjects	Language	Stress and Intonation	Articulation	Fluency
1			+	
2	+			
3	+			
4	+	+		+
5	+	+		+
6	+	+		+
7	+	+	+	
8	+	+	+	
9	+	+	+	
10	+	+	+	
11	+	+	+	

It was not possible to identify specific speech and language problems common to all 11 children. However, eight children spoke with stress and intonational patterns resembling deaf speech and 10 children had some language problems. The 10 children with language problems all had comprehension and vocabulary deficits. Seven children who were over five years of age did poorly on comprehension tasks which required prior information and tasks dependent on knowledge of word meaning (auditory reception and auditory association subtests of the ITPA, the PPVT, and vocabulary definitions). These children also demonstrated some word-finding difficulty in their spontaneous speech. Three children who were below four years of age also appeared to be delayed in receptive vocabulary development. One child who had passed the age of three scored below age level on the PPVT, while the other two children who were below the age of three did poorly on the verbal comprehension portion of the developmental scales. For example, they could not point to parts of the body or identify familiar objects by name when the requests were made by the examiner or by the mother.

Articulation errors in three school-age children's speech (two from the same family) resembled each other in that sounds which were visually similar were substituted for each other but actual errors were not consistent among the children. These children scored below age level on the Templin-Darley Screening and Diagnostic tests. Three preschool-age children's spontaneous speech was difficult to interpret and was characterized by "deaflike" articulation patterns which were not modified when speaking to hearing adults.

Three children (from the same family) had speech patterns resembling cluttering. They spoke with rapid rate and omission of syllables and words, and they made other errors in articulation and syntax. However, on articulation tests and when repeating sentences, that is, when formulation of language was not involved, their speech was considered within normal limits for their age. In addition to the three children who were considered to be clutterers and therefore tended to omit function words and morphemes in conversation, two children, aged six and seven years four months, appeared to be delayed in their grammatical development. Their speech contained numerous errors of verb tense and declensions and pronoun confusion which appeared to deviate from the norms for their age and socioeconomic status.

Six of the children with language problems were in school and reportedly had learning difficulties. One of the three children under four years of age was in a preschool program, and interestingly, only one of the school-age children had not attended preschool.

Relationship of Age to Speech and Language Development

Forty of the total population of children evaluated were under six years of age. Fourteen of these children had a communication problem, but in only four children were there no complicating factors (deafness, psychomotor retardation, emotional disturbance, or brain damage). Twelve school-age children were evaluated, and nine of these had a speech or language problem. One of these children was in the first grade and the other eight were in Grades 2–4. Two of the children came from an emotionally disturbed environment which probably contributed to their communication and school problems.

The high proportion of speech and language problems detected in the school-age children was unexpected. However, only a small number of children in this age-group were evaluated, and two of these were referred because they were having problems. It appears that in the population evaluated, speech and language problems did not disappear after the child entered school.

Sibling Status

Children who were the only or older child tended to have fewer problems than younger siblings. Seventeen (81%) of the 21 normal-speaking children living in deaf homes were the oldest or only child and four were younger hearing siblings. This is in contrast to the 11 children who presented communication problems in the absence of etiological factors other than the parents' deafness (the problem group). Among these children only five (45%) were the oldest or only child. Four of the children had older siblings with similar speech or language problems, one child had older deaf siblings, and one child had an older sibling with normal speech and language. These 11 children came from seven different families. Not surprisingly, there appeared to be some tendency for children from the same family to have similar speech or language problems.

Time Spent with Hearing Adults during the Preschool Years

Interestingly, the length of time spent with hearing adults during the preschool years varied and did not appear to be an important variable in the population examined. However, all children spent at least two hours weekly with hearing adults. Only one of the 11 children in the problem group, with no other known confounding factors contributing to their deficit, spent less than 10 hours weekly with hearing adults. Six children (from three families) had hearing grandparents living in the home with them, and three spent more than 10 hours weekly with hearing adults. There was insufficient information available concerning one child's history during the preschool years. Of the 21 children in the normal group living with their deaf parents, two children had hearing grandparents living in the home, one of whom was Italian-speaking. Eight others spent more than 10 hours a week with hearing adults and 11 spent less.

Information concerning length of time spent watching television was obtained, but was virtually the same for all the children.

Intelligibility of the Mother's Speech and Use of Sign Language

Mothers' speech was judged intelligible or unintelligible by the examiner. The mothers reported on their use of sign language with their children. Twenty-one children who were living with their deaf parents and appeared to be developing language normally came from 17 families. More than half of the 17 mothers had speech which was considered unintelligible. Regardless of the nature of their speech, the vast majority of the mothers (13 of the 17) used sign language with their children. All of the seven mothers of the 11 children in the problem group were considered unintelligible speakers and used sign language to varying degrees. Of the five mothers of children in the questionable group, four used sign language and three were considered intelligible speakers.

It appears, when comparing the normal group to the problem group, that intelligibility of the mother is an important but not essential component for normal language to develop in this population. None of the children in the problem group had mothers who were judged good speakers. More than half of the unintelligible mothers had children with problems of speech, language, or both. Any relationship between the use of sign language and oral language development was not apparent.

DISCUSSION

Of the 52 hearing children of deaf parents, at least 44% were considered to have problems of speech, language, or both, and 12% of the total sample had previously undiagnosed hearing loss requiring amplification. Thus, there appears to be a higher prevalence of communication problems in this population than in the population at large. Surprisingly, the amount of time spent with hearing adults or children did not seem to be related to speech and language difficulty. It appears that length of time spent with the hearing population tells us little about the kinds of interaction the child experiences. It may very well be that the quality of interaction with a child is more important than mere exposure to normal language.

One of the saddest problems we encountered in working with these children was convincing the deaf parents that there was in fact a problem. After a particular child's speech and language problem was identified, the parents tended not to bring their children for therapy as recommended. The mothers simply did not appear to recognize that there was a problem, probably because they could not hear it. Their children's speech and language, in every instance, was better than their own. They knew the children were having difficulties in school, but seemed not to understand the relationship between these problems and speech and language. In other words, if a child talked, they could not understand how there could be a speech problem. On the other hand, mothers of toddlers, of children learning to talk, were willing and anxious to listen to advice concerning how they should communicate with their children. Perhaps one reason why hearing children of deaf parents have not shown up in great numbers in speech and hearing clinics is because their problems are not recognized by their mothers. Furthermore, deaf mothers of preschoolers and their families are not aware of available facilities where they can seek advice concerning communication with their children before any problem occurs. The results of our evaluations suggest that it is not enough that children spend more time with hearing adults or enter preschool programs; counseling and therapy programs should be readily available for deaf parents with normal-hearing children. Regardless of whether the prevalence of communication problems is actually higher than normal in this population, it is important that deaf parents be alerted to the possibility of speech, language, and hearing problems and be encouraged to consult professionals for evaluation and advice.

A similar problem was encountered in convincing mothers that their children had hearing losses. The mothers saw their children responding to sounds that they could not hear and found it hard to understand how the child could have a hearing loss. Their disbelief was further confounded by the fact that most of them were told that their children heard at birth. There is a strong possibility that many of these children did have normal hearing at birth and their losses are progressive. Counseling deaf parents as to the nature of hearing loss and the hereditary implications, as well as recommendations for annual audiological evaluations for their offspring, should facilitate early identification of progressive or mild-to-moderate hearing losses.

While our results indicate that the prevalence of speech, language, and hearing problems in hearing children of deaf parents is greater than previously suspected, more information is needed as to why these problems occur. It appears that while intelligibility of the mother is an important, but not essential factor in speech and language development, mere exposure to other normal speakers during the early years of language development may not play a very significant role. In fact, it is not clear at this time why some children under the most adverse conditions (minimal or deviant oral input with extensive use of sign) develop oral language and speech normally and some do not. Variables such as type of education (manual or oral), grade level completed by the parents, socioeconomic status, and linguistic competence of the parents were not sufficiently investigated in this report. Furthermore, in order to counsel parents adequately in the future, more information is needed concerning those factors in the child's environment and aspects of communication between parent and child that are necessary for language to develop normally.

Effects of Sentence Context on Recognition of Words Through Lipreading by Deaf Children

NORMAN P. ERBER *and* DE A. McMAHAN

Central Institute for the Deaf, St. Louis, Missouri

Twenty monosyllabic nouns (10 animate, 10 inanimate) were presented in isolation and in three different positions in sentences to 15 profoundly deaf children to determine the effect of context on word intelligibility through lipreading. Isolated words were more intelligible (80%) than were words in sentences (46%). Animate nouns were more intelligible (70%) than inanimate nouns (33%) when used in initial position (as subjects) in sentences. Teacher ratings of children's "general lipreading ability" were correlated more highly with their recognition of words in the test sentences ($r = 0.93$) than with their recognition of words presented in isolation ($r = 0.53$). The results indicate that teachers of deaf children could enhance the intelligibility of important words by isolating them from sentences. The results also suggest that some speech-perception difficulties of deaf children could be diagnosed through lipreading tests which are scored on the basis of correctness of "key words" in sentences.

Teachers of deaf children use a variety of techniques to improve oral communication with their pupils. One common strategy, called structural change, involves manipulating the vocabulary or syntax of an utterance (Erber and Greer, 1973). For example, a teacher may rearrange the order of words in a sentence, or substitute a sentence containing different key words, in order to simplify the material. Many teachers feel that recognition of key words is the basis for comprehension of the sentences in which they occur.

Several investigators have found that both the auditory and visual intelligibility of words depend on the context in which they occur. In one well-known study, Miller, Heise, and Lichten (1951) demonstrated that normal-hearing adults, who listened to speech in noise, could understand words heard in sentences considerably better than they could understand the same words presented in isolation. Numbers and Hudgins (1948) reported that sentences were easier for deaf children to lipread than were single words (but they did not describe their procedure for scoring entire sentences). Taaffe and Wong (1957) noted that the first few words in a sentence usually were easier for normal-hearing adults to lipread than were the last few. In contrast, Blasdell and Jensen (1970), who evaluated normal-hearing children on an auditory-memory task, found that the last (fourth) syllable in a string of nonsense syllables was the one most likely to be imitated correctly. Contrary to all of these studies, Hipskind and Nerbonne (1973), whose subjects were adults with normal hearing, reported that spondaic words were no more intelligible visually when placed in sentence context than when they occurred in isolation, and that the word's position in the sentence was not a significant factor. In summary, these diverse studies of auditory and visual perception demonstrate that the context in which a word occurs can affect its intelligibility, and that the nature of the stimulus, the age and hearing level of the subjects, and the sensory modality used may all be important variables.

This paper reports a study which examined the effect of context on the visual identification of monosyllabic words by deaf children. The main purposes of the investigation were to determine (1) whether common words are easier to lipread when they are spoken in isolation or when they appear in sentences; (2) whether the position (function) of a word in a sentence influences that word's visual intelligibility through lipreading; and (3) whether children's visual recognition of words in isolation or in sentence context is related to teachers' ratings of their general lipreading ability.

METHOD

Subjects

Fifteen profoundly deaf children (nine female, six male; age range 13-16 years) from classes at Central Institute for the Deaf participated in this study. Their average hearing-threshold levels (better ear) for 500-1000-2000 Hz all were poorer than 95 dB (ANSI, 1969), and their spondee-recognition scores (better ear) all were poorer than 30% (Erber, 1974b). Each subject had been educated in an oral program for at least five years prior to this study, and all of the children used lipreading and hearing aids daily for communication. All of the subjects demonstrated normal or corrected vision as indicated by their performance on the Snellen test, and all of them had obtained at least average scores on standardized intelligence tests.

Speech Stimuli

Twenty common monosyllabic nouns (10 animate, 10 inanimate) which were very familiar to the subjects were used to construct sixty simple sentences. All contained transitive verbs, and all ranged in length from seven to 10 syllables. Each key noun was placed in an initial (subject), medial (direct object), or final (object of a preposition) position in three different sentences (see examples). Sentences of this form were chosen because the comprehension and use of certain subject–action–object constructions seems to be closely related to the cognitive development of children (Bowerman, 1973; Brown, 1973). An experienced teacher who was familiar with the linguistic abilities of the subjects helped select the vocabulary and construct the sentences.

Example (animate noun): *bird*
  The *bird* ate the bread on the ground. (subject)
  A man put the *bird* in a cage. (direct object)
  Two girls gave the food to the *bird*. (object of preposition)

Example (inanimate noun): *ball*
  The *ball* hit my brother on the head. (subject)
  That boy hit the *ball* over the fence. (direct object)
  My dog chewed the cover off the *ball*. (object of preposition)

Test Procedure

An experienced teacher who was familiar to the subjects served as the talker. Two 150-watt floodlights were positioned at mouth level 30° from the midline, and at a distance of about five feet. During test sessions, the talker sat before a black cloth screen. The subjects were tested in two groups (seven and eight subjects per group). They all sat within a ±45° angle relative to the talker and six to 10 feet from her (Erber, 1974a). They did not use their individual hearing aids and received no acoustic cues during test sessions.

The subjects viewed the presentations during two half-hour sessions separated by a short rest break. They were instructed in both written and oral form that the talker would say either words or sentences, and they were requested to write whatever they thought the talker said, even if they were not sure. An open-set format was used; that is, the subjects were not provided with a list of the response alternatives.

The talker presented each of the words and sentences once, without exaggeration and with normal vocal effort, stress, and rhythm. The talker was not told which word in each test sentence was the key word, so that she would give it no special emphasis. A pause followed each stimulus to allow the subjects time to write their responses (about 10 seconds for words and about 25 seconds for sentences). The length of this response interval was not constant; enough time was allowed to permit all of the children to complete their written responses. Timed signal lights, which were triggered by the talker, defined for the subjects the intervals during which they were to get ready, to watch the talker, and to write their responses. The stimulus materials were presented alternately: 15 sentences, five words, 15 sentences, five words, and so on. Sentences containing the same key word were randomly distributed throughout the entire sequence. Before each type of stimulus was presented, the children were shown a card indicating either *sentences* or *words*. The children received practice with similar material before actual testing began until it was clear that they understood the task.

In addition to measuring the children's lipreading performance with these materials, evaluations from their teachers also were obtained. Seven teachers who were familiar with each child's performance in the classroom were asked to rate the general lipreading ability (without acoustic cues) of each of the 15 subjects on a seven-point scale from *very poor* (1) to *very good* (7). These data were compared later with the results obtained under laboratory conditions.

RESULTS

The children's written responses were scored on the basis of correctness of key words only, regardless of whether the word occurred in isolation or in sentence context. For example, for the stimulus, "The *ball* hit my brother on the head," the response, "The *ball* hit my mother on the chin," received one point, but "The pot hit my brother on the head" was considered incorrect. Homophenous words were scored as errors, since the intent of this study was to determine a child's ability to lipread words correctly in different contexts.

Some subjective judgments were made during scoring. On 11 responses, the key word was written correctly but was not placed in the correct position in the sentence. Nevertheless, these responses were considered correct identifications of the key word. Two subjects occasionally wrote the article *a* before words in isolation. These words also were counted as correct and included in the data. However, compound words which contained the key words were considered incorrect (for example, the response *milkman* to the key word *milk*). Likewise, the creation of a morphological change was scored as incorrect (for example, -s, -ed, -ing).

A *t* test indicated that words are identified correctly more often in isolation (mean = 80.3%) than when the same words are presented in the context of sentences (mean = 45.8%) ($p < 0.005$, one-tailed test) (Figure 1). For words presented in isolation, no significant difference was found between recognition for animate (83.3%) and inanimate nouns (77.3%). For words presented in

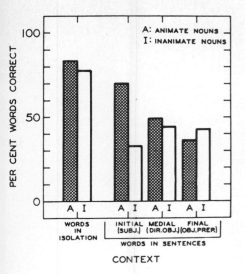

FIGURE 1. Mean visual recognition of 20 monosyllabic nouns (10 animate [A], 10 inanimate [I]) presented in isolation and in three sentence contexts. $N = 15$ profoundly deaf children.

sentences, a two-way analysis of variance showed that a word's position (function) in the sentence is not a significant variable, but that the animate/inanimate nature of the word is a statistically significant characteristic ($p < 0.01$). The interaction between a word's position (function) and its animate/inanimate nature also is a significant factor ($p < 0.01$). Inspection of the data indicates that this significant interaction is due to the difference in intelligibility of animate (70.0%) and inanimate nouns (32.7%) when they function as subjects of sentences. To illustrate, there is a strong tendency for the visual intelligibility of animate nouns to diminish as their position (function) in a sentence varies from initial (subject, 70.0%) to medial (direct object, 49.3%) to final (object of a preposition, 36.0%). In contrast, when inanimate nouns are presented in initial (subject) position in sentences, they are understood less well through lipreading (32.7%) than when they appear in medial position (direct object, 44.0%) or in final position (object of a preposition, 42.7%). In this set of stimulus sentences, the effects of word position and function cannot be separated.

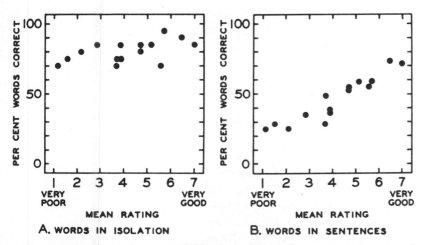

FIGURE 2. Relation between children's visual word-recognition scores and mean ratings of their "general lipreading ability" by seven teachers. (A) recognition of words in isolation; (B) recognition of words in sentence context (positions pooled). $N = 15$ profoundly deaf children.

Figure 2a, b shows that mean teacher ratings are correlated much more closely with scores for words presented in sentence context (word positions pooled) ($r = 0.93$) than with scores for words presented in isolation ($r =$

0.53). This result indicates that teachers' judgments of a child's lipreading ability are associated more closely with the child's visual perception of speech stimuli in a language context (words in sentences) than with his performance in a nonlanguage situation (words in isolation). The low correlation between the ratings and the scores for isolated words may be due partly to the lack of variance in the latter measure. That is, the recognition scores for isolated words generally are high.

DISCUSSION

Several factors may account for the difficulty demonstrated by deaf children in visual recognition of words when they occur in sentences. First, it is likely that the placement of a word within a list of other words creates "segmentation" problems for the lipreader. That is, coarticulation effects may make it difficult for the lipreader to specify word boundaries. In addition, coarticulation with segments of adjoining words may modify the appearance of the key word and interfere with its recognition (Alich, 1967; Berger, 1972). It would seem that ordering this list according to a set of rules (as in a sentence) would aid the observer in the identification of constituent words. That is, the syntactic and semantic redundancy of language should help the observer to resolve ambiguities and to fill gaps in the perceived signal (Jeffers and Barley, 1971). In fact, this effect has been demonstrated clearly for normal-hearing adults in the classic auditory study of Miller et al. (1951). But many of the important word-segmentation cues that are available to the listener in an auditory task are carried by the prosody of the stimulus sentences (for example, syllable stress, intonation contour, and so on), and this sort of information is not normally apparent to the lipreader unless he is able to receive it through a hearing aid. Instead, in order to segment words, the lipreader must rely on vision for perception of articulatory rhythm and word prominence as well as refer to his knowledge of probable word sequences. These strategies appear to suffice for many experienced lipreaders.

Unfortunately, the linguistic organization of a sentence cannot help a lipreader to identify constituent words unless he has sufficient knowledge of typical language patterns to make use of this information. For example, to a deaf child with an adequate vocabulary but with an incomplete knowledge of language structure, a sentence may be perceived as a series of (stressed) words separated by nonspecific articulatory movements. To a younger child who does not yet understand what words are, the sentence may be perceived as a sequence of articulatory movements only.

For the children in this study, words were visually more intelligible in isolation than were the same words presented in sentence context. Except when animate nouns appeared in initial (subject) position, these children apparently were unable to fully use the syntactic and semantic redundancy of the stimulus sentences as an aid to recognition of words in a series. That is, the potentially negative effect of placing a word in a list may have offset the potentially positive effect of placing that word in a sentence (a list ordered by rules). The subjects did identify animate and inanimate nouns differently in sentences. Evidently, these children have sufficient knowledge of word probabilities to know that it is more likely for animate rather than inanimate nouns to be used as subjects in sentences with transitive verbs. That is, they apparently anticipate the occurrence of animate nouns in initial positions. Informal observations suggest that this type of sentence construction is commonly used by teachers and is one of the earliest forms introduced in the classroom.

A frequent activity of teachers of deaf children is the introduction of new vocabulary. It would be valuable for teachers to know the best linguistic context in which to place a new word for optimal comprehension through auditory or visual modalities. The results of this study indicate that words in isolation may be visually more intelligible to deaf children than are words in sentences. Thus, to increase a child's visual identification of an important word, a teacher should isolate the word while pairing it with the associated object or activity. For example, the teacher might say, "Ball!" (points to ball) "Throw the ball to me!" or alternately, "Throw the _ball_ to me!," emphasizing the word _ball_ to effectively isolate it from the other words in the sentence. Teachers have been observed to use techniques of this sort in their oral communication with deaf children (Erber and Greer, 1973). Yet, to increase a child's knowledge of the way in which words are joined to form sentences, and to familiarize him with the patterns of language, a teacher also should try to use connected discourse during oral communication with her pupils (Simmons, 1964; 1966). Perhaps the best strategy is a compromise approach directed to both vocabulary growth and language development. This sort of orientation would include both the use of single words to label objects and events and also the use of sentences to describe the relation between language and the child's experience.

Sentence-recognition tests commonly are used to evaluate lipreading performance (see Jeffers and Barley, 1971). These tests are valid in the sense that the stimuli are similar to those which normally are received in conversation, and they are useful for obtaining a general impression of a child's lipreading ability. In our experience with this testing format, however, the sentence errors of some deaf children have varied in unusual ways, and neither main idea, correct syntax, nor number of words correct have been found to be completely appropriate criteria for scoring the written responses. In some cases, the scorers have found it difficult to specify the perceptual or linguistic nature of the error, and interjudge agreement occasionally has been poor.

A test of key-word recognition, such as the one used in this study, samples a deaf child's ability to extract information from sentences while avoiding most of the difficulties in scoring whole-sentence responses. Figure 2a, b indicates that teachers' ratings of a child's general lipreading performance are related much more closely to the child's recognition of words in sentences than to his recognition of isolated words, although the recognition scores generally are higher for isolated words. Therefore, it appears that a test which requires recognition of important (key) words in sentence context would be suitable for the assessment of lipreading performance of deaf children.

The key-word approach to lipreading evaluation is clinically feasible and has diagnostic potential. This testing format could be used to examine the relation between lipreading proficiency and certain characteristics of stimulus sentences. For example, a child may demonstrate an inability to identify key nouns in sentences longer than 10 syllables. A clinician could use this sort of information to diagnose a child's lipreading problems and to construct practice materials to help the child overcome his communication difficulties.

The Tadoma Method:

A Tactual Approach to Speech and Speechreading

ROSE M. VIVIAN

The Vibration Method of teaching speech and speechreading was first used in Norway in the 19th century. It was rediscovered in the U. S. by Sophia Alcorn and renamed Tadoma Method, and, beginning in 1932, was used exclusively to teach the deaf-blind at Perkins Institute. Using this method, the teacher shows the pupil how to place thumb and fingers on the speaker's face and neck to get the maximum tactual clues. The method can be tailored to suit the needs of children who have varying degrees of residual and auditory handicaps. A keen kinesthetic sensitivity is necessary for tactile development, which eventually leads to speechreading and the production of speech.

THE usual mode of teaching speech and speechreading to the deaf, today, places the greater emphasis on the use of vision, with only incidental help from vibration interpretation or kinesthetic application. This development was a natural one, since the size of classes makes impossible a mass of adoption of any other method requiring greater individual teaching. In considering the child who lacks the efficient use of both his vision and hearing, the emphasis is and has been forced on the more comprehensive and personally involved tactual or vibration approach. Since these children require individual and personalized teaching, the problem of teacher-child ratio need not arise.

Very little has been written in recent years on the Vibration or Tadoma Method of teaching speech and speechreading, thereby, causing an invaluable teaching technique to lie dormant except in isolated instances. This tactual approach was first used, according to available records, in Norway during the latter part of the nineteenth century.[3] It is sometimes referred to as the Hofgaard Method in honor of the first teacher known to use it.

A tactual approach was newly discovered or revived in this country by Miss Sophia Alcorn when she was asked to teach two deaf-blind children, Tad Chapman and Oma Simpson. It was from the first names of these children that she derived the title, *Tadoma*, for the method which she later adapted for deaf-sighted children.[2]

When Miss Inis B. Hall became the first head of the then newly-established Deaf-Blind Department at Perkins School for the Blind in 1932, the Tadoma Method was used *exclusively* with students capable of learning speech, and has continued to be used to the present day, for both blind and partially-sighted deaf children. Before this date, deaf-blind students in this school had been taught communication through print or fingerspelling in the hand. Two excellent living examples from the group of students who produced intelligible fluent speech and acquired an ease of speechreading through vibration, are Leonard Dowdy, taught by Miss Hall; and Juanita Morgan, taught by Mrs. Maurine Nilsson Gittzus.

The Vibration Method

The vibration method is a means by which an individual, who is partially or totally visually and auditorially deficient, is given every opportunity to feel the muscular movements and the vibrations of sounds, and to develop the ability to interpret them.

The child[*] places his thumb on the lips of the speaker and his fingers lightly on the cheek—spreading from the cheekbones down to the jawbone just below the ear.

In a recent research project conducted in this department, the following observation was noted and warrants further special attention.[4]

"...the two thumbs were placed over the lips extending from the chin to the upper lip, the fingers were spread out, fanwise, across the cheeks, and reached down to the neck.

"...the adult subjects experimented with various hand positions. All subjects evolved the same hand positions. The fingers were widely spread, the little finger of the right hand resting lightly on the hollow below the thyroid cartilage. The thumb spanned the lips. The remaining fingers of the right hand rested on the upper neck and cheek. The left hand was placed in a similar position but with the thumb on the corner of the mouth. The little finger did not extend as far down the neck."

The teacher should introduce the child to one position, but will wisely allow him the freedom and flexibility to discover the most comfortable and effective position to meet his own individual needs.

The deaf child with sight can benefit by placing the thumb on the side of the speaker's mouth or just below the lower lip, instead of directly on the lips and thus be able to visually speechread as well as gain supplementary tactual clues.

Before continuing to the teaching process it is important to emphasize that the tactual method is by no means easy. It is tiring, tedious, and slow. It should be used often and regularly and in every possible teaching situation. The best results are obtained only by constant and continuous use. Thus, it is taxing for both the child and the teacher. The teacher must believe in it and not inwardly or outwardly repel physical contact, for the child immediately senses the hesitation by the teacher and reacts accordingly. The child's ultimate acceptance or rejection of the method will directly reflect the teacher's attitude, just as in any other teaching experience.

The Teaching Process

The following suggestions are based on experiences with children who are

---

[*] For the sake of simplicity, the writer shall refer to the individual as *child*, though this method can be adapted to child, adolescent, or adult, assuming the tactual sense is intact.

114

intact except for deficiencies in the effective use of sight and hearing. It has been most helpful for the child who is totally blind and profoundly deaf. It can be tailored to suit the needs of children with varying degrees of visual and auditory handicaps.

The beginning student should receive a full and varied school program. All the experiences should provide opportunities to gain or increase inner language and learning readiness. Within the program should be exercises related to the tactual approach for speech and speechreading.

Awareness to Vibration

Vibration is ever present, but we are not generally aware of it unless it is especially powerful or unless our attention is drawn to it. Since we depend on all our senses and are especially oriented to visual and hearing distraction, we are not more conscious of its presence. Those who lack vision and hearing need other means to compensate for these lacks and become more tactually sensitive. It is through this developed sensitivity to vibration that the approach is made to teach speech and speechreading. Every opportunity possible should be used to develop in the child the ability to discriminate *and* interpret vibrations within the environment with the ultimate attention focused on the teacher's face for speech vibrations.

The teacher should saturate the child with vibration. The child should be encouraged to place his hands on the teacher's face, preliminary to formal lessons, while she is talking, singing, or reciting nursery rhymes. At the appropriate times, call the child's attention to the vibrations made by a plane flying low over head, a nearby passing train or heavy trucks, the stomping of feet on a wooden floor, or the playing of musical instruments. Place the child's hands on the teacher's head, chest, and back as she speaks or hums. He will enjoy discovering the variety of sources of vibrations. It can be fun, as well as learning, when this is treated as a game.

Imitation Facility

The child's ability to imitate is very important. It is through discriminate imitation that the normal child learns from the time of his birth. He imitates what he hears of the speech from the adults who surround him and what he sees of their deeds and actions. So, too, the deaf-blind child. This skill is developed, and those who have not had previous opportunities for imitation ex-

periences need specific training.

Start from gross motions to the more minute movements. The following are suggested exercises:

1. Walking, running, jumping, stopping, and starting. Stepping over objects, under objects, through openings, around openings, and other variations. The teacher should lead the child through these activities, perhaps with the child close behind, with hands resting on the teacher's waist.

2. Gross body movements standing in one spot using arms and legs bilaterally and cross laterally. Teacher and child face each other and child feels the movements made by teacher and then imitates them.

3. Head motions. Teacher and child positions same as #2.

4. Facial motions and expressions. Positions same as #2.

5. Mouth and cheek motions. Positions same as #2.

6. Tongue gymnastics. Positions the same as #2. The child must feel free to place his fingers in teacher's mouth to feel tongue positions.

Tactile Development

A keen kinesthetic sensitivity is necessary. This skill can be developed by utilizing the innumerable educational items found in the retail stores. The teacher with ingenuity or friends with ingenuity and carpentry ability can make a variety of items which will help the child develop discrimination, reasoning, and tactile ability. The following are some of the skills which can be developed through sense training:

Tactual recognition and discrimination,
Sequence perception,
Reasoning,
Concentration,
Motor control manipulation,
Following directions, and
Stimulating curiosity

Basic rhythm skills can be started very simply by placing the child's hands on the teacher's face while the teacher produces sound. The child indicates presence and absence of sound, loud and soft sound, voice volume, and high and low voice pitch. These exercises can be extended to playing on the piano and can be continued by following any well-planned rhythm program found in most schools for the deaf. A comprehensive knowledge of rhythm skills can be appreciated best when the child has learned to speak in sentences. Correct pitch, inflections, and rhythm patterns make speech more intelligible.

As early as possible the child should be introduced to proper breathing habits. Exercises should be directed toward development of the correct breathing process, and sustaining power of breath. Instructions for breath training should be and generally are included in the Speech Course as part of the Teacher Training Program or information on correct breathing can be found in most textbooks concerned with speech production.

Speechreading and Speech Production

A period of several months, sometimes longer, is not only necessary, but is recommended before any demands are made on the child for voice production. This block of time may be called a period of adjustment and acceptance, and it relieves the child of pressure and tension. It also allows the child considerable time to become thoroughly familiar with vibration, the recognition of basic elements, and interpretation of beginning sounds and some whole words. Both hands of the child should be placed on the teacher's face, at first, and as the child becomes more proficient, he should be allowed to use one hand. Be sure that he has opportunities to use either hand, not one, habitually.

Vowel sounds, then breath sounds, followed by voice consonants are presented to the child. As each sound is introduced through vibration the same sound is presented to him in braille or print, again, according to his individual need. Concurrently, at another time of the day, he is introduced to whole word objects and commands, preferably with contrasting initial sounds. The teacher should especially note that all sounds and words should not be grossly exaggerated, but said rather slowly with good volume, moderate pitch, and flexible relaxed lip movement.

Obviously, the beginning period should not be hurried. A very firm basic knowledge is necessary before proceeding to more complex blends, phrases, and sentences.

If the child has usable sight, gently encourage the child to close his eyes or use an eye cover for part of each lesson to help him devote his complete attention to developing and refining his tactual sense. This request, too, will be received by the child in direct reflection of the teacher's attitude and manner.

Speech Production

When the child is ready to produce speech sounds, the teacher should make sure that the child has correct tongue

3. LINGUISTIC DEVELOPMENT

placement and mouth position for each sound to avoid establishing poor speech habits. The child should have one hand on the teacher's face and one on his own face for purposes of comparison with and imitation of the vibrations and muscular movements he feels on the teacher's face. Speech lessons may, at first, be involved with single speech elements. However, if the child spontaneously articulates whole words, he should be encouraged to do so with a great display of adult praise and pride. Again, the teacher is cautioned to note the correct positions in reproducing the whole word.

There are three important points to remember in using this method or for any learning development. They are:

1. Lay a firm foundation.
2. Be slow in progressing to the next step.
3. Provide a variety of experiences and tasks.

The whole process of vibration speech-reading and production is a taxing one. Intense concentration and attention is necessary. Memory retention for position and muscular images is also most important. Discrimination skill is called for to make appropriate associations with specific vibrations.

All these facts add up to exceptional mental effort during and after the beginning learning steps. Consequently, the environment should be pleasant and relaxed, and the lesson periods should be short but frequent. But this method also offers mental stimulation and a teaching challenge. A conscientious and well-trained teacher who is willing to spend the time and effort, will find the results profitable and satisfying.

REFERENCES

1. "Speech Developed Through Vibration," Alcorn, Kate. *The Volta Review*, Nov. 1938.

2. "The Tadoma Method," Alcorn, Sophia, *The Volta Review*, May, 1932.

3. "The First Case In the World: Miss Petra Heiberg's Report," Anders Hansen, *The Volta Review*, Vol. 32, No. 5, May, 1930.

4. *Hofgaard Method of Speechreading:* An Experimental Study of the Reception of Speech Through Touch. Term Paper. Church, C., Cyphers, R., Horner, C., Raeburn, R., May, 1964.

5. "The Value of Vibration in Teaching Speech to the Deaf," Daley, Jane E., *The Volta Review*, 1938.

6. Gittzus, Mrs. Maurine Nilsson—1942-1954. The writer is indebted to Mrs. Gittzus for her personal instruction, inspiration, and guidance in the vibration method of instruction. 1943-1954.

7. Haycock, Sibley, *The Teaching of Speech.* pp. 19-20. Washington, D. C.: The Volta Bureau, 1957.

NOTE: This paper presents a short description of the vibration or tactual method. Its purpose is to familiarize the general public and interested professionals with the system. Anyone wishing to know specific details or related information may feel free to contact the writer at Perkins School for the Blind.

Are We Raising Our Children Orally?

Audrey Ann Simmons, Ed.D.

Perhaps we should rephrase the question in order to focus more pointedly upon its meaning. Rather than asking, "Do we raise our children orally?", perhaps we should really address ourselves to the question, "Are we raising children who talk?"

meaning of oralism

The word *oral,* with all of its derivations, has many connotations in professional and nonprofessional circles these days. To avoid the problem in semantics perhaps I should define what I mean by *oral, oralism, orally,* etc. To me, it is a way of life, a philosophy, yet also a process. To me *oralism* is not something given to a hearing impaired child within the confines of a classroom. Unlike reading, math, social studies, or spelling it is not something that can be tutored. Drills and exercises can sharpen some skills, but without all the other components they do not help the child to be *oral.*

"*Oral*" means to be able to *speak* the mother tongue. This linguistic act is made up of components of pronunciation, articulation, intonation, rhythm, vocabulary, word order, word endings, sentences—sentences of varying kinds and lengths. But most importantly, it is made up of ideas, of meanings.

environment

During the past decade we have learned a great deal from the psycholinguists about how our language is learned. Without exception they focus upon the important and even critical role of parents in developing language in their children. To be sure they are quick to say that learning to speak is probably the most difficult intellectual accomplishment a human being is called upon to perform, but they promptly add that the child's thinking grows with the mastery of language. Nevertheless, they point out that it is the parents' style of "teaching" that governs that development. Under no circumstances do they think of that "teaching" as some-

"Are We Raising Our Children Orally?" Audrey Ann Simmons, Ed.D., *The Volta Review.* ©1971 The Alexander Graham Bell Association for the Deaf, Inc.

thing done with certain materials at given times in a day. At no time do they even consider that the process of learning to speak the mother tongue can be accomplished during the hours of 8:30 to 3:00 five days a week for 32 weeks per year in a school setting. They are unanimous in their thinking that language learning goes on hour in and hour out from the instant of birth, in the home.

Probably it is not by accident that the term *mother tongue* has been given to the first language learned and spoken by the child. When both parents are present in the home, it is the mother who is with the child for most of the time and whose influence upon the child is greater. It is unfortunate for our hearing impaired children that the roles of the parents are not reversed because of the acoustic characteristics of fathers' voices. More of the auditory clues are available to the child when the father is the speaker rather than the mother. Nevertheless, she usually serves as the primary model for the child's attempts at imitation of the language patterns. The acquisition of language by the child is essentially a learning process dependent upon feedback between parent and child.

communication between parent and child

The dialogues between mother and child have a flavor of their own. If it is a hearing child, the mother is programming in sentences and vocabulary which are longer and more complex than the child himself is using. For the most part, they are the kinds of sentences and are at the level that the child will produce a year later. Too frequently, if the child is deaf, the material is filtered. The mother of a hearing impaired child often reduces the material to its barest essentials and gives her child simple redundant sentences for models, e.g.,

> Grandmother will come.
> She will fly in an airplane.
> We will meet grandmother.
> We will go to the airport.
> We will drive in the car.
> She will be happy.

Descending to the child's output level is only rubber-stamping his language. Such rubber-stamping is reflected in the language used by older children. Instead of giving the same language over and over, do you use different language for the same situation? When he wants to play with the toy airplane, what do you say? You have lots of possibilities, you know.

> Here is your airplane.
> Do you want to play with your airplane?
> Can you make the airplane fly?
> There are two wheels on the airplane.
> A pilot flies an airplane.
> There is a tail on the airplane, etc.

If he is older and working on a model plane you might be using:

> Is that a jet plane?
> You can see that it doesn't have a propeller.
> Do you know that jet planes use a special fuel?
> The newest jet plane carries almost 500 passengers.

Conversely, do you see that the same language or concept gets applied to many situations? *Big* and *little* might be used when the child tries on daddy's hat or lifts the bowling ball, but the concept of relative size needs to be extended, e.g., cookie, car, pizza, dog, bird, truck, etc.

To continue with the plane, you can establish which is bigger, the 747 or a fighter plane. Which flies faster? Which holds more passengers?

Both the quality as well as quantity of language stimulation that the child receives influences his speech. Children who live in narrow and unstimulating environments, having only a limited number of close personal contacts, will show a more limited language development than children who are exposed to varied and stimulating experiences. It should be remembered that children growing up in affluent American suburbs often live in narrow and unstimulating environments.

It is significant that certain unique language patterns occur with hearing impaired children leading to the term "deafisms." Studies have shown that though the deaf child is able to use more sophisticated language as he grows older, he does *not* show a proportionate growth in the accuracy of the language he uses.

Could he be living in a narrow, unstimulating environment in which language is accepted regardless of quality or quantity? Probably we should think of his linguistic age rather than his chronological age and program into him appropriate language. If we worked at the role of input and its influence, I doubt that we would be receiving from hearing impaired children such stories as:

> A girl throw a ball to boy.
> The boy bat a ball.
> A boy bat a ball to the window
> and broke the window. Mother
> boy heard broke window. Mother
> saw a broke the window. She
> went to see ball game.

Surely a hearing impaired child needs at least the same amount of help as linguists have shown that hearing children receive. From the protocols of Brown and his associates we find that 2-year-old Adam tried to repeat what his mother said, however he reduced it in length. For example, he said, "Fraser unhappy," after his mother's, "Fraser will be unhappy," and, "Mummy soup," from, "Mummy is going to have her soup."

In turn Adam's mother expanded his utterances for more imitation. He was found to say on one occasion, "See truck, Mummy." Mother responded with, "Did you see the truck?" He responded, "No I see truck," and she said, "No, you didn't see it. There goes one."

Notice how the mother is tuned in to her child. She follows his lead. The child initiates the language to which Mother *listens* and then expands. As Van Uden [1] described it:

Mother plays a double part as the speaker in a theater: she speaks what she herself wants to say and she seizes the clumsy speech of her child molding its form. She finds, led by nature, the crystallization point of language: conversation. The mother converses with her child all day. Notice that the mother is never emphasizing the language forms (or vocabulary) quite detached from the content and the situation. pp. 95-96

3. LINGUISTIC DEVELOPMENT

Van Uden proposes that this system be continued with the deaf child through seven or eight school years. It would seem, then, that the influence of parents is not restricted to a particular age, but rather continues throughout the child's language learning years. Surely the child who described a picture as I quoted (and did it orally) had had benefit of little conversation between adults and himself. He was oral, but was he communicating?

affective quality

The learning of the mother tongue is not only a linguistic task, but is also a deeply emotional experience for the child. For the child raised in an environment where the input is restricted, the emotional content of the communication is of particular significance, since nonverbal cues must be the primary method of obtaining meaning. The real meaning of the parent's messages are conveyed not only by the few words she utters, but by the silent language of her facial expression and general behavior as well. Because of the child's sensitivity to extra-verbal cues which have been developed as a result of restricted verbal communication, the child perceives how his mother feels about things and especially about him, without the words. Too often he interprets the dissatisfaction portrayed in his mother's face as dissatisfaction with him. We are asking the hearing impaired child to observe minute movement and slightest sound and derive meaning. A facial expression is many times easier to interpret. He can read meaning into the parent's posture, the look in her eyes, her movement. If we are to raise our children to speak, let's not let our nonverbal speaking be of a quality that would discourage their efforts. Let them experience as much adult affection and support as their hearing peers do.

Along with Wyatt [2], I would like to say that the optimum condition for successful speech learning is a continuous, undisrupted, and affectionate relation between mother and child, manifested in frequent and appropriate communication. Such communication is appropriate for the child if the mother takes her cues from the child's behavior and his verbalizations. Then she provides the child with a corrective feedback. A sentence such as "She went see ball game" would be immediately corrected to, "She went to see the ball game," so that the child gets feedback.

cognitive ability

The question of the role of language in the development of thought has come in for increasing consideration in the current era. A large number of psychologists, both in the United States and Russia, have shown that children learn more rapidly when they name things or talk about problems as they go along. Verbal ability and intelligence are inseparable, they believe. While speech at first serves largely a social function—to express the child's immediate needs and moods—it soon becomes an instrument for thought.

As your child grows in language, do you continue to change the quality of your conversation? Do you shift from "Who" and "What" questions to those that ask, "How are things alike or different?" "What was the evidence for?" "What was an alternative move?" etc.? Surely you move on to categories and generalizations and aren't letting the child refer to "milk" as "white" and "butter" as "yellow" or the "library" as "many many books" as several children I know do.

The research, limited as it is, seems to tell parents not to be overly afraid of complexity in their speech. Be interesting to your child, the authorities imply, and, for goodness sake, don't talk down.

advantages

Parents have special advantages they should be aware of and use. They know the changing interests of each child. Hobbies can serve as wonderful launching pads for supplementary reading and enriching trips to museums or historical sites for vocabulary building. Parents have the opportunities to take advantage of interests at the moment when these interests are at their peak: a walk with the child because he is excited about rocks, a book about dogs because he loves dogs, a ball game because he is learning the game.

Attention from parents is welcomed by children. Conversation about any subject has charm and impact. Take the child's lead and talk *with* him, not *to* him or *at* him.

When parents teach it is not thought of as teaching. Parents can pack in a lot of information when the children's guards are down. As an author of a magazine article put it, it is the parents alone who can teach their children that learning is something more than a scramble for grades. Learning is an end in itself, and an end that brings an abiding joy.

Parents have an edge in offering incentives and rewards. If the child is allowed to stay up a quarter of an hour or so later to finish a conversation, this privilege will magically be mingled with the delights of talking. Being brought downstairs in pajamas so that daddy can enjoy the story, too, adds to the story value.

Parents can work on a flexible schedule. They can pack a sudden wallop when a child is in a receptive mood, and wisely drop it when he is too fatigued to pursue it.

conclusion

You did ask me a question, and I haven't answered you directly. You are the only ones who can do that. If *orally* means using spoken language and if *raising* means providing an environment in which teaching the mother tongue is the aim, I believe you can answer in the affirmative. If you observe the following, I believe you are heading in the right direction.

1. Use conversation early and constantly.
2. Model the language for the child's self-initiated efforts long before you initiate the topic.
3. Warmly and affectionately expand his efforts.
4. Use repetition and variety.
5. Keep the input you provide ahead of his output.
6. Encourage his thinking with language by providing the appropriate words and eventually the questions.
7. Recognize you can be a teacher in the sense that no one else can.
8. Talk to him and then, importantly, *with* him.
9. Let his speech move mountains and, most of all, get your attention.
10. Recognize your advantages and use them.

Let nobody tell you that your child cannot learn to talk!

BIBLIOGRAPHY

1. Van Uden, A. *A world of language for deaf children, Part I,* St. Michielgestel, The Netherlands: St. Michielgestel School for the Deaf, 1968.
2. Wyatt, Gertrud L. *Language learning and communication disorders in children,* London, England: The Free Press, Collier, 1969.

Education of the Deaf: A Perspective

It was estimated twenty years ago that approximately three deaf children out of four are educated in segregated residential schools rather than in public schools. It seemed practical and realistic to remove deaf children from the mainstream of education, as the deaf represented a comparatively smaller population in the area of exceptional children. New awareness has altered the ideology behind that reasoning, and more deaf children are educated of not in public school systems, then closer to the "norm" of education facilities.

The educational problems of the deaf are such, that the best of facilities in the classroom environment should be available. The rooms and general atmosphere should be cheerful, with a good amount of illumination provided for the speech reading and other visual learning aids. Modern technological equipment, such as audiometers and hearing aids should be at hand. Motor expression has been demonstrated to be an effective form of communication for the deaf child, therefore facilities for such activities should be provided. Likewise music activities are a form of beneficial therapy for the deaf child, and should be considered in curriculum planning.

Certainly the process of educating the deaf is not a simple task. With the use of modern technological and medical advances however, educators may increasingly raise the academic functioning level of all deaf children.

Education
and Communication

H. L. Owrid

Contrary to the song which said, "An apple for the teacher," teachers today have come to expect brickbats. At every level those who work in education have met attacks on their ideals, their aims and their methods. Very often these attacks are stimulating. Like the apple they are a source of invigoration and creation. But destructive criticism is sometimes linked with suggestions for change in order to give a misleading appeal to new proposals which would seem much less attractive if they were considered solely on their merits. The present situation is painted in the gloomiest of lights and is contrasted with a bright and imaginary future in which today's problems will be nonexistent. We should remember when we are asked to subscribe to this tempting prospectus that Utopia meant Nowhere.

It was suggested to me recently that I might be interested in commenting on an article which, to my mind, follows precisely the pattern of misguided and exaggerated criticism of some educational methods combined with an unfounded optimism about alternative methods. The article* by Professor McCay Vernon is based on experiences of people with hearing impairments and associated handicaps in the United States. (As an Englishman I do not have personal acquaintance with the American scene and I apologize in advance for any points I make which do not appear to be relevant when considered against the background of work with the hearing handicapped in the United States. I hope that readers will accept my presumption by recalling that many of the problems encountered as a result of deafness are common to all countries and especially to those countries which have high levels of education and technological civilization.)

I must emphasize my initial admiration for Professor Vernon's immense labors in the publication of important data on the nature of the disabilities and the problems of handicapped people. With much of what he says I am in complete agreement, and yet I will contest strongly many points in his article about the education of hearing impaired children. The focus of my discussion lies in those views of Professor Vernon which, drawing principally on explicit statements, may be summarized as follows:

Deaf people possess (nonverbal) intelligence which does not differ essentially in its distribution from the normal pattern. That is to say the numbers of deaf people with high, average, and low intelligence are similar in proportion to those in the general population. In spite of this similarity, deaf people are poorly placed in employment when compared with the general population. The poor vocational levels of deaf people reflect their poor educational achievement, and this low level of educational attainment is a consequence of present-day education and its failures. The potentialities of deaf people as represented by their nonverbal intellectual levels can be realized by changes in educational methods and, in particular, by the use in education of manual communication.

In examining and disputing the argument set forth here I wish to consider first one or two general issues on deafness which are raised by Professor Vernon's views, and I will then turn more directly to the questions of education.

deafness and deaf children

Professor Vernon places great stress on his statement of the meaning of deafness. The distinction between his definition and some definitions of audiological deafness is, he says, a crucial one; and the failure to grasp this difference has led to confusion, misunderstanding, and denial of deafness. According to him, a person is educationally and socially deaf *when he cannot understand conversational speech in most situations* and when the onset of hearing loss is prelingual or early in life.

In this definition I have italicized the criterion of comprehension of speech which, it will be noticed, is a very strict one. Many of those whom we in England would call partially hearing (the hard of hearing in the United States) are deaf, according to Professor Vernon's measure. They may be able to follow conversational speech, provided that reasonable care is taken to make conditions favorable, but are not able to do so in most situations. Moreover, it is a definition which is inappropriate for children since young children with relatively slight impairments of hearing may, by Professor Vernon's definition, be considered deaf. Yet, since he is speaking of educational deafness, it is surely most important that the definition be readily applicable to young children. If Professor Vernon does not wish to regard as deaf those sufferers from impaired hearing to whom I have referred, then his own definition is, in turn, partial and confusing. As I see it, the danger of the definition is this: we know that any group of people defined as deaf in these terms will include very many for whom considerable auditory experience of spoken language can be made available provided that those who are in contact with them are convinced of its value. To neglect such experience through and because of the visual orientation of manual communication is to throw away a most valuable resource for the development of language.

---

*"Sociological and Psychological Factors Associated with Hearing Loss," McCay Vernon. *Journal of Speech and Hearing Research*, September 1969, pp. 541-563.

4. EDUCATIONAL RESOURCES

I would argue further that to apply any equally stringent criterion as a measure of the linguistic progress of a person with impaired hearing would be unhelpful. I believe that even where extensive use cannot be made of spoken language in the majority of situations, it is still of great value to have at least some access to spoken language in a limited number of situations. It is not only half a loaf, but even a slice, which is better than no bread at all.

deafness and additional handicap

Professor Vernon's article states that there is no causal relationship between hearing loss and IQ. I am in complete agreement with the principle which is implicit in this statement, although I am rather doubtful about its expression. P. E. Vernon (1969) and other investigators have shown by cross cultural studies that it is virtually impossible to measure intelligence without the influence of environment intervening during the measuring processes. Hearing impairment certainly entails environmental deprivation. Consequently our acceptance of Professor Vernon's view carries the proviso: it depends on what one means by, and how one measures, IQ. Nevertheless, we do not doubt that for the majority of hearing impaired children learning and problem solving abilities are not reduced within those areas which are free from the deprivational effects of deafness. Unfortunately the question of the learning difficulties of hearing impaired children is more complicated than the straightforward question of the relationship between deprivation of hearing and intellectual capacity.

In most schools for deaf children in England there are pupils who have disorders which are additional to their hearing disabilities. In many instances these secondary disabilities create difficulties for the children, for their parents, and for their teachers, which may be as grave as, or graver than, those difficulties which are consequent upon the impairment of hearing. The disabilities usually have a marked influence upon different areas of the children's learning and, in particular, they frequently affect communicative capacities in all aspects. These children form a minority of pupils in the schools. It seems likely that there are more children in the residential schools who are handicapped in this way. Although they are a minority, the impact on the life of the schools which stems from their problems is disproportionately large. What is true in this respect of schools for deaf children in England is likely to be true also for any country in which there is longstanding provision for education of the deaf. Yet Vernon's article argues that the deaf and hard of hearing population has essentially the same distribution of intelligence as that of the hearing population. This argument can only be sustained contrary to data which have been furnished by a number of studies, not least by those of Professor Vernon himself. In the January 1970 issue of the *American Annals of the Deaf* Anderson and Stevens (1970) provide figures returned by 43 residential schools for the deaf in the United States showing the number of enrolled pupils whose intelligence quotients were below 83, that is, more than one standard deviation below the mean. This number was 1,345. The authors do not provide the total number of pupils in these 43 schools but an estimate on the basis of other figures given suggests that the total enrollment was rather less than 10,000 pupils. On this evidence, therefore, almost 14% of the pupils suffered mental retardation according to the definition used by the authors.

A second example is from Professor Vernon's table of studies in the article under discussion here (Vernon, 1969), where figures are given for six residential schools having a total population of 1,600 pupils. Of these pupils 19% have Performance Scale quotients below 83. That is virtually one pupil in every five. Even when allowance is made for the possibility of a disproportionately high presentation of multi-handicapped children in the residential schools, the figures indicate an appreciable difference from the general pattern of the distribution of intelligence. Moreover, since these figures relate to pupils whose quotients are below 83, they do not include those children who, though having higher quotients than this, are also afflicted by other disorders which interfere with learning. It is strange that Professor Vernon, who knows this problem so well, should not take this into account in his general argument. It seems to me that to minimize a matter of such educational significance is helpful neither to the children nor to their teachers.

Even when, in criticisms of education, the children who have additional handicaps are left out of the account, and even if consideration is restricted to those children whose disabilities are solely a result of impaired hearing, it is altogether superficial to assume that educational progress—and, in particular, *verbal* educational progress—of children with severe impairments of hearing can be brought into line with their progress in nonverbal learning simply by a manipulation of teaching and communicational techniques. Present-day experience and a history which has seen the application of many different educational procedures both suggest that the obstacles to education and communication which are imposed by severe deafness are not so easily removed.

deafness and education

In Vernon's article, the most concentrated attack is upon present educational provision for hearing impaired children. The blame for what is seen as a failure to realize educational and vocational potential is laid principally upon educational shortcomings. For example, it is reported that approximately 80% of the deaf are employed in manual labor as contrasted with half of the general (United States) population, and that only 17% of deaf people are found in white collar work compared to 46% of the general population. Vernon claims that "this is due primarily to failure of the educational system to provide the deaf person a chance to develop his intelligence constructively and to use it vocationally (Vernon, 1969 a, p. 551)."

The vocational pattern represented in Vernon's article is not a new one. Rudolf Pintner (Pintner, Eisenson, & Stanton, 1941), on the basis of evidence accumulated some 40 years ago, reported that the chief occupations of the deaf were in semi-skilled and unskilled level occupations. Elsewhere in the same chapter it is stated: "In the vocational world at present the deaf take a lowly place. They find it hard to get jobs and to keep them." Pintner's interpretation of the reasons for this pattern was very different from that of Professor Vernon. Perhaps because he was much nearer to a time when manual methods had generally predominated in the education of the deaf, Pintner was not optimistic about the possibility that manual communication would grant access to the English language. He argued that, because of limitations in their abstract verbal intelligence and in academic achievement, deaf children should be provided with an education which would lay the emphasis on "the motor, the mechanical, the concrete." Language learning, he advocated, should be subsidiary and ancillary to making, building, and doing. The trend of present-day society is such that those people who are verbally restricted are those who find it increasingly difficult to find opportunities in professions, trades, and work of all sorts. Consequently, the type of emphasis in education which Pintner suggested is one which would simply increase vocational difficulties for the hearing impaired.

This trend toward the limitation of employment opportunities is one which I personally deplore. It seems to be a tragic waste that those people having pronounced verbal handicaps, due either to deafness or to some other disability, should be prevented from earning their living by making a satisfactory and satisfying use of their talents. It is not only unfortunate for the handicapped themselves, but is also a weakness in society, that opportunities should be so narrowed as to drastically limit the range of pursuits which gives scope for individual differences in the expression of abilities. The problem is obviously not one of hearing impaired people alone. Many other workers are also affected; and there are, too, many indications of concern that society should be moving so rapidly in this direction. Some would argue that, if developed societies of the Western type are to survive and to retain their undoubted advantages, they must adapt much more readily and flexibly than hitherto to the needs of their members. The problem of satisfactory vocational outlets for many hearing impaired people, as well as for many others who suffer disadvantages in other ways, will only be resolved by adaptations made by society as a whole. It is nevertheless clear that the general public, which constitutes the majority of society, will make its adjustments much more readily if met half way. I am therefore in full agreement with Vernon's article's emphasis upon the need to improve the verbal achievements of the hearing impaired. In the context of communication with society at large I would think that the most necessary verbal skills are those of spoken language, both comprehension and expression; and I am doubtful that the suggestions made by Professor Vernon which impinge most directly on communication would be effective in enhancing these particular verbal skills. As far as can be determined from the article, one of the chief ways to overcome the educational problems of deafness is by "a combined oral and manual approach," and this approach would be sufficiently effective to eliminate the gap between the potential (i.e. nonverbal intelligence) and (academic) achievement.

This aspect of Professor Vernon's case demands careful scrutiny. First of all, there is no precise definition of what is meant by a combined oral and manual approach. Those writers who have argued the most coherent case for manual methods have stressed the need for a manual method which follows precisely the grammatical and lexical form of the English language. This is clearly true of Stephen Quigley (1969) in his study of fingerspelling. In so far as Quigley approves of manual communication, it is the Rochester method, in which every word is to be spelled out as it is spoken. This is also true of Hans Furth (1966) in his advocacy of a manual method which is principally conducted by signs. "The child," he writes, "would sign according to the English syntax, not according to the popular sign language in common use." Elsewhere in the same text he writes: "The signing which is proposed . . . would be English in which frequently used words or morphemes would have simple, gesture-like signs. Some spelling would obviously be necessary and some manual signs for syntactical features now completely neglected in the conventional sign language would have to be devised."

Advocates of these systems appreciate that in order to develop a knowledge of the English language, even in written form, the manual means of communication must itself conform to the English language. What they tend to disregard is the evidence that the facility with which deaf children acquire manual signs is dependent on the lack of grammatical structure in this medium. They also overlook or minimize the difficulty which parents of deaf children would have in acquiring any manual system which did adhere precisely to the structure and vocabulary of their native language.

There is nothing in Professor Vernon's article to indicate that he has in mind manual methods which are strict transpositions of the English language of the types discussed by Professors Quigley and Furth. Instead, his references to manual methods are in general terms. He writes of "the language of signs and fingerspelling," by which means deaf persons are able to communicate fluently. Surely it is precisely these means which are available to, and used by, the great majority of children in public residential schools for deaf children at the present time.

We know from published figures* that the largest single educational category of hearing impaired pupils in the United States is that of the public residential schools. I do not think that anyone would dispute that this category is contributing proportionately to the group of deaf school leavers whose academic performance gives concern to Professor Vernon. These are children who are likely to be most readily conversant with unsystematic signing and fingerspelling because they use these means so extensively in communication with each other and with supervisory staff in the long hours of the day which are spent out of the classroom. Yet these children have problems of verbal and educational underachievement which are at least as great as those of children who have not the same fluency in manual communication.

It is well known that in learning language, normal-hearing children develop the language of their environment without any deliberate teaching by parents or teachers. When these children go to school, they rapidly adopt the language patterns of their schoolmates; and where these patterns differ from those of teachers and parents, it is generally the patterns used by a child's peers which will prevail. This is so even for children in day schools who continue to have frequent daily contact with their parents. There is no reason to doubt that similar processes exist for hearing impaired children so that, particularly in residential schools, they will be very much influenced by the communication patterns of their fellow pupils. That this does happen is made plain by the data on communication behavior of deaf children in public residential schools published by Tervoort (1961), and Tervoort and Verberk (1967). These works make clear that the communication of deaf children in these circumstances is predominantly visual, that is, by manual communication and by facial communication including lipreading. Any hearing which the children possess is likely to be playing no operative part in communication. Teachers may have this fact brought home to them if they have

---

* Directory of Programs and Services. *American Annals of the Deaf*, April, 1971, Vol. 116, no. 2.

observed, as I have, the occasional hard of hearing child in a residential school for deaf children. Such a child is likely to communicate with his deaf schoolmates without the use of voice, though he will produce his usual voice when addressing the hearing members of the school.

It is true, of course, that some residential schools do reach very high standards of communication in spoken language even among the pupils themselves. Achievement here is usually linked with certain typical features: an unswerving and dominating belief in the values of spoken language to hearing impaired children; a high representation of staff ready to communicate with the children by spoken language at all times; an emphasis on the importance of spoken language in the children's lives, which gives it as high a place in out of class hours as in school time; and cooperation with parents to ensure that the home communication environment is complementary to that of the school. For a variety of reasons the large public residential schools for deaf children do not usually have these characteristic features and are likely to be in an ambiguous situation in respect to development of communication skills in their pupils. Such schools cannot satisfy those whose aim is oral communication because, despite whatever happens in the classroom, so much of the vital communication between children in leisure hours is by manual means. On the other hand, the residential schools are ostensibly teaching spoken language to the great majority of the children and, as a consequence, critics of oral communication point to the children's lack of oral communication abilities as evidence of oral failure. If we add the further problem which these schools face in the presence of substantial numbers of multi-handicapped pupils, we can scarcely be surprised if the verbal and educational attainments in the schools are depressed. Many teachers would argue that, in spite of the obstacles to scholastic achievement which are presented by the conditions in which children and teachers are functioning, the schools do serve the children well in other respects: in sympathetic understanding, in companionship, in release from stress, in creative activities and, in many instances, in providing an education for children to whom other educational institutions are unwilling to grant admission.

Failure of aural rehabilitation of deaf children is a main theme in Professor Vernon's article. I certainly agree that there has been, and is, a continuing failure to provide for many hearing impaired children the auditory experience which is essential if the hearing which many of them retain is to be functional in their development of language. It is my belief that the influence of manual communication tends to reduce the auditory experience made available to deaf children.

I have considered, in this article, aspects of Professor Vernon's article which relate most closely to the education of hearing impaired children. I have disputed the foundations of some of the criticisms in the article and consider that they are often unfair. I regard the proposals for reform in the education of the hearing impaired as neither new nor likely to have the effect that is being sought. I believe that the handicap of severe deafness particularly in its influence of verbal communication is such that quick remedies are not likely to be effective. I think that an education in which the primary verbal emphasis is on spoken language skills is more likely to lead hearing impaired people to satisfying occupations in which they can communicate adequately, at the very least, with the hearing people they will meet.

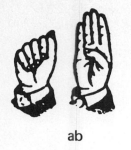

ab

ad

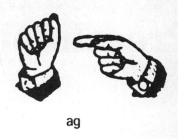

ag

am

an

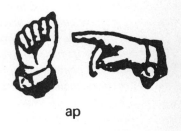

ap

BASIC PHONETIC ELEMENTS IN THREE-LETTER RHYMING WORDS

ar

as

at

ay

ax

131

Curriculum for the Preschool Deaf Child

Leahea F. Grammatico and Sophia Dhimitri Miller

Although educational literature has for decades provided description and rationale of various curricula for use with young children, little has been written regarding direct application of this knowledge to programming for preschool hearing impaired children. A curriculum framework developed by Hilda Taba has been adopted for use with the preschool deaf children at Peninsula Oral School in Redwood City, California, because accomplishment of its major objectives can be effectively combined with the development of communication skills. Thinking, knowledge, attitudes, and skills — the four main elements of the Taba curriculum — begin to develop during the preschool years as the teachers relate them to specific behavioral objectives and provide the learning experiences to stimulate their growth. The following presents the basic principles of the Taba curriculum and describes how they are applied and adapted at the Peninsula Oral School.

Often a preschool curriculum initially attempts to teach language through specific, unrelated words, which the hearing impaired child cannot easily put together and use. The child is given separate lessons in speech sounds and in auditory training, but little attention is given to teaching him how to think. In general, preschool teachers seem to have defined their curriculum program by its content rather than its broader goals. Since the 1930's, studies on curriculum have been available which administrators and teachers could apply to the preschool deaf child's education, but seldom has a specific method of application been recorded to be shared among educators.

general principles of the Taba curriculum

The curriculum design at Peninsula Oral School is based on the studies of Hilda Taba (1962, 1967), who defines curriculum as "a plan for learning and a plan for teaching something to somebody by some process." Her plan contains five major elements: 1) the objectives to be attained, 2) the selection and organization of content, 3) the selection and organization of learning experiences, 4) the formulation and organization of teaching strategies, and 5) evaluation. This program enables the teacher to focus on developing these basic components — thinking, knowledge, attitudes, and skills — which are pertinent to all levels of education from preschool through college.

According to learning theorists such as Piaget and Bruner, thinking is learned developmentally (Taba, 1962). The data that Piaget accumulated on children's behavior showed distinctive characteristics of intelligence developing at four different age levels: 1) *sensorimotor* — 0-2 years, 2) *preoperational* — 18 months to 7 years, 3) *concrete* — 7-11 years, and 4) *formal* — 11 years and older. Piaget maintains that children will progress through all of these stages in this order, but at various rates.

basic cognitive tasks to develop independent thinking

If learning to think is developmental, it should be taught systematically. Taba describes teaching strategies for developing three cognitive tasks leading to abstract thinking: 1) concept formation; 2) interpretation, inference, and generalization; and 3) application of principles. She has ingeniously constructed logical sequences of questions which cause the child, through the process of answering, to develop his mental skills.

One cognitive task establishes a foundation for the next. Concepts are formed as students respond to questions which require them to enumerate items, to group them, to identify their common characteristics, and to subclassify them.

Teachers tend to be concerned with giving information to students and then having the pupils give it back — often in the same frame of reference in which it was originally presented. When the child is asked to transfer the memorized information into a closely related framework but is unable to do so, the inability is often attributed to his deafness rather than to inadequate teaching of thinking. Little use is made of what a deaf child *already* knows.

Piaget found that classification and seriation abilities are acquired independently of language (Riccuti, 1965); it has also been determined that profoundly deaf children as young as 18 months of age can freely classify items on the bases of color and shape. It is thus possible and advisable to teach young children to use the information they have and to organize and reorganize this information according to similarities and differences. At *every* age it is important that a child be able to classify the items for himself, see relationships between items, and indicate why he grouped them in a particular way. It is also important for the teacher to direct the child's attention to *other* characteristics of the items so that they may be regrouped in different ways. As Shindelus and Durkin point out in the teacher's guide for *People in Families* (1962), "The important thing to aim for is a climate in which the teacher's suggestion is given no more status than that of the students', but is simply offered as another alternative to be considered."

The second cognitive task in developing thinking skills requires the child to compare individual items by asking himself the same questions about each, to explain what he sees, and finally to arrive at generalizations. Providing experiences through which children can learn to generalize is one of the most important elements of a curriculum. Without the inhibiting notion that there are only "correct" answers, the children can more easily apply their generalizations to other materials and experiences.

The third cognitive task, application of principles, involves three steps: predicting and hypothesizing, explaining or supporting the hypothesis, and verifying it. This process of predicting consequences by generalizing from known facts induces more divergent ways of thinking than do either of the other cognitive tasks.

generalizing from facts to acquire knowledge

Taba's curriculum plan subdivides *knowledge* into three components: basic concepts, main ideas, and specific facts. Basic concepts are comprehensive abstractions expressed in single words (e.g., interdependence, change, cooperation). They occur and recur in connection with different classroom activities and can be developed methodically with increasing complexity. Main ideas are expressed in word groups or sentences. They help the teacher determine relevant facts, thus narrowing the subject. The facts themselves support and develop the main ideas.

When the teacher selects and organizes her curriculum content, she begins with basic concepts, decides what her main ideas are to be, and then

4. EDUCATIONAL RESOURCES

chooses the facts to support, explain, illustrate, and develop the main ideas. The children's learning process is, in a sense, the reverse of this: the teacher should provide the facts (with the aid of books, toys, etc.) and allow the children themselves to generalize from the facts to the main ideas.

developing attitudes and skills

To a large extent, children's attitudes are learned by imitation, with the teacher serving as their model. Their values are also developed by exploring their own feelings and then transferring those feelings to others. The teacher can continually capitalize on situations, personal conflicts, or learning materials such as books, songs, pictures, etc., to expand the children's awareness.

At the same time that thinking, knowledge, and attitudes are developed, the child is also acquiring certain skills — motor, academic, and social. These skills, in turn, enable him to arrive at more sophisticated objectives.

applying the Taba curriculum to the education of preschool deaf children

We chose to use the Taba curriculum with preschool hearing impaired children because it seemed best suited to the development of communicative skills: listening, language, speech, and cognition. The four general objectives of the Taba curriculum (thinking, knowledge, attitudes, and skills) do not, of course, specify what the children are expected to accomplish. Behavioral objectives do. On the preschool level our behavioral objectives include the child's developing listening skills, watching, imitating, using language spontaneously, developing concepts, making comparisons, inferring, expressing feelings (his own and others'), thinking independently, and producing correct speech sounds.

concept formation

Preschool deaf children can learn concepts with the aid of simple tools or materials such as construction paper and random 2 x 4-inch pictures of familiar objects: ball, blackboard, ice cream, dress, cake, monkey, hat, blocks, eggs, shoes, bike, apple, roller skates, swing, turkey, dog, watermelon. After the pictures are presented to the child (e.g., "Here's an apple. You can bite an apple."), he is given four pieces of construction paper and is encouraged to group the items by placing each of them on one of the four pieces of larger paper. Duplicate pictures are presented so that the child may freely classify on the basis of his mental framework.

One child in a preschool class grouped the pictures in the following manner:

Group 1	Group 2	Group 3	Group 4
blackboard	ice cream	dress	monkey
ball	cake	hat	ball
swing	eggs	shoes	dog
roller skates	apple	roller skates	
bike	turkey		
dog	watermelon		

His explanations for these groupings were: "Play with," for Group 1; "Eat," for the second group; "Wear," for the third; and, for the last group, "Monkey play ball," and, "Dog play ball."

After the child has grouped the items and indicated his rationale for the various groups, the teacher should offer some appropriate language for him to use in describing these categories. However, the *child* must perform the grouping operations himself; the teacher must not impose *her* categories.

developing divergent thinking skills

A technique for helping the child acquire divergent thinking skills (as opposed to those skills which lead to "right" and "wrong" answers) is to cut various shapes from colored construction paper and ask the child what he sees in the shapes. From a paper triangle, for instance, a child may visualize a pointed block, a Christmas tree, or a wigwam. When the child is old enough to draw, the teacher might cut out a shape, paste it onto a piece of paper, ask the child what he sees, and then ask him to draw a picture using the shape. Sometimes the child will have the words to express what he sees; however, if he doesn't, he might use gestures. Again, the teacher can provide the language needed for the child to express himself verbally. In this way, she is not only stimulating thinking, but is teaching language as well.

Simply matching object to object, object to picture, or picture to picture does not lead to the development of a vocabulary that is very functional, nor does it lead to thinking that is very productive. From the outset, the child should be taught to connect descriptive verbs and adjectives to the nouns or objects.

While presenting a picture of a bike, the teacher might say, "Wouldn't it be fun to ride a pretty bike like this one? Do you have a bike? What color is the bike you ride? When you ride your bike, do you ever fall down?" After talking about three or four items, the teacher might ask, "What do you ride?" When the child responds with the word, "bike," the teacher would reinforce the response: "Yes, you ride a bike." As the children progress, the teacher can elicit divergent responses by asking questions like, "What other things do you ride?"

Posing questions that have several possible answers can teach problem solving. For example, the teacher might say, "Our room is too hot; what can we do about it?" Or, "I want to stick the cotton onto the paper; what do I need to make it stick?" To an older child she might say, "This hearing aid doesn't work; what do you think is the matter with it? What should we do?"

The children are not asked to memorize facts but, all along, are led to make comparisons. For instance, in one lesson the teacher might talk with the children about cars, then about airplanes. From all of the information they've gathered, the children will extract the ways in which cars and planes are similar. Or, the teacher may hold up an apple and an orange to compare them. Much later on, the children are able to compare vowels and consonants, recognizing — among other things — that they are all letters of the alphabet.

Children can be taught to make inferences from such questions as, "Where is Mommy? What do you think she is doing?" "What will happen if I stick this pin in the balloon?" At first it will be necessary to give some of the language to the child as he tries to formulate his response. Then, as he acquires more expressive language and comes to realize that there is more than one answer, he will not only reply with the learned answer but will also offer his own ideas.

attaining curriculum objectives

Ways to arrive at the objectives of the curriculum must be carefully planned. The knowledge that is taught at the preschool level is *language*. This language is concerned with the child's surroundings and experiences: his home, family, school, body, the people he encounters, food, clothing, illnesses or injuries, holidays, toys, transportation, animals, etc. Lessons planned around such topics will make use of the children's *common* experiences and will thus be more relevant to them.

4. EDUCATIONAL RESOURCES

Some of the basic concepts we have chosen to teach are *change, cooperation, similarity, interdependence, causality,* and *sequential order of events.* We do not, of course, expect that any one basic concept can be developed fully in a single unit or, for that matter, from *all* of the child's preschool experiences. Rather, these concepts continue to develop throughout the child's education. As the child's experiences broaden and his intellect develops, he is provided with opportunities in different contexts to develop a greater understanding of the basic concepts. For example, the idea of *change* can be taught at the preschool or primary level by presenting the class with opportunities to share in the experience of change: concrete experiences of ice melting, jello hardening, water evaporating, milk souring, food forming mold, flowers withering, seeds sprouting, cucumbers being made into pickles, children growing, etc. "Interdependence of family members" taught in the first grade is the foundation for understanding "interdependence of nations" in the twelfth grade.

emphasizing useful language

The preschooler must come to recognize that language will ultimately help him to satisfy his physical and emotional needs. The teacher may determine what specific language to teach the child by focusing on a main organizational idea, such as: "We all have families," "We all need shelter," "Children go to school," "People live according to certain rules," "We all have work to do," "We travel in different ways for different reasons," or, "Certain living things survive in various ways."

To show preschool children that language can lead to gratification, we begin by using three sentences repeatedly in many different contexts: "I want that," "What happened?" "Help me." These sentences can be used in numerous and varied situations, and they can be easily expanded. For instance, "I want that," can be extended to, "I want milk," "I want chocolate milk," and, "I want milk and a cookie." Hearing impaired children should begin to use connected language as soon as they have a working awareness of words.

Because normally hearing babies hear the same language over and over again before they begin to use it, we have tried to exercise a similar language control for the hearing impaired child. However, there can be no prepared list of nouns to teach the child since verbs and adjectives might well determine the nouns that the child needs. Useful sentences for establishing language control through repetition are: "Let me see," "Open it," "Pour it," "Stop it," "Put it back," "I don't want. . .," etc.

Language control is initially established by the content of the curriculum — which must be carefully coordinated with the child's learning experiences. The learning activities should be organized sequentially, should be built on previous learning, and should challenge the children to take what they have learned in one context and apply it to another through transfer of learning. The experiences should be designed to encourage the learner to inquire and to exercise independence of thought. The teacher might provide such experiences through discussions or through materials such as books and toys. By offering learning experiences that do not contain or focus on single solutions, the teacher can accommodate differences in ability, personality, and background.

learning to express personal feelings

Emphasizing words that convey feelings should be part of every plan for learning. The mental processes involved in developing attitudes differ from those involved in making inferences, developing abstract ideas, and forming hypotheses. The hearing impaired child can be made aware of attitudes by the teacher's use of such phrases as, "You have a happy smile," "You look delighted," "Johnny is in a bad mood," "The wolf is angry," "I'm not angry — I'm furious," "Johnny needs to be loved." The teacher should provide situations in which the children are able to explore feelings; for instance, she might ask them how they think a particular character in a story feels. A problem situation involving personal conflict encourages the child to relate the situation to his own life and to decide how to resolve it; e.g., "The little boy doesn't want to share his bicycle but his mother says he must. What should he do? How does he feel?"

building skills

Tearing, cutting, coloring, playing with clay, and painting are all skills that preschool children need to practice as a foundation for reading, writing, and number skills. Speech activities at this level should emphasize syllables, words, phrases, sentences, loudness, intonation, and pitch. The alphabet builds words, words build sentences, and sentences convey ideas. The child should be assisted in developing skills at his own rate and should not — simply because he is deaf — be led to skip levels of natural development. In order to compensate for the inability to hear, many deaf children have been expected to read and write before they have developed language. If a child does not know that words have meaning, how can he be taught to read?

At the beginning level it is possible to implement all four objectives of the curriculum (thinking, knowledge, attitudes, and skills) by using an object such as a toy pig and descriptive information from a familiar story, song, or rhyme:

1. The teacher says, "Here is the pig that says, 'Wee, wee, wee,' all the way home."
2. She then asks the child to identify the pig. "Show me the pig that says, 'Wee, wee, wee,' all the way home." If the child does not respond, she holds out her hand and repeats the request, perhaps varying the language slightly: "I want the pig that says, 'Wee, wee, wee,' all the way home."
3. After the child has given the pig to her, the teacher repeats: "That's the pig that says, 'Wee, wee, wee,' all the way home."
4. Next, the teacher eliminates the noun from her language in order to elicit it from the child: "What says, 'Wee, wee, wee,' all the way home?"
5. After the child has learned to reply, "Pig," the teacher says the full sentence and asks the child to repeat it.
6. The teacher presents the toy pig along with other animals and other objects and asks the child to group them however he likes. If he places all the animals in one group, she may say to him, "Yes, they're all animals." But the child may have another classification in mind. The teacher does not impose her own classification scheme since she is interested in finding out how the *child* is thinking.

This sequence, with variations, could extend over a period as long as two years. During that time, the teacher may have pointed out physical characteristics of the animals and talked about what pigs eat, where they live, and how they act. The child may have been told the story of the "Three Pigs," seen books about farms, and perhaps even visited a farm and seen a live pig. The child might now be given pictures of many *different* animals and be asked to subclassify them or, in other words, to reorganize his information; e.g., certain animals live on land or in water, have feathers or fur, produce food or pull equipment — whatever the child himself happens to note.

At the beginning, of course, not just farm, zoo, wild, or domestic animals are chosen, but a random sampling of each to avoid limiting the classification and subclassification possibilities. With this one basic process, then, a teacher can fulfill several curriculum objectives and most of the behavioral objectives while developing communicative skills such as listening, language, speech, and cognition.

Such a curriculum provides an outline for certain teaching-learning strategies and yet allows for differences in individual teachers and students. It is hierarchical in nature, enabling an increase not only in content but also in the development of abstract thinking skills.

The very complexity of Taba's system is a major obstacle in using it. Charles Silberman in *Crisis in the Classroom* (1970) points out the dilemma:

> If the analytic system is sophisticated enough to reflect the varieties and complexities of classroom interchange, it is too cumbersome to use (and certainly too cumbersome to be easily mastered); if it is simple enough to be easily used, it provides a simplistic picture of classroom interchange.

Granted that the system cannot be *easily* mastered, nevertheless it *can* be mastered by anyone given proper guidance. However cumbersome its use, it allows the teacher and children to share a more sophisticated and more satisfying approach to preschool education.

REFERENCES

Riccuti, H. Object grouping and selective ordering behavior in infants 12 to 24 months old. *Merrill Palmer Quarterly,* April 1965.

Shindelus, M.J., & Durkin, M.C. *People in families – teachers' edition: The Taba program in social science.* Reading, Mass.: Addison-Wesley Publishing Co., 1962.

Silberman, C. E. *Crisis in the classroom.* New York: Vintage Books, 1970.

Taba, H. *Curriculum development: Theory and practice.* New York: Harcourt, Brace, and World, Inc., 1962.

Taba, H. *Teachers' handbook for elementary social studies: Introductory edition.* Reading, Mass.: Addison-Wesley Publishing Co., 1967.

A Parent-Oriented Nursery Program for Preschool Deaf Children*

DAVID M. LUTERMAN, D.Ed.

A nursery program involving parents of preschool deaf children is described. The program involves the very active participation of the parent in the therapeutic process including administering therapy under the therapist's supervision. Some techniques described include: the parent's working with another child; program extension; hearing children in the nursery setting, "Father's Day" and evening meetings for fathers; "Other Children's Day"; and "Word for the Week." Several of the problems of the program involve the orientation of the staff and parents to the parent-centered nature of the program; the pervasiveness of the "middle-class" value system; and dependency of the parents on the program. The major difficulty noted is a lack of adequate measures of the variables under examination. Despite the limitations noted, the program appears to promote a great deal of growth in both parents and children.

THE NEED FOR EARLY INSTRUCTION of the congenitally deaf is generally acknowledged, although formal programs for the child rarely begin before the child is 3 years old. There are several programs in the United States in which the parents of very young deaf children are actively enrolled in the program so that they can learn to work effectively at home with their children. One of these is a program of parent education within an academic speech and hearing environment initiated in 1965 as a part of the services provided by the Robbins Speech and Hearing Center of Emerson College in Boston.

The Program

The program ran for two academic semesters, with eight families beginning enrollment each semester. During the first semester, the parents attended on a two-mornings-a-week basis. For one of the two mornings, the parents ob-

* This program has been supported in part by Federal Grant No. OEG 1-6-062069-1591 from the Department of Health, Education, and Welfare, Office of Education.

served their child in the nursery and in the individual tutoring sessions. On the other morning, the parents attended a group discussion class while the child remained in the nursery. There were also evening sessions one night a month for the fathers. The children were between the ages of 18 months and 3½ years, all deaf, but otherwise normal as determined by pediatric, audiometric, psychometric, and otological examinations given prior to the families' admission to the program.

Facilities. The facilities included a spacious (20' x 30') room, fully equipped for nursery school, with a large one-way vision mirror and a microphone-speaker arrangement contiguous to a large observation room. Two small therapy rooms with adjacent observation booths were in close proximity to the nursery. A large conference room, located elsewhere in the building, was used for the parent group meetings.

Nursery. The staff of the nursery consisted of a head teacher, trained in early childhood education, and two graduate assistants enrolled in a speech pathology and audiology curriculum. The format of the nursery was informal, with language stimulation given under natural free-play situations while the children were exploring various media. When observing the nursery, the parents were aided by other staff members who pointed out aspects of the children's behavior and the techniques of natural language stimulation being employed in the nursery. The parents completed an observation form on their own child during one half-hour period of the morning.

Tutoring. Each nursery day the child was seen for a half-hour individual tutoring lesson which, in general, followed that of the Tracy Correspondence Course, with individual modifications. The tutors utilized materials and techniques that were well within the cap-

abilities and budgets of the parents who were observing the tutoring and completing an observation schedule. After each session, the tutor and parent discussed the session, with emphasis placed on the therapy goals and the techniques employed to control the child's behavior. At some point during the semester (approximately 2 months after the start), the parent administered the therapy while the tutor observed. At the end of the session the tutor discussed the lesson with the parent. In general, the tutors were supportive of the parent and gave constructive criticism gently and somewhat indirectly as the parent was able to handle it.

Group Discussion. In the weekly group discussion class, the technique employed was generally nondirective, i.e. the parents were encouraged to find their own individual solutions to the problems under discussion. The role of the discussion leader was to set the topic and insure that the discussion centered on the topic. Specific parental questions were seldom answered directly by the leader, but would be thrown back to the group for further discussion. No attempt was made to "lecture" to the parents, although factual information was provided to the group when necessary. Some of the topics discussed were: feelings and attitudes, goals, problems of child management, and problems of educational placement.

Evening Meetings. Once a month both parents attended a group meeting in the evening. There were five such meetings during the first semester. This aspect of the program was reserved for the more formal lectures which followed presentation of two of the Tracy Clinic parent-information films. Guest speakers then presented their subjects: an otologist discussed the medical aspects of deafness; a psychologist commented on emotional needs of deaf children; a representative of a school for the deaf outlined the programs available for deaf children in Massachusetts; and a demonstration lesson was taught to a class of 11- to 12-year-olds from one of the local schools for the deaf. The fifth evening meeting was reserved for an evaluation of the program. The parents were provided with literature on deafness which, combined with the lecture material, served as the basis for much of the discussion in the morning meetings.

Once a month, group discussions were held for fathers only. These followed the same format as the morning group discussions, but were generally of longer duration and of a more informal nature.

The nursery, tutoring, group discussions, and evening meetings constituted the basic program. Within this program, the staff and parents evolved techniques which appear to have merit in furthering the goal of increased parental education. These procedures are not a permanent part of the program; they have evolved from the group discussions of the parents and the staff conferences. None of these procedures, as yet, has been subjected to vigorous scientific investigation, but they are under constant review by the staff and parents.

Second Semester. At the completion of the first semester, the parents felt the need for more time to solidify what they had learned, and so they requested that there be an extension of the program. Consequently, a second semester was initiated in which each parent came on a once-a-week basis to teach his own child under the supervision of the therapist. A group discussion was held in the morning on a once-a-month basis at which time the therapist provided the lesson. There were also evening meetings once a month when the Tracy parent-attitude films were shown and discussed. A requirement of the second semester was that the parent also enroll in an existing child-centered program in the community. This was done to help ease the transition from the parent-education program to the community facilities, and also to provide the child with more direct professional contact other than the once-a-month sessions available in the program extension.

Working With Another Child. When the parents had begun to administer the therapy, they had started with a child other than their own. Parents had been paired by the staff, and both parents had observed the child in therapy and remained for the conference with the tutor. The parent-therapist had then been gradually introduced into the therapy situation and had taught several lessons to the "other deaf child."

The staff and parents observed that

the procedure appeared to yield the following benefits:

1. It encouraged a more objective attitude toward their own child's behavior because the parents did not know the other child very well, and had to observe him very carefully to plan a lesson for him. This helped them realize that they had not really been looking at their own child's behavior very carefully.

2. It increased the parental planning for the lesson. When working at home with their own child, the parents had tended to extemporize since their knowledge of their own child was obviously greater than of "the other deaf child."

3. It demonstrated to the parents the individual differences of deaf children.

4. It helped the parents to know one another better and facilitated the forming of a group.

Hearing Children in the Nursery. Two hearing children of approximately the same age were placed in the nursery with the eight deaf children. The purpose of this procedure was to help the parents distinguish between behavior that is consistent with normal 2-year-olds and behavior that is due to deafness. Because of the nonverbal nature of the 2-year-olds, there was no difficulty in integrating the hearing children in the nursery. As the hearing children matured and therefore became increasingly verbal, the contrast between the deaf and hearing children became more apparent. This led to a greater realization, on the parents' part, of the degree of language handicap imposed by deafness.

Our experience with the hearing children has suggested that there should be only one nondeaf child in the program to further his need for interaction with the deaf children. He should be one of the youngest in the group to help compensate for the language handicap of the deaf children who will, on the other hand, be physically more adept and therefore able to act in many instances as protectors and teachers for the younger hearing child.

Other-Children Day. Another frequently recurring problem reported by the parents was that they had relatively little time to spend with the siblings of the deaf child. Moreover, the siblings, particularly the older ones, did not understand the problems of deafness and inadvertently interferred with the deaf child's progress. Consequently, during "other-children day" the parent had no responsibility in the nursery, but instead was required to spend the morning with the deaf child's siblings. Those parents with children older than the deaf child were expected to remain in the observation room with them for one morning to point out some of the special problems of their deaf sibling

in the nursery and in the individual tutoring. (This procedure was tried during a special summer program and will probably be incorporated in the regular program.)

Word for the Day. On the day the parents observed in the nursery, the nursery assistants were responsible for demonstrating techniques of working on a specific word in a free-play situation. They were not permitted to use any standardized materials, but had to use homemade materials. Initially the words were selected by the nursery staff, but as the parents became more sophisticated, they were made responsible for selecting the words.

To further promote the parents' utilization of the child's play activities, the parents also assumed the role of nursery assistants—that is, they spent the morning in the nursery working with all of the children. They planned the day's activities with the nursery teacher prior to their working day, and executed the plan under her supervision. It seemed to the staff that teaching the parent to operate in an individual therapy situation was not sufficient to accomplish our goal of teaching parents how to utilize everyday situations for the teaching of their own children. The nursery experience gave them a wider and more natural setting to stimulate language than did individual therapy sessions.

Problems

A minor difficulty in a program of this nature is orienting the staff to the parent-centered concept of the program. Most of the academic training centers train teachers to work with the child, so that most tutors find it difficult to think in terms of the non-speech-handicapped parent. It is most important to indoctrinate the staff (and the parents) in the concept that it is indeed the parent who is enrolled in the program, with the child functioning as the raw material for the parent's learning experience. In some instances, the parents did not realize that the therapists were actually doing demonstration lessons for their benefit rather than providing therapy for their children. Consequently, when the parents became enrolled in the outside child-centered program during the second semester and came into contact with therapists working directly with the child, they became (for a while) disenchanted with the therapists in our parent-centered program.

One of our most fundamental problems was the middle-class orientation and values of the staff as opposed to the diverse backgrounds of the parents. Because of this, parents from lower socio-economic backgrounds would at times be disdainful of some of the ideas discussed; e.g. the Tracy information films depicting the progress of a family with one child living in their own home. Parents from a lower socio-economic background would not accept the ideas presented because they did not seem to relate to these parents' life situations. In a similar vein, much of the discussion about child-rearing practices was rejected by these parents. They also found it difficult to identify with the characters in the Tracy parent-attitude series of films. It is doubtful how much these parents were able to obtain from our overall program. While they tended to be very appreciative of the staff's efforts on their behalf, it was the staff's impression that their behavior was not materially affected by this program.

One danger in this program is that the parents tend to become dependent on the personnel, which is, of course, the antithesis of the goal of the program. The parents themselves receive so much personal attention that child-centered programs suffer in comparison. Parents in the first group became extremely reluctant to leave the program and tended to bring up very minor problems just to maintain the staff's interest. It is vitally important that the parents gain the self-confidence to make their own decisions and to move out into other programs where the professionals may be much too busy to give them a great deal of attention and time.

The major difficulty in the entire area of education is the absence of adequate measures. In the present program, the variable under examination is the degree to which these children will be able to develop to their fullest potential within a parent-education program, and this is not readily susceptible to scientific attack. We can document changes in parental attitudes and changes in the behavior of the children, but we cannot really determine if similar changes might not have occurred in a child-centered program. Moreover, the potential of the child is difficult, if not impossible to measure; and of course, the degree to

which the child is achieving his potential is not easily ascertained with current measures. A further problem of measurement is determining the extent to which improved parent attitudes are being translated into improved methods of managing the children. Examination of existing literature suggests that no satisfactory tests of these factors are currently in existence.

Evaluation

The ultimate objective of our program is to produce more capable deaf children through early parental education. The final evaluation must be deferred until the children are placed in schools. The staff has observed a great deal of growth and change in the children and in many of the parents. Almost all the children are doing specific lipreading and the majority of them are using speech meaningfully. In addition they demonstrate an increased capability in social and play situations, and are currently being prepared for the more structured environment of school.

The parents have been very enthusiastic about the program. No parent left the program, and all reported that they would enroll again if given the opportunity. Based on staff observations and reports of the parents, there are several areas in which the program appears to help all parents:

1. The Initial Confusion. By the time the parent enters the program he has generally met a large array of professionals and has generally been given conflicting advice and information, but has not had the time to reflect and absorb the information provided. This program, by providing a consistent point of view and allowing the parents ample opportunity to discuss their conceptions and misconceptions, appears to help parents resolve a great deal of the confusion. Another source of confusion lies in the feelings of guilt, embarrassment, and fear that parents bring to the learning situation. Because they

are allowed to discuss their feelings and are helped to accept them, the parents are better able to organize their behavior.

2. Getting the Problem into Perspective. Related to the confusion is the feeling of being overwhelmed by the extent of the problem. This is translated into a very tense parent, who, when viewing her deaf child, tends to see the deafness and not the child. By meeting with other parents and thereby losing the feeling of being alone with their problem; by discussing the problems involved in having a deaf child in the family; and because of their contact with the matter-of-fact attitude of the staff, the parents begin to relax. As their tensions decrease, the parents are better able to meet the needs of their deaf children, and they can, as one parent expressed it, begin to "enjoy their children now."

3. Speech vs Language. One of the fundamental problems parents encounter comes from the fact that they do not recognize that the deaf child is primarily a language-handicapped child. The very emphasis placed by the staff on the difference between speech and language, and the reciprocal nature of both, helps the parent to become language oriented, so that he no longer asks, "when will my child begin to talk?," without any regard for his child's comprehension of the language involved.

4. Parental Appreciation of Therapist. A fourth factor common to all parents who participated is an appreciation of the difficulties and training necessary to become a good therapist. Several of the parents have commented, "It all looked so easy until I tried to do it." This increased appreciation will hopefully, be transferred into a better working relationship with other professional people working with their children.

The assistance of Mrs. Alan Dolmatch in preparation of the manuscript of this article is gratefully acknowledged.

Acquisition of Lipreading in a Deaf Multihandicapped Child

C. Merle Johnson
James H. Kaye

Operant techniques were used to develop lipreading in a nine-year-old deaf boy who had failed to respond appropriately to previous speechreading training. Remediation was initiated with two experiments: the first entailed a reversal and the second a multiple baseline. A component analysis revealed that both tokens and social reinforcers presented simultaneously or separately were effective in shaping lipreading. In addition, the child learned to lip-read either voiced or nonvoiced names of objects.

Operant conditioning has been demonstrated effective in teaching numerous tasks to children exhibiting various disorders. In the area of speech and language development, the use of behavioral principles has been instrumental in ameliorating deficits for these children. For example, Stark et al. (1973) described reinforcement procedures in the modification of language and behavior of the nonverbal child during speech therapy. Operant discrimination training using tokens as reinforcers has been successfully employed in teaching retarded children to point to appropriate objects subsequent to verbal cues (Guess, 1969; Bricker and Bricker, 1970). In addition, Doehring (1968) demonstrated that various populations including deaf children, children with learning disorders, and normal children could learn to associate nonverbal sounds with appropriate pictures.

Multiply handicapped deaf children are a population that can greatly benefit from the technology developed from operant principles. Garrard and Saxon (1973) prepared a multihandicapped deaf child for hearing therapy using behavior modification. Johnson and Kaye (1974, 1975) demonstrated that multihandicapped deaf children can be taught to lip-read the names of objects based on oral discriminative stimuli. However, except for these few experiments, behavioral principles have seldom been applied in the area of speech and language training for multihandicapped deaf children. Specifically, operant conditioning has not been employed by clinicians in teaching speechreading to multihandicapped deaf children.

This study was designed to develop and maintain speechreading of four groups of words in a deaf multihandicapped child. Operant techniques used in this study involved a contingency reversal in the first experiment and a multiple baseline in the second experiment. The difference between this study and previous speechreading studies was that the experimenter manipulated verbal stimuli, schedules of reinforcement, and the various reinforcers utilized to shape speechreading.

DESCRIPTION OF SUBJECT

Rusty was a nine-year-old deaf boy who had been diagnosed as emotionally disturbed and mentally retarded. He obtained an intelligence quotient of 45 on the Ontario School Ability Exam (Amoss, 1936) and received a social quotient of 41 on the Vineland Social Maturity Scale (Doll, 1965). Using pure-tone averages for the better ear plotted on the basis of the 1964 ISO reference thresholds, he evidenced a profound bilateral sensorineural hearing loss which progressed from 60 dB at 250 Hz to 95 dB at 1000 Hz. For frequencies beyond 1000 Hz there was no unaided response. When Rusty was fitted with a Radioear 980 hearing aid, his pure-tone audiogram was 35 dB at 500 Hz, 40 dB at 1000 Hz, and 50 dB at 2000 Hz.

Rusty had been removed from his deaf oral special education class at the teacher's request and referred to a local mental health agency because of behavior disorders. Subsequently, he was placed in the Kalamazoo Valley Multihandicap Center where behavior modification strategies and American Sign Language (ASL) techniques were used to shape appropriate classroom behaviors. He was placed on the center's token economy and it appeared that tokens were reinforcing to him. Later, his academic skills were significantly raised to a level required for successful functioning in a special education classroom. However, speechreading, as a part of his receptive language skills, had not been developed and this behavior was a prerequisite for returning the child to a special education classroom.

EXPERIMENT I: REVERSAL

All sessions of the study took place at the subject's classroom desk. The experimenter and child sat facing each other with the desk between them, and Rusty wore his hearing aid each session. The experimenter pronounced the names of six fruits in a random order at normal conversational levels while plastic imitations of the fruits were lying on the desk. During each session, each of the six fruits was named 10 times for a total of 60 presentations. Rusty was to point to the fruit named. Responses were scored correct only if his first response was appropriate and occurred within 10 seconds.

The sequence of procedural steps used in this experiment is described below and shown in Figure 1. The figure shows the number of sessions devoted to each step in the research.

Baseline. A shaping procedure was not required to evoke a pointing response by Rusty during the first session. During baseline the experimenter simply recorded each response, giving the child no indication whether it was correct.

Reinforcement. All correct responses emitted by the child during the first reinforcement step were reinforced with tokens and praise while incorrect responses were not reinforced. Praise for correct responses consisted of smiles accompanied by enthusiastic statements in ASL such as "Good boy," "That is right," or similar phrases. The incorrect responses were followed by a limited time-out in which each error was followed by the experimenter terminating eye contact and withholding attention for approximately 20 seconds.

Reversal. The contingencies in this phase were the opposite of those in the previous phase. All correct responses emitted by the child were placed on limited time-out and all incorrect responses were reinforced with tokens and praise.

4. EDUCATIONAL RESOURCES

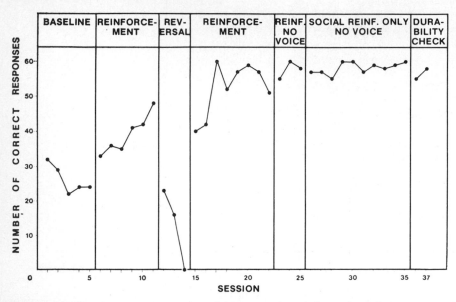

Figure 1. Number of correct responses out of 60 presentations during each of the seven steps of experiment I starting with baseline.

Reinforcement. The contingencies and consequences in this phase were the same as in the previous reinforcement phase. All correct responses were reinforced with tokens and praise, and incorrect responses were not. The preceding reinforcement-reversal-reinforcement sequence was conducted to demonstrate the effectiveness and selectivity of contingent reinforcement and time-out.

Reinforcement, No-Voice. In this phase the contingencies did not change, but the presentations of the auditory stimuli did. When the experimenter made his verbal presentations, he silently mouthed the names of the fruit instead of voicing them. Mastery of this situation would require Rusty to lip-read and not attend to sounds.

Social Reinforcement Only, No-Voice. In order to make the experimental setting approximate the classroom setting that the child eventually would enter, two manipulations were made by the experimenter in this phase. The first was omitting the tokens as reinforcers and the second was reducing the density of social reinforcement. Whenever Rusty emitted a correct response, he received praise only. After two days of this procedure, the reinforcement schedule was changed from continuous reinforcement (CRF) to a fixed ratio 2 (FR 2) in which every second response was socially reinforced instead of each one. Two sessions later the schedule was changed to a FR 3 and in Session 31 it was changed to a FR 4. A FR 5 was initiated in Session 33 followed by a FR 6 in the next session.

Durability Checks. Durability checks were taken two and three months after the completion of the experiment. These were single sessions with the same contingencies and consequences in effect as in Session 35.

Data Analysis. Since Rusty was familiar with the fruits and other food, the high correct responding percentage during baseline was not surprising. The initial reinforcement procedure for correct responses yielded an increase from 33 to 48 in the number of correct responses in just a few sessions. The next manipulation, a reversal, resulted in a decrease in the number of correct responses per session from 47 to zero in just three days. In the following phase, the reinforcement procedure for correct responding was reinstated and the number of correct responses rapidly rose again and reached 100% correct three days after the commencement of this manipulation. The no-voice condition in the next phase failed to decrease the number of correct responses per session. Reducing the reinforcement density in the last phase did not show a significant change in Rusty's correct responding percentage. The single session durability checks produced correct response percentages of 92 and 97% respectively.

EXPERIMENT II: MULTIPLE BASELINE

In the second experiment the experimenter pronounced the names of nine colors each of which was printed on a 3″ x 3″ card. These colors were divided into three groups (Group 1: brown, green, purple; Group 2: red,

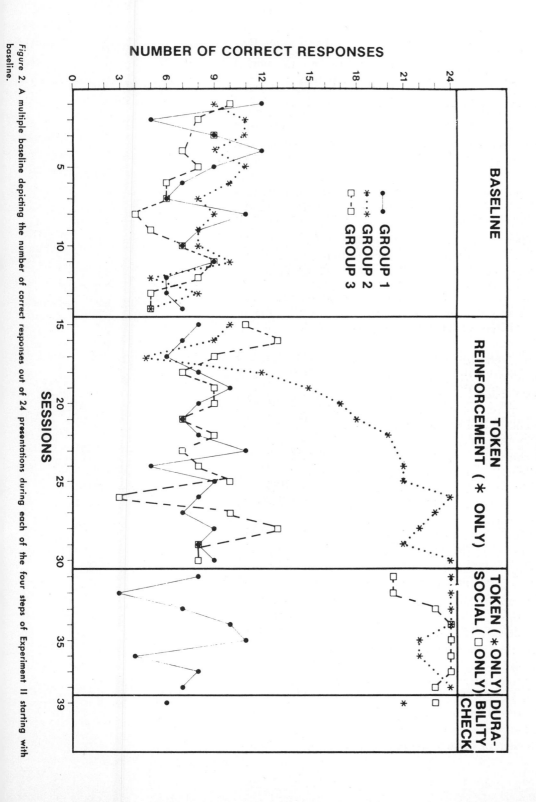

Figure 2. A multiple baseline depicting the number of correct responses out of 24 presentations during each of the four steps of Experiment II starting with baseline.

white, blue; Group 3: black, pink, yellow), and one group of cards at a time was placed on the desk. The three groups were always presented in the same order, but the three colors within each group were presented randomly for a total of eight presentations per color each session. Response correctness was defined as in the first experiment.

The sequence of procedural steps used in this experiment is described below and shown in Figure 2. Again, the figure shows the number of sessions devoted to each step in the research.

Baseline. Neither correct nor incorrect responses by the child were reinforced during baseline and the experimenter simply recorded each response as in baseline of the first experiment.

Token Reinforcement. In this phase, all of Rusty's correct responses to Group 2 stimuli were reinforced with tokens delivered by hand from the experimenter. Tokens were delivered without the simultaneous pairing of social reinforcers. Incorrect responses in Group 2 and all responses in Groups 1 and 3 were not reinforced with tokens or praise.

Token-Social Reinforcement. During this phase correct responses to Group 2 items continued to be reinforced with tokens. Correct responses to Group 3 items were socially reinforced by the experimenter with attention and praise. Incorrect responses and all responses made to Group 1 items received no reinforcement of any kind.

Durability Check. One month after the completion of this experiment, a durability check was made with the same contingencies in effect as in the previous phase.

Data Analysis. The mean percentage of correct responses to Group 1 items which were never reinforced was relatively stable for the four phases of this experiment. However, training items that received token reinforcement or social reinforcement improved as shown in Figure 2.

CONCLUSIONS

The two experiments in this study demonstrate the effectiveness of a reinforcement approach to teaching lipreading. The data from the first experiment revealed that tokens and praise increased correct responding in the reinforcement phases as well as decreased correct responding in the reversal. In addition, praise maintained lipreading and did not have to be presented each time a correct response was made. Presentations of tokens and praise were separated in the second experiment and it was found that either was effective for increasing the percentage of correct responses. The durability checks from both experiments demonstrated that the child maintained the previously reinforced behaviors even though no one taught him lipreading during the two interims.

This study presents further evidence that the systematic and consistent application of reinforcers can develop and maintain relatively complex discriminatory behaviors in individuals who are both mentally and physically handicapped. Furthermore, the techniques described are relatively simple and could be easily applied to deaf mentally handicapped or emotionally disturbed individuals. This necessitates further research to determine whether lipreading training of this kind influences an individual's daily lipreading activities.

Picture Perfect

DORIS W. NAIMAN

■ Individual use of a camera is a joyful and effective way to help deaf children increase interpersonal communication. While taking the photographs and while showing them, children are stimulated to interact more with other children at school and with parents and siblings at home.

New York University's Deafness Research and Training Center conducted a photography project with children ages 9 through 16 in four classes at New York City's Public School JHS 47 for the Deaf. Financed by grants from New York University's Deans' Committee, the Polaroid Foundation, and Marge Neikrug of Neikrug Galleries, the project produced results positive enough to encourage teachers to use this technique.

The project included children in regular classes and children who had been placed in special classes because they exhibited patterns of maladaptive behavior severe enough to interfere with their ability to function and learn in regular classes for the deaf. The behavior of the children in special classes ranged from extreme lack of control and hyperactivity to almost complete unresponsiveness and withdrawal from interaction. Many had developed neither language nor a way to communicate.

Individual student photography with cameras seemed a promising approach because it offers a nonverbal, nonacademic way in which children can achieve success, express themselves, and communicate.

WHAT WE WANTED TO DO
The overall objective was to provide an additional mode of communication for the 20 deaf children involved in the project. Specific behavioral goals for each child were set for the first four weeks of the project. These included:
1. To learn how to operate the camera.
2. To take at least 20 photographs at school.
3. To take at least 20 photographs at home or outside of school.
4. To show the photographs to classmates and teachers.
5. To show the photographs to family and friends at home.
6. To talk, write, sign, or pantomime about the photographs to classmates and teachers.
7. To talk, write, sign, or pantomime about the photographs to family and friends at home.

In preparation for the project, conferences were held with administrators and teachers to discuss objectives for the children, suggested approaches and activities, and procedures for evaluation. Workshops were held with the participating teachers and classroom educational assistants to teach the use of the camera and techniques for presentation to the children.

WHAT WE DID
Each camera was shared by two children. They took turns using the cameras at various times during the school day designated by the teacher. Each child had use of the camera out of school on alternate weekdays and weekends. Film allotment was two rolls per week per child, for a total of 16 exposures per week. Both black and white and color film were provided, and flash cubes were available as needed.

Photographic activities took place daily. Children received individual instruction on how to take and develop photographs. Using a Polaroid camera made it possible for the children to develop their own pictures at once. During the first week all cameras remained on the school premises and picture taking was confined to the general school area. For the remaining three weeks, the children were allowed to take the cameras outside of the school.

The children were allowed to photograph whatever they wished. Teachers encouraged the children to show their photographs to other children, to take their photographs home, and to tell about their photographs using all modes of communication, including talking, signing, writing, and pantomiming. Teachers suggested special activities such as making individual booklets of photographs, mounting photographs, writing stories about them, and arranging an exhibit for parents and other classes.

HOW WE ASSESSED SUCCESS
The extent to which each child achieved the project objectives was assessed by means of the following evaluation instruments:

1. *Teacher report forms* were filled out daily by the teacher to record the child's ability to use the camera, number of photographs taken in and out of school, frequency in

showing photographs, and efforts to describe pictures and experiences.

2. *Questionnaires* for teachers, educational assistants, and parents were filled out at the conclusion of the project to provide information from individuals closely involved with the children regarding their perception of the children's interpersonal communication as related to the photography experience.

3. *Structured interviews* with the school's principal, assistant principal, and media specialist were conducted in the two weeks following completion of the project to provide information from observers less closely involved regarding their perceptions of the effectiveness of the photography experience.

Data gathering procedures, which included the use of anecdotal records, contributed valuable information about the following questions:

• Are there differences in response to the photography project by children who have been identified primarily as presenting behaviors that are withdrawn, hyperactive, or aggressive?

• Are there differences in response to the photography project by children of different age levels?

• Are the photographic activities helpful in increasing the length of time that children are able to spend working at a task?

DID IT MAKE A DIFFERENCE?
Among the 20 children involved in the project, 19 achieved all of the specific behavioral objectives set. All the children learned to operate the camera; 16 children learned in one day, 4 required two days. Most of the children took as many photographs as their film allotment allowed.

All the children regularly showed their photographs to classmates and teachers. Of the 12 mothers interviewed, 8 indicated that taking photographs at home and showing pictures taken at school increased their communication with their child.

Teacher ratings indicated that 18 children showed a significant or outstanding increase in their interaction with peers, expression of feelings, and communication of ideas. These children used varying combinations of speech, manual communication, writing, and pantomime.

In addition, 17 children regularly communicated about their finished photographs either on their own initiative or in response to questioning. The other 3 children communicated about their pictures only with much encouragement from the teacher, but in spite of this reluctance, 1 of the 3 still showed a significant increase in interaction and expression of feelings according to her teacher's rating. The teacher commented, "This girl is rather shy. To get children to pose for her, she had to really make an effort to communicate. It has helped her a great deal. She loves taking pictures."

INCREASE IN SELF ESTEEM
Teachers and parents described what they perceived as a rise in the self esteem of many of the children as a result of the project. Mastery of photographic equipment and techniques contributed to a general feeling of competency; for some of the children who had a long history of failure, the project provided success at a task for the first time. Reports of inner city photography projects have shown similar results and indicate that because photography projects tend to create a chain of successes, they also tend to encourage young people to try new things and to increase their feeling

of "being somebody who can do things" (*Manual for Photo Project Leaders*, 1969).

The children were pleased with their new role as photographers and with having others view them in this role. One 9 year old boy who had in the past avoided any interaction with other children approached a boy on the playground and asked to take his picture. Other children gathered around him and the usually withdrawn boy visibly enjoyed the new experience. Performing an attractive activity in the midst of his peers gave him more social confidence and greater ability to approach unfamiliar situations.

An 11 year old boy was so excited about taking photographs that he was able to relate to people in ways that were entirely new for him. When his teacher asked him if he wanted to go around the neighborhood with a student teacher to take pictures of whatever he wished, the boy seemed thrilled. He immediately turned to the student teacher (whom he did not know), told her his name, and asked her name. In his enthusiasm he led her on such a run down Twenty-Third Street that she reported she should have been prepared with sneakers and a sweat band. He guided her to a neighborhood park where, abandoning his shyness, he proceeded to position her for the picture he wanted to take. He saw two children with their father, who offered to take his picture, but the boy indicated that he wanted to be the photographer himself. He then took two pictures of the family and gave them to the man, smiling at the family and pleased at the whole event.

OPPORTUNITIES FOR MAKING CHOICES
The children's freedom to decide what photographs they wanted to take and how they wanted to take them played an important part in adding to their feelings of self worth, personal power, and competence. Most of the time the children did not take shots randomly; rather, they purposefully chose what they wished to photograph and, in many cases, carefully planned the picture. The children had an opportunity to decide, choose, and create—processes that build confidence for any child, but especially for these deaf children who need every opportunity they can get for independent action.

One boy took five pictures during a 45 minute stroll in the neighborhood, apparently snapping whatever appealed to him as he walked along. His pictures were of a car he liked, a construction worker on a scaffold, a lawn mower, a street cleaning machine, and a man with a McDonald's emblem on his blazer pocket. Another boy deliberated at length about what to photograph. On one occasion, after spending a little while scouting the neighborhood, he picked out a bicycle shop, walked over and asked the proprietor if he could take his picture, and proceeded to do so.

On a class trip one boy decided to take pictures of flowers. The teacher commented on his high degree of concentration to get just what he wanted and his care in making sure the camera was focused properly and adjusted for proper lighting. Several children took many different shots of the new school building being erected next to their school. They watched the construction from their classroom windows and took photographs from the windows and from different angles on the sidewalk outside.

LANGUAGE DEVELOPMENT
Although the primary focus of the project was on helping the children increase interpersonal communication, there were additional positive results. The children enjoyed writing about their photographs, and progress in written language

and in reading was observed in all of the classes. One little boy related long stories about his pictures, about what people were doing, and how they were feeling. His teacher helped him write down the stories, which he kept in a little book. Many of the children kept similar personal books of their photographs with written descriptions. They enjoyed rereading their own books and showing them to the other children.

The teachers also arranged partially structured photographic activities planned for language development. As part of a unit on which the class was working, one teacher assigned each child to go around the neighborhood with a student teacher and take pictures of various kinds of stores. On a field trip to the Staten Island Zoo the children took pictures of the ferryboat and the animals. Subsequent discussions and language learning activities centered around the photographs. The children were eager to talk, write, and read about their own pictures and their recollections of the day.

"FAMILY PORTRAIT"

Among the children's parents, two-thirds reported that the photography activities increased their communication with their child. Being able to take photographs at home and then take them back to school helped some children make their life an integrated whole instead of separate school and home compartments with no communication tying them together.

One 9 year old girl with limited language skills had never been able to tell her class anything about her home life. When she was asked about home her comments had been limited and unclear. After she took the camera home she eagerly brought back pictures of her family and her apartment and tried to explain them to the other children. Some children daily carried their pictures back and forth between school and home. One little boy who had almost no verbal language always pasted his pictures on a sheet of paper, wrote a sentence for each picture with the teacher's help, and then carefully put the papers in an envelope to take home.

A BROAD EXPERIENCE

Not the least valuable feature of the photography project was the pleasure and eagerness with which the children participated. A happy experience has reason enough for being, especially for children who have difficulties functioning satisfactorily in a traditional school program. But in addition, the teachers were able to handle resourcefully the children's high interest in taking photographs and to make the experience pay off in communication and language growth as well as pleasure.

REFERENCE

Manual for photo project leaders. Rochester NY: Eastman Kodak Company, 1969.

An aspect of Indian culture that astonished the colonists, we are told, was the concept that the gods had a special concern for the mentally and physically handicapped and that all creatures on earth were obliged to share it.

The more prevalent feeling, a legacy from the Middle Ages, was essentially one of rejection. It was thus perhaps inevitable that the initial moves to provide education for the handicapped entailed removing them from everyday affairs. Those offered any help at all were normally placed in an "asylum," a word which, along with "feeble-minded" and "deaf and dumb," quickly acquired pejorative connotations. The effort was nevertheless a major step forward, and it began in the New World with Americans who traveled to Europe to study the pioneering techniques beginning to emerge there.

One such was Thomas Hopkins Gallaudet. Not only a teacher but a teacher of teachers, he became so interested in the communications problems confronting people who could not hear that he went to Paris to visit a school for the deaf that had been started by a young priest named the Abbé de l'Epeé. When Mr. Gallaudet returned to the United States he brought with him a deaf man who had been trained at the school, Laurent Clerc, and in 1817 they established the Nation's first formal educational institution for the handicapped—the American Asylum for the Deaf, located in West Hartford, Connecticut. Mr. Gallaudet was in time to gain an international reputation for his leadership in the education of deaf and other handicapped children, and he is memorialized today by Gallaudet College in Washington, D.C., the only liberal arts college for the deaf in the world.

Another importer of European techniques for educating the handicapped was John D. Fisher, who had gone to Paris to study medicine. There he became fascinated by the work being done in a residential school for the blind that had been started by Valentin Hauy. After his return to the United States in 1826, Dr. Fisher described that work so persuasively that three years later the Massachusetts State Legislature voted funds to

Deaf education proponent Thomas Gallaudet, for whom Gallaudet College is named

establish in Boston the New England Asylum for the Blind (soon thereafter renamed the Perkins School for the Blind and subsequently relocated in its present site in Watertown). The initial director of the school was a physician named Samuel Greeley Howe, and his contributions and those of Dr. Fisher also were to be

or Special Education

From the left: Helen Keller; her tutor, Anne Sullivan; and Alexander Graham Bell.

Students—from 1893 and today—of Gallaudet College, since 1864 the world's only liberal arts college for the deaf.

memorialized—in their cases by the accomplishments of two remarkable women who had been born both blind and deaf.

The first was Laura Bridgman, who began her instruction at Perkins in 1837 when she was seven years old. Her success not only in learning to read and write but as an extraordinarily effective teacher brought new hope to the parents of handicapped children around the world. One such parent was the mother of six-year-old Helen Keller, who read about Laura Bridgman's achievements and sought help from a graduate of Perkins Institute named Anne Sullivan. With Anne Sullivan's help and her own indomitable determination, Helen Keller became the author of several books, a much-sought-after lecturer, and one of the most admired public figures the Nation has ever known.

Spurred by such examples of what could be done, other institutions for youngsters suffering various handicapping conditions began to come into existence. Most clung to the practice of separating the handicapped from society in special schools, but appearing here and there were arrangements which, while segregating handicapped youngsters from other children, at least made it possible for them to remain with their families. In 1871 a day school was established in Boston for deaf pupils, for example, a class in Providence in 1896 for the retarded, another in Chicago in 1899 for crippled children.

One of the most effective spokesman for this approach was Alexander Graham Bell, who proposed to the 1898 convention of the National Education Association that programs for the handicapped be established in the public schools. Such

children, he said, would "form an annex to the public school system, receiving special instruction from special teachers who shall be able to give instruction to little children who are either deaf, blind, or mentally deficient, without sending them away from their homes or from the ordinary companions with whom they are associated." Dr. Bell was addressing the conference not as the celebrated inventor of the telephone but as a speech expert from a family of speech experts. He had among other things successfully undertaken the instruction of a deaf boy named George Sanders in Salem, Massachusetts, and it was in the Sanders home that he made his first telephone experiments. When it became clear that his invention would bring him wealth, Dr. Bell wrote to his mother, "Now we shall have money enough to teach speech to little deaf children."

A Structured Program of Learning for Moderately Retarded Deaf Adults

ANNETTE P. TAYLOR
BARBARA E. POLLOCK

A structured experimental teaching program for two mature, moderately mentally retarded deaf patients in a state mental hospital and school was designed to see how subjects with this combined handicap would respond. Results of the 8-week program conducted on a one-to-one pupil-teacher basis indicated that these two individuals were highly motivated to learn when the instruction was meaningful to them and was related to their environment.

DURING THE SUMMER of 1966 an educational program was developed for two mentally retarded deaf women who had not been exposed to a structured learning experience for approximately 15 years. The women were hospitalized and, because of their manual communication, were unable to function in and benefit from the usual rehabilitation programs. They had been considered to be unsuitable candidates for individual therapy or highly structured small-group work but were now scheduled for intensive therapy in an attempt to stimulate their learning potential and improve their communicative skills. The project was undertaken through the combined efforts of the Speech and Hearing Clinic and the Education Department at Laurelton Pennsylvania State School and Hospital.

Communication therapy for individuals of severely diminished intellectual function and advanced age has traditionally been conducted informally, aimed at restricted achievement levels. This approach has been largely unsuccessful for patients characterized by the combination of mental retardation, deafness, and advanced age. This pilot study attempted to determine the effectiveness of a highly structured teaching program with this type of patient. It was not an experiment in the sense of a highly formalized analytical design and procedure, intended to arrive at unequivocal conclusions regarding the effectiveness of one teaching method over another. Rather, it was an initial attempt to find some way of getting through to these patients.

Personal History

Subject A is 44 years old, has been institutionalized at Laurelton State School and Hospital since she was 16. She had attended a school for the deaf in Pennsylvania until the time of her admission to Laurelton. When she was dismissed from the school because of her reported inability to benefit from further education, she had achieved a slow third grade academic achievement level and was considered a persistent behavior problem. Tests given in 1961 indicated that she functions at a borderline level of intelligence; her full scale IQ measured on the Wechsler Adult Intelligence Scale is 83.

Subject B, 31 years old, attended a school for the deaf from the age of 8 to 14. School officials reported that her hearing impairment was an additional handicap rather than the basic cause of her ineducability. She has been a patient at the Laurelton State School and Hospital for 15 years. The Grace Arthur Performance Battery given in 1961 indicated a full scale IQ of 61.

Audiologic Data

Subject A has a profound binaural sensorineural hearing loss as a result of influenza contracted when she was 3 years old. She wears a body-type hearing aid that apparently serves to amplify gross environmental noises.

Subject B has a binaural hearing loss of profound degree, possibly congenital. She is unable to benefit from amplification.

Educational Program

An 8-week summer program, initiated in 1966, was designed to stimulate and improve the acquisition and use of communicative symbols. The symbols included manual signs, fingerspelling, reading, writing, speechreading, numerical concepts, and a minimum of oral speech production. Through the cooperation of the Speech and Hearing Clinic and the Education Department at Laurelton State School and Hospital, a speech and hearing specialist and a classroom teacher worked as a team with these subjects for 16 hours weekly. Daily classes were arranged, with academic sessions lasting for 2 to 2½ hours each morning. Three afternoons a week the women were seen in a home economics suite that served as the setting for social learning situations.

The California Achievement Test, Primary Form, was administered to them in July at the start of the educational program and again at its end in September. Although this test is not designed for deaf students, it was selected because of its availability, ease of administration, and diagnostic uses. The time limits were not adhered to; certain liberties were taken and some sections eliminated where it was felt that the test would not apply to deaf students because of hearing loss and communication difficulties.

The program of instruction based on the California Achievement Test performance was planned to provide for the individual needs of the students. It soon became evident that these needs varied so widely as to necessitate individual instruction. Subject A often became impatient when held back because of the slower progress made by the other student, and for this reason classes became centered on individual instruction, with each teacher working on a one-to-one basis with each student.

Time concepts taught were minutes, hours, days, weeks, months, and years; this included the identification of seasons and holidays. The numerical concepts involved were illustrated through pictures and written words and their corresponding symbols.

Language arts centered on learning the names of environmental items. Each object was labeled—from desks and windows inside the classroom to the trees and flowers outside. The students were taught to sign, fingerspell, read, and write the nouns as they appeared in the class lessons. Speechreading was continually encouraged.

During the afternoon meeting the materials from the morning sessions were adapted for use in social situations. The clinicians were fortunate to have access to the home economics suite of the school where facilities included a model apartment with kitchen, dining room, living room, bathroom, and bedroom. Typical social occasions were simulated such as preparing, serving, and eating a meal or a snack; and introducing guests. The subjects took turns acting as hostess and guest.

Toward the end of the program the women were taken on a field trip to a nearby community where they toured a bank, post office, drug store, and department store; ate lunch in a restaurant; and visited historical sites.

Subject A revealed no difficulty with visual discrimination when she was shown the teacher-prepared materials covering concepts of alike-and-different, larger-and-smaller, more-and-less, and opposites. She could discriminate between the letter and number forms.

An attempt was made to utilize subject A's more extensive vocabulary by directing her efforts toward the development of some basic language and mathematical skills, i.e. punctuation and capitalization, put to use in letter writing; addition and subtraction; telling time; recognition of coins and their value (used in making change) ; and learning to read for information and understanding so that she could follow directions and answer questions.

Subject B lacked the vocabulary to express herself by any method. She was encouraged to increase her spatial concepts, and to develop and expand her vocabulary. Efforts were concentrated in areas of visual discrimination, forming letters, counting, and associating number symbols with number words. Emphasis was placed on names of objects in the classroom and of people.

Results

During the initial administration of the California Achievement Test, it was observed that the students had difficulty comprehending directions and understanding what they were expected to do. Subject B was least sure of herself and frequently looked on Subject A's test booklet for reassurance. The examiners believe that a great many of Subject B's answers constituted guessing. Her low performance in class supports this. Scores for both subjects, on the pre- and post-tests are presented in Table I.

In comparing the test scores, one must keep in mind that this test was designed for "normal" children and that much of what was learned by these students could not be measured. Scoring was difficult, particularly in spelling, because manual signs often convey a concept rather than a particular word form, and fingerspelling must be substituted where a sign is lacking. Such words had to be omitted from the test list, but doing so obviously does not present a realistic picture of the students' ability in this area. The scores indicate that the women made progress, especially when one considers that less than one-tenth of a point improvement should be expected from normal students doing a full day's work over an 8-week period.

TABLE I

California Achievement Test Score Results

	Pretest	Post-test
Subject A		
Reading vocabulary grade placement	1.4	1.7
Reading comprehension grade placement	1.6	1.6
Total reading grade placement	1.7	1.7
Arithmetic reasoning grade placement	1.3	1.5
Arithmetic fundamentals grade placement	1.2	2.0
Total arithmetic grade placement	1.3	1.7
Spelling grade placement	2.9	2.9
Subject B		
Reading vocabulary grade placement	1.3	1.2
Reading comprehension grade placement	1.2	1.4
Total reading grade placement	1.3	1.2
Arithmetic reasoning grade placement	.9	1.2
Arithmetic fundamentals grade placement	.8	1.0
Total arithmetic grade placement	.9	1.0
Spelling grade placement	1.4	1.4

By the termination of the program, Subject A was able to read and write in complete sentences, using accurate grammar and punctuation. When the program began, her sentences were characterized by omission of words and reversals in both spelling and word

order; punctuation was nonexistent. Her vocabulary increased from approximately 30 to 65 written words, and her speechreading ability improved slightly. She became eager to learn oral speech and did manage to articulate a few conversational phrases well enough to make herself understood. Her attempts at production of spontaneous language showed a wide variety of errors and omission of words and word endings.

The progress of Subject B was far more limited than that of Subject A. Her learning centered predominantly on time concepts. By the end of the program she was able to grasp the meaning of yesterday-today-tomorrow and the calendar concepts of weeks, months, and years. On the other hand, she could not, no matter how much she tried, comprehend the clock nor the simplest arithmetic computations. Her vocabulary and spelling as expressed in the finger alphabet and manual signs did increase; but because her retention from day to day and from week to week was so poor, an accurate estimate of the amount she actually learned cannot be made. She did not advance to reading, writing, or speechreading.

Discussion

Although this program was administered on an exploratory basis, it was apparent that these women want to learn and that they can be taught if methods of teaching are simplified and patiently presented. It is interesting to consider the mental and chronological ages of the subjects and the fact that neither student had been exposed to any type of learning situation for approximately 20 years prior to this program. Their attendance was regular, and they often requested to continue working beyond the end of a session. A positive attitude was maintained by the subjects throughout the program. They did not appear to become discouraged or frustrated by the difficulty of a task but worked persistently to accomplish a desired end.

The students expressed anxiety at the termination of the summer program because they feared that once again they would have no teachers. They wanted to learn, and to learn precisely what was offered. The clinicians received numerous comments and reports from cottage personnel and other staff members regarding the new social behavior exhibited by these women. For the first time since their institutionalization years earlier, they spoke such phrases such as, "Hello, how are you?" "Fine, thank you," and "Goodbye." The subjects were able to communicate more fluently with their hearing peers by means of writing and reading, and they felt more socially acceptable. For the first time, both students appeared on time for meals because Subject A had learned the clock concepts and was able to direct Subject B to the appropriate places at the correct hour. Hence, an unexpected change in behavior resulted from the program, because of the students' ability to function in and relate to their social environment. They were highly motivated to learn, especially to learn to communicate, because it was apparent to them that through communication they could relate to their environment.

This program indicated that learning can transpire in instances where the learning process has been in limbo for many years as a result of lack of appropriate stimulation and experience; and that programs of intensive and structured therapy can be meaningful for the moderately retarded deaf adult. These patients should not be simply set aside and forgotten. Further studies are warranted using controls and methods that would be applicable to research procedures in an attempt to improve and expand available methods of educating the mentally retarded deaf.

The Value of Music
in Teaching Deaf Students

Cora Jo Moore Hummel

This article is a brief summary of a study made to show how music has been used with the deaf in the past and what its potentialities are in the future. The research was done in partial fulfillment of the requirements for the degree of Master of Arts in Education of the Deaf in the Graduate School of Texas Woman's University, Denton, Texas. According to the literature, music has been used with the deaf in teaching sound perception, improving speech, building more adequate language, and encouraging self-improvement. The major emphases in these categories are presented. At the conclusion are some recommendations for further work in this area, and an extensive bibliography of the literature written on the uses of music with the deaf.

Although the idea of including music in an educational program for deaf pupils may seem paradoxical, it has been advocated by authorities in the field of education of the deaf, and a number of schools for the deaf have used music with varying degrees of success. For more than a century people have written about the benefits of music for deaf pupils, but its actual use in education is still in its infancy. Because the literature on this subject is scattered over many years and is divided into two fields—music therapy and the education of the deaf—it has not been easily accessible. In doing the research for my master's degree at Texas Woman's College, I brought together the references in books and articles written on this topic, making them readily available to those who are concerned with the education of deaf people, and to deaf people themselves.

early records

The earliest substantial and scientifically oriented instance of using music with the deaf that I found recorded is that of Itard, an eminent otologist working in Paris in 1802. He carefully observed the responses of six deaf students to the auditory stimulation of bells, a drum, and a flute [1].

In 1848 Bartlett recorded his struggles in teaching a deaf girl to play the piano. He concluded from this experience, according to Turner, that definite "intellectual gratification and cultivation was inevitable when music was taught to the deaf" [2].

1. Max Goldstein, *The Acoustic Method for the Training of the Deaf and Hard of Hearing Child*, St. Louis, Missouri: Laryngoscope Press, 1939, p.12.
2. W. W. Turner, "Music Among the Deaf and Dumb," *American Annals of the Deaf*, II, October 1848, pp. 1-5.

4. EDUCATIONAL RESOURCES

Two sources from the mid-nineteenth century, Castel and Ludlow, indicate that some work was done in devising an apparatus for conveying music to deaf individuals by means of color [3].

In 1893 instructors at New York Institution for the Instruction of the Deaf and Dumb found that the deaf students could march to the beat of a drum and could successfully participate in a field-music corps. In reference to this band, May wrote that there "seems to be something in the vibration of music that exercises the nerves of audition and vitalizes them" [4]. By 1927 the Illinois State School for the Deaf and the Tennessee State School for the Deaf also had bands made up of deaf students [5]. Research shows that, particularly during the early part of the twentieth century, many educators of the deaf promoted the value of the piano in teaching speech to deaf pupils.

new concepts

More recently new concepts have come to the forefront. These include Guberina's Verbotonal Method which creates speech structures based on the rhythm of nursery rhymes and the rhythm of body movements [6]; Uden's combination method of hearing and feeling which integrates both vision and sound perception into motorism [7]; and an adaptation of Orff's method of teaching music to children, which emphasizes rhythm and creativity [8].

various uses

Although the literature reflects different and sometimes contradictory attitudes, several general views are apparent. One is, as Birkenshaw states, that music should be used "primarily as a means to an end. The prime goal is not to attain musical perfection . . ." [9]. Generally, those who write about deaf people singing refer to singing as a type of choral speaking or chanting with some pitch variance and expressive tone.

Another major emphasis expressed consistently in the literature is that music is an effective teaching aid because it is a fun thing. Music, as stated by Giovanni, "lends variety and interest to lessons which by nature must be repetitive. Music also creates an atmosphere of relaxation so necessary in teaching a deaf child" [10].

7. A. van Uden, "Instructing Prelingually Deaf Children by the Rhythms of Bodily Movements and of Sounds, by Oral Mime and General Bodily Expression—Its Possibilities and Difficulties," *Proceedings of the International Congress of Educators of the Deaf and of the 41st Meeting of the Convention of American Instructors of the Deaf,* Gallaudet College, 1963.

8. Lois Birkenshaw, "Teaching Music to Deaf Children," *The Volta Review,* LXVII, May 1965, pp. 352-358, 387.

9. ———, "A Suggested Programme for Using Music in Teaching Deaf Children," *Proceedings of the International Conference on Oral Education of the Deaf,* II, 1967, p. 1233.

10. Sister Giovanni, "Music as an Aid in Teaching the Deaf," *9th National Association of Music Therapy,* 1959, p. 88.

3. Fitz Hugh Ludlow, "The Music Essence," *American Annals of the Deaf,* XVII, April 1872, pp. 94-126.

4. Elizabeth May, "A Military School for the Deaf, and Its Band of Deaf Musicians," *The Volta Review,* XIII, September 1911, pp. 201-2.

5. "A Brass Band That Can't Hear the Snappy Music It Makes," *The Literary Digest,* XCII, March 26, 1927, p. 52.

6. Petar Guberina, "Verbotonal Method and Its Application to the Rehabilitation of the Deaf," *Proceedings of the International Congress of Educators of the Deaf and of the 41st Meeting of the Convention of American Instructors of the Deaf, Gallaudet College,* 1963.

A majority of the articles pertain particularly to the value of music in teaching speech to the deaf. Most of these articles emphasize music as an aid in teaching rhythm. Some, however, deal with other aspects of speech. Uden claims success in teaching specific pitch, even half-step intervals. He attributes this phenomenon to the type of amplication he utilizes, as well as to the technique of explaining to the child that the fine differences he hears are in reality different pitches. He relates these pitches to the music scale. Other writers place special emphasis on teaching voice quality and proper breathing.

The use of music in teaching and testing sound perception is another area emphasized. In addition to feeling the vibrations of music, the deaf individual can now perceive music through the auditory channel. This new role for music in auditory training is made possible through developments in acoustical equipment which enable the child to make more extensive use of his residual hearing.

In the area of specific language development several writers report that music helps the deaf child to increase his vocabulary, to develop correct grammatical usage, and to practice speechreading.

Authorities also agree that music is valuable in the realm of self-realization. This involves therapeutic movement, social dancing, and musical instrumental skill, all of which can bring pleasure to the person and help him develop self-assurance.

current research

There are several leading figures who are continuing research in this area. For instance, Uden is preparing a book entitled *The Education of Deaf Children: A World of Sound for Deaf Children*. This should be valuable as a teaching aid since, according to Dale, Uden is "probably the world authority on music for very young deaf children" [11]. Also, although not yet released in the United States, there is a short film with a sound track about Orff's work with "rhythmical musical education" with children whose hearing is impaired. Orff is a musical composer whose works are well known for the rhythm and the musical sound of words. Birkenshaw, as a consultant in North America for Orff's method, is someone else who is likely to contribute more to the literature on music and the education of the deaf. Guberina's theories, which include the use of music, have been creating interest and should continue to do so. He, too, has a film showing his work. Every effort should be made to encourage further research in this area and to publish progress reports. Clearly, there are numerous possibilities for using music as a supplement to the core curriculum for the deaf.

suggested research

Several recommendations can be made for further research in this subject. One suggestion is that a bibliographical list of songs for the deaf be designed. An inquiry could be made among teachers of the deaf to determine the extent of their training in this area and to discover the specific purpose for which they use music with the deaf, if they use it at all. Investigation could be made of music therapists and dance therapists regarding their training and experience with the deaf. Another study, perhaps, could review the literature pertaining to the values of music in working with the hard of hearing and the

---

11. Dion Murray Crosbie Dale, *Applied Audiology for Children*, 2nd ed., Springfield, Illinois: Charles C Thomas, 1967, p. 130.

adventitiously deafened, as there are numerous articles written from that point of view. A study which should appeal particularly to the music therapy student is an extension of Traughber's program of testing specific abilities of the deaf in discriminating music stimuli [12].

While these avenues are being examined, educators of the deaf should use music as advantageously as possible. It is apparent from studying the available literature that, as Birkenshaw aptly states: "a well-organized course of music, particularly one based on a creative approach stressing rhythm, speech and movement, can be a valuable extra aid in teaching the deaf" [13].

12. Sam H. Traughber, "Discriminations Made on Musical Stimuli by Children Institutionalized for Deafness," (unpublished master's thesis, Murray State College, 1957).

13. Birkenshaw, *op cit*.

JAWS IN THE CLASSROOM

Jean Andrews
Ann Dexheimer

■ Peter Benchley's bestselling novel *Jaws* sparked a unique class project—the construction of a 6 ½ foot papier-mache shark—and motivated students to undertake various reading activities. This popular thriller became an effective reading text for eight intermediate students at the Maryland School for the Deaf and provided many practical and useful teaching strategies.

MOVIE-BOOK RELATIONSHIP
The hottest item of conversation among summer returning students at the Maryland School was the movie, *Jaws*. Capitalizing on *Jaws* "mania" in the Intermediate III Department, a reading unit was developed using this box office sellout as a beginning. Finding appropriate reading material that parallels student reading level and taps pupil interest is never an easy task. The coordination of the printed version of a book with the story content of the movie is one solution to the reading teacher's dilemma of finding suitable material.

Current research on the reading habits of deaf adults shows that they tend to select books that have been adapted into movie form (McLaughlin & Andrews, 1975). After viewing the film, many deaf adults read the book. In an attempt to tie student interest to trends in the adult deaf community, we developed a unit on *Jaws* around a nucleus of reading skills, idiomatic expressions, and problem solving.

COMPREHENSION SKILLS
Each student had seen the film version of *Jaws*, so all pupils were familiar with the main idea of the story. The movie was the visual frame of reference with which to compare the printed words in the book. Discussions centered around a comparison of the movie and the chapters read in class. One student remarked, "I like the book better than the movie. It explains more action."

VOCABULARY SKILLS
Deafness denies the adolescent the use of much of the "hip jargon" common to his hearing peers. Using a current bestseller in the classroom as a reading text gives these students the opportunity to experience the vernacular of the 1970's, that is, the idiomatic expressions used in conversation today. The printed word has more meaning because the students have had the visual experience of the film. The combination of film and print increases comprehension of specific idioms that otherwise might appear meaningless to these students.

After each *Jaws* chapter had been read, groups of new words and idioms were listed on the blackboard. The reading teacher gave the American Sign Language equivalent for each English expression. Students discussed the meaning of the new words in the context of each chapter. When the general definition gleaned from the paragraph did not suffice, a more specific definition was found in the dictionary. The study of vocabulary thus became a curious venture into more specific comprehension of the story, rather than a tedious experience.

Students kept a record of the new vocabulary in order to use the words in their original chapter synopses. These chapter synopses became an effective testing tool. Instead of a traditional ex-

The design of the shark is discussed before molding the body out of chicken wire.

"Jaws in the Classroom," Jean Andrews, Ann Dexheimer, *Exceptional Children*, Vol. 9 No. 1, Fall 1976. ©1976 The Council for Exceptional children.

am in which a pupil's memory of the material is evaluated, the chapter synopses were reviewed to discover how well the student could use the material he had learned.

THE GREAT SHARK

The 45 minute daily reading class was divided into two activity periods. The first 20 minutes were spent reading and discussing the novel. During the second half of the period, the pupils moved to a workroom to construct a 6 ½ foot papier-mache replica of a great shark. The motor activity of shark building gave meaning to the verbal labeling of shark descriptions and actions in the book. This hands-on activity was also a relaxing diversion from the printed word, which for deaf students can become quite tedious.

OTHER SUBJECT AREAS

Jaws provided a reservoir of ideas for teachers in different disciplines. For example, the science class investigated the habits of sharks, and coordinating the content gave students the realization that all knowledge is related. The following are some practical teaching ideas with brief descriptions of student activities during the study of *Jaws*.

Reading

1 *Direction following.* While constructing the papier-mache shark, students had to read the directions on a wheat paste package in order to determine the correct mixture of paste and water and the procedure for applying newspaper strips to the chicken wire frame.
2 *Library reports.* Research papers were assigned on various topics. One student described the differences and

likenesses among three sea creatures: dolphins, porpoises, and sharks.

Mathematics

1 *Word problems.* Using information from the novel, students composed mathematical word problems. These examples were exchanged with fellow students and used as an evaluation technique for math class.
2 *Geometry.* Geometric shapes were discovered and analyzed through the basic design of the shark. For example, the body suggested a cone shape, the fins were triangles, and the eyes were half spheres.
3 *Cost of materials.* The cost of chicken wire, wheat paste, and paint was subtracted from class funds. The class sold copies of chapter synopses to other teachers and students when the project was completed. The cost of materials was subtracted from the profits earned from the sale of the *Jaws* pamphlet.
4 *Measurement.* A metric ruler was used to measure the length and width of the shark's body parts. This information was then used to compute ratios to determine actual body proportions of the shark.

Art

1 *Spatial relations.* Using sign language, one student described to the class the spatial relations of the shark. The reading teacher then provided the English equivalent: "The broad head tapers to a thin cylindrical body, then branches out into a fanlike tail."
2 *Shapes.* Shapes were described with body parts. Cone:body; triangle:fins and teeth; sphere:eyes, half circle:jaw.

The class discusses math word problems based on the novel.

3 *Chromatics.* White and black paint were mixed to produce the neutral gray color of the shark.

Science: Discussion Topics

1 Living habits of sharks.
2 Behavioral patterns of sharks; how sharks eat and sleep.
3 Ocean temperatures and currents.

Social Studies: discussion Topics

1 The effect of the beach closing on the economy of a tourist town.
2 What to do in an emergency situation, e.g., drowning, shark attack.
3 The do's and don'ts of swimming in a shark infested area.

Value clarification: Discussion Topics

1 Loyalty and fidelity in personal relationships.
2 Appropriateness and inappropriateness of certain slang expressions.
3 The emotional effects of abusive language; is it used to convey meaning or merely to "let off steam"?
4 City government corruption, lying, bribery, misuse of town funds, blackmail, integrity of elected officials.

GET YOUR FEET WET

The combination of a best selling novel and an award winning film provided impetus for deaf students to explore new and imaginative learning experiences. *Jaws*, the book and the movie, made a splash in secondary curriculum that has implications for the use of companion media as teaching tools.

REFERENCE

McLaughlin, J., & Andrews, J.F. The reading habits of deaf adults in Baltimore. The American Annals of The Deaf. 1975. 120, 497-501.

Four students finger spell their class project: J-A-W-S.

New Realizations
In the Light of The Pure Oral Method

Anthony van Uden, pr.

Contrary to some beliefs, deaf children do possess and utilize a real mother tongue. Through the "maternal reflective method," students at St. Michielsgestel in The Netherlands have achieved a high degree of success in speech, with near normal tempo, and high levels of intelligibility and rhythm. The method is special: the teacher does not try to make the child imitate; but she encourages the child to speak, then imitates the speech of the child herself, thereby beginning with the child's speech movements rather than his perception. The focus is on oral conversation from childhood. The ability to read receptively is developed through conversations, diaries, and storytelling. Grammar is taught by the reflective language method based on conversing and reading, with the aid of reflecting exercises to help the child discover for himself the aspects of grammar. Since the accent-group is here considered to be the true basis of sentence structure, rhythm is thus a significant help to children in constructing correct sentences. Fingerspelling is not used, because it lacks normal rhythm and does not compare as an aid to lipreading with what sound perception can offer.

THE PARADOXICAL combination of "teaching" and "mother tongue" is the central and perhaps the most difficult problem in the education of deaf children.[1] In the course of my work at St. Michielsgestel, I have developed some procedures for teaching deaf children their mother tongue. I have called the overall method we use at this school "the maternal reflective method." In this paper, I shall discuss some of my experiments and procedures, in the hope that these may be of help to teachers and parents of deaf children.

Before I begin, a few definitions are in order. When I speak of "prelingually deaf children," I have two major criteria in mind. First, I am thinking of children whose deafness was inaugurated before the age of 2 years, 6 months. I refer to the period from before birth to 2 years, 6 months as the prelingual period. Second, the hearing loss of the children to whom I refer exceeds 90 dB on the ISO Fletcher Index (Uden 1951, 1960). In other words, they are profoundly deaf.

Furthermore, when I discuss lipreading, it is always (except where specifically indicated otherwise) understood that amplification is being utilized. As far as we now know, prelingually deaf children can understand speech only by lipreading. However, the perception of sound—both hearing and vibration sensations—functions to enhance the lipreading ability of most deaf children. I shall expand upon this statement presently.

One final definition. In our school, about 25 percent of the children are multiply handicapped. We have developed a series of tests to diagnose those children already in the kindergarten, and other tests to show methods by which these children may be helped (Uden 1968). I have in mind especially the so-called "minimal brain dysfunction" children to whom Lemke (1954) and Prechtl (1959-1963) first drew attention. However, I must make it very clear at the outset that I am not speaking about multiply handicapped children in this paper. I do not mean unduly to exclude them from the pure oral method, of course. Special measures, however, will be necessary for the management of these children; measures with which I shall not deal at this time.

some background information

Throughout my discussion, I will refer repeatedly to home training (Ewing 1943; Löwe 1952) and sound perception (Ewing 1934). These are not, of course, new approaches to the education of deaf children. In fact, we have been utilizing them in our institute for, respectively, 14 and 28 years. They will, however, form the constant background of our explanations. For this reason, I mention them now.

I would also like to mention several "possibilities" we have encountered in our work. It is possible to protect deaf infants from also becoming "dumb." It is possible too, that deaf children can be brought to a lipreading readiness and a successful wearing of hearing aids and "vibration-aids" from birth onwards. Moreover, what is, in my opinion, most important, the parents of deaf infants can raise these children in a well-balanced way. Although (unfortunately) the ultimate is seldom reached, most of our children do enter kindergarten "facially directed," as I have called it. In addition, it is possible that deaf children can possess, on the average, a spoken vocabulary of some 300 words by their fifth birthday, and of 600 by their sixth. Finally, it is possible that deaf children can, technically, speak all the syllables and "syllable-linkages" of their mother tongue by the

[1] See my book, *A World of Language for Deaf Children:* Part I: Basic Principles. St. Michielsgestel. The Netherlands: Institute for the Deaf, 1968, p. 13.

4. EDUCATIONAL RESOURCES

age of 6. It is with these possibilities that we at St. Michielsgestel begin our work.

the "from mouth to mouth" method

We have found that before their ninth birthdays many deaf children can repeat from mouth to mouth all—even the most difficult—words, without the help of any extraneous aids. For longer words, this "mouth to mouth" method works in the following way. A word like "personification," to take one example, is not immediately repeated by some deaf children. We begin our teaching by breaking the word down into several shorter components.

For example, we might give him this form: "cation" (beginning with the accented part). We then present him with "personifi." Finally, we say the whole word: "personification." The child repeats this a few times by heart. Then he writes it down—he almost always manages at least a phonemically correct spelling, if the teacher has done her job. At first this method may be time-consuming. But once the children have learned it, "speaking-thinking," as well as the entire learning process, is speeded up considerably.

I believe that this approach should be less and less necessary as the child becomes older. This may be illustrated by one of my recent experiments,[1] in which I composed a test of ten 18-syllable sentences. These are said to the child once in clear rhythmic grouping. For example:

We gaan van daag *alle*maal/ met de *au*to/ *op* en *neer* naar *Eind*hoven.

(We are *all* going/ by *car*/ to and *fro*/ to *Eind*hoven.)

The child is to repeat the whole sentence immediately, without the help of a written form. (See Table I.)

As you can easily see, the older deaf children exhibited considerably more ability to repeat entire utterances immediately upon perceiving them.

tempo of speech

We believe that many of our children speak with essentially normal tempo. This is easily demonstrated by another of my experiments. I measured the

---

[1] Some of the experiments I mention in this paper are still provisional, "pilot" experiments. However, they mirror our daily experiences.

TABLE I

Age of Deaf Children	Avg. # Syllables Correct
8 years old	9.3 S.D.* 3.8
9 " "	9.1 " 6.2
10 " "	11.7 " 6.0
11 " "	14.0 " 3.3
12 " "	15.6 " 2.0

* S.D.: Standard Deviation

tempo of several 50-minute class conversations by boys and girls aged 9, 10, 12, and 16. An analysis of the results of this study showed that the children spoke 2.15 syllables per second (S.D.: 0.67). For purposes of comparison, I also measured the tempos of the speech of the teachers in class conversations, and that of normally hearing television actors. The teachers averaged 2.45 syllables per second (S.D.:0.72), while the actors produced 2.90 syllables per second (S.D.:0.89).

These results dramatically illustrate the fact that these children did not significantly differ in the tempo of their speech from that of their teachers or the actors in question. Nor did we find any significant differences among the various age groups of the children. Unfortunately, I could not make a comparison with class conversations by hearing children.

intelligibility of speech

To test the intelligibility of the speech of some of our deaf children, I devised the following experiment. The deaf youths in the study ranged in age from 11 to 20 years, while the normally hearing youths ranged from 13 to 18 years of age. Each deaf youth sat opposite three hearing youths, and spoke one-syllable words from a Dutch P.B. list. (The deaf children had read over the words prior to the experiment and any mispronunciations had been corrected.) During the experiment, as in normal conversational situations, the listeners could see as well as hear the deaf youths.

After each word, the hearing listeners wrote down what they understood. We computed the average number of words which the hearing students correctly transcribed. We found that a total of 55 percent (± 16) of the words were correctly understood. This means that 68 percent of the deaf youths

scored between 39 percent and 71 percent intelligibility on the test. No significant differences were found among the various age groups.

Rhythm is one of the most important aspects of speech intelligibility. This is especially true in the case of multisyllabic words and sentences. Hudgins (1942) found that intelligibility and rhythm were highly correlated. I utilized a speech-intelligibility test consisting of one-, two-, three-, and four-syllable words to test for rhythm. I found, on the average, that the rhythm of speech by the deaf children I tested was correct in:

93% of the one-syllable words
73% of the two-syllable words
83% of the three-syllable words, and
82% of the four-syllable words.

These appear to be good scores for the children studied. In passing, I might note that the intelligibility and rhythm of the children's speech generally remain on a high level even after they have left school, provided they meet a lot of hearing people. We often find, in fact, upon meeting old pupils again after some years, that, if anything, their speech appears to have become clearer.

utilizing sound perception

At St. Michielsgestel we make use of a special method of teaching deaf children to speak which was developed between 1942 and 1947 by Sister Rosa (1942-1949) and Prof. Reichling (1949). The teacher begins by attempting not so much to make the child imitate her as to imitate the speech of the child herself. She evokes the child to talk in a completely relaxed way, catches what the child offers, and imitates it. The starting point is always the speech-movements of the child, not his perceptions.

An essential component of this method is the utilization by the child

162

TABLE II

PART A

Hearing Loss (Fletcher, ISO)	P.B. Lists	Spondee Lists
90-99 dB	23% ± 14.4	31% ± 18.3
100-109 dB	11% ± 8.1	17% ± 9.3
110-119 dB	2% ± 1.3	3% ± 2.3
Vibration cases	0.2% ± 0.	0%

PART B

H. Loss (Fletcher, ISO)	Choice from 5 one-syllable words	Choice from 3 spondee words	Choice from 10 spondee words	Choice from 30 spondee words
90-99 dB	98% ± 1.3	98.3% ± 1.3	96% ± 3.0	53% ± 13.8
100-109 dB	82% ± 15.2	100% ± 0	96% ± 3.7	54% ± 18.7
110-119 dB	78% ± 17.0	85% ± 10.3	62% ± 15.5	33% ± 20.8
Vibration cases	79% ± 19.3	79% ± 17.7	45% ± 18.1	34% ± 23.0

of all sound perception cues available to him. This includes both hearing and vibration-feeling. The latter is especially helpful for those few children who have no residual hearing. For the vast majority of deaf children who do possess some hearing, vibration-feeling complements this hearing. In fact, vibration can be felt by the skin in all parts of the body, although it seems to be most effectively perceived in the interior part of the ear. In addition to this stress on sound perception, we have used from the beginning what is now called the cybernetic method (Uden 1960). Our children not only hear their speech, but also see it by means of mirrors and "feel" it by means of microphones and headphones.

In evaluating the roles played by lipreading and sound perception in the understanding of speech, we must distinguish between perception with unlimited choice (choice at random) and perception with limited choice (multiple choice). It should be clear that for deaf individuals lipreading serves to limit the possibilities from which sound perception then "chooses." The easier this choice becomes, the greater the understanding.

I devised an experiment, which is still in progress, to measure speech perception. The test items of this study consisted of one-syllable words from Eggermont's (1956) P.B. list, and two-syllable (spondee) words (Uden 1960). We included spondee words

because it has been found (Egan 1944, Davis 1961) that for hard of hearing people the scores on spondee words are nearly equal to the scores on entire sentences. The tests were given to deaf youths aged 11 to 16 years, who utilized sound perception through group hearing aids. The number of youths involved in each test ranged from 84 to 144.

The results will be presented in Table II in two sections: (A) choice at random—sound perception only, no lipreading; and (B) multiple choice —sound perception aided by seeing the written form of the word without lipreading.

Part A of Table II indicates that slightly higher scores were obtained from all children, except those with no residual hearing, on spondee words than on one-syllable w o r d s. The greater rhythm and intonation present in spondee words may account for part of the observed discrepancy.

With respect to Part B, essentially the highest rates of comprehension were attained when the children had to choose among three two-syllable words. Their performance in this sec-

tion was closely followed by their comprehension in choices between five one-syllable words. Those children with higher dB losses scored lower with choices among 10 spondee words, while children with lesser losses did not seem affected by the wider choice offered in this section. All children scored poorly when forced to choose from 30 spondee words.

These tests convincingly demonstrate that sound perception is of greatest use when visual cues have narrowed the number of possible choices. What about the other side of the question: Is lipreading enhanced by the presence of ample sound perception (Uden 1962; cf. van Dongen 1962)?

To answer this question, I devised a test contrasting lipreading with sound perception against lipreading without this aid. My results are summarized in Table III.

From Table III it can be seen that in all cases the use of sound perception increased lipreading scores. The benefit was significant for all groups at the 1 percent level. I believe that these scores only hint at the benefit gained from utilization of sound perception in everyday conversational situations.

In concluding this section of the discussion, I want to mention that we at St. Michielsgestel feel no need for fingerspelling. On the contrary, we believe that fingerspelling cannot compare as an aid to lipreading with what sound perception can offer. Perhaps with fingerspelling a child's vocabulary might initially grow at a faster pace, but in my opinion, this initial gain is overshadowed by the long-range gain in oral cognition and behavior which comes from constant and continuous utilization of sound perception.

developing oral cognition

The central focus of all our efforts at St. Michielsgestel is education

TABLE III

Hearing Loss (Fletcher, ISO)	Lipreading words from a Dutch P.B. List	
	without sound perception	with sound perception
90-99 dB	79% ± 11.0	89% ± 9.3
100-109 dB	81% ± 9.3	94% ± 3.8
110-119 dB	64% ± 19.0	80% ± 9.5
Vibration cases	53% ± 10.3	69% ± 10.4

4. EDUCATIONAL RESOURCES

EXAMPLE 1

A child of two years is looking at a field.

Child	Mother
"Look, Mother, Seep!"	"Oh, what a sweet little sheep."
" 'ig seep an' little seep!"	"Yes, the big sheep is the mother of little sheep."
"Mama? . . . Look! 'ig seep an' little seep walk. . . ."	"Don't you see the big sheep. . . ."
"Dog, oh dog, look a dog! Not allowed!"	"The dog is naughty! . . . That is not allowed, is it. . . ."
"Go away dog!"	"Yes, go away dog, the dog must go." and so on.

toward oral conversations from childhood. Thus, our children are taught one language only: the oral mother tongue. We have come a long way in the last 20 years toward reaching our objectives. We have not, however, yet reached our target because we do not have the means. That it is indeed possible to reach these objectives has been demonstrated to me at St. Joseph's School for the Deaf in St. Louis, and the Clarke School for the Deaf in Northampton, Massachusetts. If only we had the necessary means!

How can one get into conversation with a deaf child? The way a mother treats her hearing child gives us the answer. I have often heard it said that a hearing child learns his spoken language spontaneously of his own accord. This assertion is not strictly correct, as close observation of the mother's behavior will reveal. My own observations of my sisters and their children (Uden 1955, 1967) showed me that in fact the mother is busy all day long teaching her child the mother tongue (see also Bellugi and Brown 1964). Example 1 shows the process in action.

What is it that the mother does without completely realizing it? She *catches* what the child says, or rather, what the child *wants* to say, and gives it back in the correct form. Specifically note in Example 2 what the mother does with the child's sentence fragments.

Looking at these examples, one immediately observes that the child leaves out quite a lot of small words—in much that same way that our older deaf children often do—and the mother keeps filling them in. The mother, then, always uses completely normal language in her conversation. I believe that this process is the key to a good oral education, indeed to all language education. None of us speaks only to fill air—that is, we do not verbalize for the sake of verbalizing. We say what we *want* to say, and nothing else.

Consequently, when we want to enter into conversation with a child, we should look first of all for what the child wants to say. We give the "need to say something" the correct form. Then we let the child reproduce this correct form as soon as he can. If he cannot immediately do this, we write it down for him. In this way,

we can quickly and easily begin a real exchange of thoughts with the child, i.e., a conversation.

What would happen if we failed to establish such integral, germane conversations with deaf children? The child would learn a lot of abstract "oralism" but he would not learn how to converse orally. He would look for other means to express himself with his friends. This surrogate means often takes the form of signs, more and more signs. As a result of this schism between the language he uses with his teachers and that he uses with his peers, he grows up with a form of bilingualism.

If, however, we utilize the maternal reflective method consistently, the child will converse orally both with his teachers and with his friends. In this way the child learns to communicate effectively with all the people he encounters. I was once told: "Deaf children do not feel the urge to say anything." If this is true of a child, then obviously one has *played* too little *with* the child. If we change our orientation from one of simply teaching the child words to one of playing with him, he will certainly want to say something.

Allow me to illustrate my meaning with a few verbatim reports from discussions recorded in two "difficult" classes. Example 3 shows conversation in a class taught by Sister Margaret. The children, all five years old, had recently visited a fair.

All the children have diaries in which class conversation should be recorded. These sentences are also written on the blackboard. Throughout the discussion, the teacher makes short notes from the conversations for the children's diaries. For example:

We have been on the dodge 'ems. M's mother has also got a car. This, though is not a dodge 'em! M. said: "All the children came back in my mother's car." All the children rode in the car of M.'s mother. What a pity! The teacher had to walk it.

This is roughly understood and read by the children. In the higher grades, the procedures remain essentially the same, although, of course, the chil-

EXAMPLE 2

Child	Mother
"seep"	"a sheep"
" 'ig seep"	"the big sheep"
"little seep"	"the little sheep"
"dog"	"the dog"
"not allowed"	"that is not allowed"

EXAMPLE 3

Children

"Cars . . . (Making the sign of bumping)

"Mama." (Pointing to another child)

"All car . . . Mama all."

"Walk, you."

Teacher

"Yes, there were dodge 'ems at the fair."

"Yes, M.'s mother was also at the fair."

"Yes, you all left in your mother's car."

"We had to walk it. What a pity. The car was full."

and so on.

This sample shows that the teacher has manipulated the chronological order of the actual conversation, using such transitional terms as "interrupted . . . were talking . . . then . . . however" to integrate the various sentences. The children will frequently encounter constructions of this sort in their later reading.

The diaries, of course, represent the first reading materials for the younger children. Reading begins *synthetically* —"from the whole." Only later will the children approach reading analytically.

From the preceding discussion of our teaching techniques, it will be apparent that our method can be compared with the behavior a mother uses with her hearing children. The primary purpose of the entire method is to enter into conversation—oral conversation—with the deaf child as soon as possible. Not only do the children use the oral language in speech, they also use it in their thought processes: one thinks in the language in which he converses. This is why I cannot condone Shuy's (1955) and Kröhnert's (1966) contention that deaf children do not possess and utilize a real mother tongue.

In support of this statement, I offer the results of an oral-fluency test which measures the percentage of words used by a child that are "visually-dependent" (names of objects, etc). I asked a number of deaf children to say as many words as possible in two minutes. During the test I watched for any signs being used by the children. My results are summarized in Table IV.

I did not observe any signs. Although the children may use a few signs among themselves, they were able to avoid all signs during this experiment. Of course, none of the children tested were multiply handicapped. I have observed that signs are most frequently used by the multiply handicapped children — they almost compel the others to sign to them. As for the normal deaf children, those who are more "visually-dependent" in their oral fluency generally are more inclined to use signs. I hope to validate this observation more scientifically by actually measuring the frequency of occurrence of signs in the everyday behavior of the children.

dren's language is more advanced. In Example 4 I recorded the following verbatim report from a fourth form class taught by R. Vermeulen. The children's ages ranged from 10 to 11 years; these were slow learners.

The children in this class will keep diaries which closely resemble those used in the preschool class of Sister Margaret, except that these are in normal language rather than in programmed, "purpose" language. This excerpt is a sample:

Peter interrupted the conversation between the teachers and Leo. They were talking about a real pistol. Then Peter said: "My father has got one!" This, however, was not a pistol, but a gun. He received it for his birthday.

EXAMPLE 4

Children

"Bert has got a real pistol!"

"No, sir, make up."

"I made it up."

"No, sir!"

"His father."

"My father has got one."

"No, a gun."

"He has got a gun."

"Because birthday . . . previous birthday 1963."

"He got it for birthd. . . ."

"He got it for his birthday."

Teacher

"Is Bert carrying a real pistol?"

"Say that correctly."

"Is Bert allowed to carry a real pistol?"

"It is not allowed to have a real pistol. Who prohibited this?"

"Has your father got a real pistol? Is he a policeman?"

"Say: He has got a gun."

"A real gun?"

"Say: He got it for his birthday."

"Say: He got it for *his* birthday."

"But for what purpose did your father get a gun?"

and so on.

teaching of language

How does a deaf child learn the system—grammar—of his language? The teacher of the mother tongue (what a paradoxial combination) challenges the hearing child to discover this system himself by analogy from what he already knows (Lewis 1947). How well can deaf children be expected to do this? We believe it is really quite possible in certain respects, namely by utilizing what we have called the reflective language method (Uden 1955, 1957, 1968). This method rests on the twin foundations of conversing and reading. Suitable "reflective exercises" are provided, stimulating the child to

4. EDUCATIONAL RESOURCES

TABLE IV

Age of Children	Median # Words	Median % "Visually Dependent" Words
6;6 to 7;5	24	80%
7;6 to 8;5	37	60%
8;6 to 9;5	49	30%
9;6 to 10;5	56	25%
10;6 to 11;5	65	20%
11;6 to 12;5	66	20%
12;6 to 13;5	79	10%
13;6 to 14;5	79	10%
14;6 to 15;6	85	5%

discover aspects of grammar himself. For example, these exercises might include: "Find the accent-groups," "Underline the adjectives," and "Find the plural words."

The child will probably first learn a rule through his *reading*. These newly discovered rules can then be applied in his conversation and in his writing. Understanding the rule precedes its application. Consequently, it is absolutely necessary that the child read! The more the child hears what I have called "receptive reading," the more reflective exercises can be utilized.

Ability to read receptively is developed through conversations, diaries and telling stories. In daily conversations the children learn increasingly to enter into each other's worlds. The diaries are especially important. At about age six, diaries begin to become more differentiated as each deaf child compiles his own diary. The children exchange diaries from time to time and read what other children have written. Letters are also included in the diaries.

It is easier for the children to understand stories they are told than to read because facial mime, gestures, the rhythm of the living word, and the surrender of the listener to the storyteller all function to increase understanding. In fact, during the telling of a story, communication is really two-way, not just one-way, especially for deaf children because the teacher must check continuously to ascertain that her children are following the story.

It is definitely possible for 80 percent of our children to begin reading regular books by the age of nine or ten. The 20 percent who may not be ready

by this time quite possibly would not have been ready even had they had normal hearing. However, we use essentially the same methods with these children that we use with the others. By the time they actually begin reading books, all the children have firm foundations for reading which were developed through conversation, diaries, and storytelling.

effect of "accent-grouping"

We put very heavy stress on *rhythm* training in daily conversations (Uden 1957). From childhood on, deaf children can and should learn to speak in "accent-groups" with correct intonation and stress. Intonation (and especially accent-grouping) represents the only essential basis for control of syntax and sentence structure. Any other means is, in my opinion, merely supplementary (Uden, 1968).

For a full appreciation of my meaning, it is essential that you understand the denotations of these terms. Syntax is based on two polar constructions: the accent-group and the "pincer construction." The latter is found primarily in German and Dutch, and less frequently in English and French. An accent-group basically is a group of syllables which possesses one heavy stress (or accent). A few examples will help clarify this:

"A student, highly intellectual," contains two accent groups ("a student" and "highly intellectual"), but no pincer constructions. By contrast, "A highly intellectual student" consists of one accent group with a pincer construction. Another example of a clause containing a pincer construction is: "His knapsack was so heavily crammed," which contrasts with "His

knapsack was crammed so heavily." The latter contains no pincer constructions.

It is difficult adequately to define what I mean by "pincer construction." It is not, in my opinion, a logical and semantic structure, but a rhythmical one. Perhaps I can best illustrate this by analogy (Uden 1960). When Mozart brings together the various components of a theme in one of his symphonies, he increases both tension and unity. In much the same way we join parts of two or more accent groups into one pincer construction, thereby increasing tension and unity. It is humorous the way we hearing adults make many slips of the tongue in producing such pincer constructions. For example, take: "His knapsack was so heavily was crammed." We are so accustomed to keeping the parts of small accent groups together that we almost automatically repeat "was" before "crammed." Deaf children who are well trained in rhythmic speech often make similar slips. I have already collected more than one hundred examples, e.g.:

Mijn moeder gaat morgen gaat naar huis
   (My mother is going tomorrow going home)
Blijf jij altijd hier blijven?
   (Stay you always here staying?)

"Gaat naar huis" ("going home") and "hier blijven" (here staying) were both spoken as rhythmic accent-groups.

It has been our experience—and I hope to prove it experimentally—that rhythm, far from being a disturbing factor in constructing correct sentences (the above example notwithstanding), is actually a great help. If the deaf child can learn to speak rhythmically, he will approach more and more the standard, correct ways of constructing sentences in his language. It is my view, then, that the accent-group is the true basis of sentence structure. For this reason alone, fingerspelling is inadequate as a means of teaching language because it lacks normal rhythm.

We also have some evidence that rhythm training can substantially affect memory and thinking processes in deaf children. In an examination (1956) I found that rhythmically well-educated deaf children could remember a sentence better when they had spoken it rhythmically than when they had only written it down. Broadbent (1958) and Conrad (1965) have distinguished between "short-term memory" and "long-term memory." The latter extends over a period of several minutes, hours, or days, whereas the former is of short duration. Speech, of course, is here one instant and gone the next. To recall what a friend of yours has just said, your short-term memory must function effectively. In this connection, I might note that Conrad (1965) found serious deficiencies in the short-term memories of the deaf children he tested.

I believe that rhythm is a crucial factor in short-term memory. My examinations—which have not yet been published—show deaf children with no rhythm training to be two or three years behind hearing children in rhythmical development. It should be realized that such a serious deficiency in short-term memory, that is, in rhythmical grouping of words, also affects thinking. This may be why so many deaf children and adults resort to trial-and-error problem solving instead of thinking things through thoroughly. I believe that deaf children should be trained from childhood to code their thinking rhythmically, and that rhythm training should be an essential part of a deaf child's education. We achieve this partially through dancing and music in our "Geluidsmethode" — "Sound Perception Method" (Uden 1947, 1952). A thorough rhythm-oriented education, of course, can only be achieved through the use of the pure oral method.

conclusions

No one can deny that our deaf children have to live mainly in a hearing world. Even if they should marry other deaf persons, they remain essentially in the hearing society, especially if their children should be hearing. We have found that deaf parents of deaf children insist just as much as—in certain cases even more than—hearing parents that their children receive an oral education.

We are convinced that we can make the deaf most happy when we educate them in such a way that they can associate easily and conveniently with hearing people. However, the education that we provide must of necessity be the very best we can possibly produce. Of all handicapped children, deaf children are the most vulnerable. If their education does not achieve the ultimate, the oral method will fail in many cases. This failure may push the child into a deaf ghetto. So it must be all or nothing!

Even in our so-called welfare states deaf children still do not receive all that to which they are entitled. May the hearing society not only invite them, but meet them with every possible means—mostly with love—God willing!

REFERENCES

Bellugi, U. and Brown, R. *The Acquisition of Language, Child Development Monograph*, 1964.
Broadbent, D. E. *Perception and Communication*, New York, 1958.
Conrad, R. and Rush, M. L. "On the Nature of Short-term Memory Encoding by the Deaf," *Journal of Speech and Hearing Disorders*, 1965, pp. 336-343.
Davis, H. and Silverman, S. R., editors, *Hearing and Deafness*, third edition, New York, N.Y. 1970,
Dongen, Rev.Br. Ach. *What Horen Onze Dove Kinderen van Spraak*. Jaarverslag, St. Michielsgestel, 1962, pp. 54-77.
Egan, H. *Articulation Testing Methods*. Cambridge, Mass., 1944.
Eggermont, J. "De Klankfrequente in het hedendaags gesproken Nederlands," *De Nieuwe Taalgids*, 1956, pp. 221-223.
Ewing, I. R. and Ewing A. W. G. "Hearing Aids in Schools for the Deaf," *The Teacher of the Deaf*, 1934, pp. 171-173.
Ewing, I. R. "Deafness in Infancy and Early Childhood," *Journ. of Lar. and Otology*. London, 1943.
Fletcher, H. and Steinberg, J. C. *Articulation Testing Methods*. Bell System, New York, N.Y., 1929.
Heider, F. and Heider, G. M. *An Experimental Investigation of Lipreading*. *Psychol. Monograph*, 1940, Vol. 52, pp. 125-153.
Hudgins, C. V., and Numbers, F. C. "An Investigation of the Intelligibility of the Speech of the Deaf." *Genet. Psychol. Monograph*, No. 25, 1942, pp. 289-392.
Krohnert, O. *Die sprechliche Bildung des Gehorlosen*, Weinheim, 1966.
Lemke, R. "Das Enthemmte Kind mit Choreatiforme Symptomatik," *Psychiatr. Neur. Med. Psychol.*, 1954-55.
Lewis, M. M. *Language and Society* London, 1947.
Lowe, A. *Haus-Sprach-Erziehung fur Gehorgeschadigte Kleinkinder*. Berlin, 1952.
Prechtl, H. F. R. and Stemmer, C. J. "Ein Choreatiformes Syndrom bei Kindern," *Weiner med.* Wochenschr, 1959, 22.
Prechtl, H. F. R. *Het Cerebraal Gestoorde Kind*. Groningen, The Netherlands: 1963.
Rosa, Rev.Sr. *Cursus in Leren Spreken*. St. Michielsgestel, 1942-1949.
Schuy, C. *Die Sprachliche Situation des Taubstummen*. Sprachforum, 1955, pp. 146-159.
Uden, A.M.J. van. *Voelmuziek en dans voor Doofstommen*. St. Michielsgestel, 1947. *Een Geluidsmethode voor Zwaar en Geheel Dove Kinderen*. Idem, 1952. *Cursus Taaldidactiek*. Idem, 1955-57. "Moglichkeit und Verwertung der Lautempfindungen bei Taubstummen Kindern," *Neue Bl. f. Taubst. Bi*, 1955, pp. 153-172. "Tonwahrnehmung und Sprachformenunterricht bei Taubstummen," *Heilpadag.* Werkblatter, Luzern 1957, pp. 111-126; 169-172.
"Erfahrungsbericht uber Drei Jahren Hausspraerziehung Tauber Kleinkinder" *N.Bl.f.T.Bi.*, 1959, pp. 76-82.
"Gehorlosenschule und Schwerhorigenschule als Verschiedene Schultypen," *N.Bl.f.T.Bi.*, 1960, pp. 161-173.
"Motoriek en Verwerying van een Klankentaal," *Het Gehoorg Kind*, 1960, pp. 179-216.
"Cybernetics and the Instruction of the Deaf," *Proc. Intern. Cong. on Cybernetics*, Oct. 1960.
Spraak-verstaan, Jaarverslag, St. Michielsgestel, 1962, pp. 43-53.
"Das Gegliederte Ziel der Haus-sprach-Erziehung," In: *Bericht uber die Arbeitstagung:* Fruh-erziehung Horgeschadigter Kinder. Berlin-Aachen, 1963.
"A *World of Language for Deaf Children*," Part 1: *Basic Principles*.
A Maternal Reflective Method. St. Michielsgestel, and Washington, D.C., 1968. Unpublished experiments, 1969.

Classroom Observation Under Conditions of Simulated Profound Deafness

Normal-hearing teachers and audiologists continually seek new ways to improve the oral communication skills of profoundly deaf children.* But because they do not perceive speech in the same way that deaf children do, normal-hearing persons are not likely to appreciate fully the receptive difficulties which these children encounter in an oral environment.

The technique of role-playing often has been used to provide insight into situations where direct experience is difficult or impossible to obtain. Likewise, several attempts have been made to simulate the effects of hearing loss in order to gain a better understanding of this problem. Some normal-hearing investigators have occluded their ear canals (Hebb, Heath, & Stuart, 1954), while others have used masking noise to eliminate auditory sensation (von der Lieth, 1972). But most studies and demonstrations have used low-pass filtering of speech to simulate the effects of hearing impairment (Harford, 1964; Glorig, 1971; Ross, Duffy, Cooker, & Sargeant, 1973). Although low-pass filtering may produce a sound quality that is similar to that heard by *severely* hearing impaired listeners, the method probably grossly overestimates

---

*Profound deafness implies an inability to understand speech by ear alone. It usually is associated with average hearing threshold levels poorer than about 95 dB (ANSI, 1969) for 500-1000-2000 Hz.

 "Classroom Observation Under Conditions of Simulated Profound Deafness," Norman P. Erber and M. Lynn Zeiser, *The Volta Review*, Vol. 76 No. 6, 1974. ©1974 The Alexander Graham Bell Association for the Deaf, Inc.

the acoustic information that is available to those who are *profoundly* deaf (Erber, 1972a, 1972b, 1974b).

Profoundly deaf children seem to perceive little more than the time and intensity patterns of acoustic speech signals (Erber, 1972a, 1974c). Several studies have suggested that they do not *hear* at all but instead detect amplified acoustic signals through vibrotactile receptors in their ears (Boothroyd & Cawkwell, 1970; Nober, 1970). Thus, to an oral child who is profoundly deaf, vision (speechreading) is the principal source of speech and language information (see Erber, 1974b). For these children, the acoustic output of a hearing aid probably provides vibrotactile stimulation only.

An important step in improving oral instruction for deaf children is to understand the special conditions under which they perceive speech. This report describes the experiences of two normal-hearing adults who used special equipment which deprived them of auditory stimulation, but which enabled them to perceive speech visually and vibrotactually. With this limited sensory input, they observed classroom instruction in order to experience some of the conditions under which profoundly deaf children learn to communicate orally.

the observation procedure

Two observers participated in the study: a research audiologist and a teacher at Central Institute for the Deaf (CID). Both were very familiar with teaching strategies, amplification equipment, and the sensory capabilities of deaf children. In addition, both had previously participated as subjects in several studies on visual and vibrotactual perception of speech. The teachers who were observed varied widely with respect to age (23-53 years) and experience (1-32 years), and they employed many different teaching styles. The children in their respective classes represented a wide range of ages (4-16 years), hearing threshold levels (52-127 dB average, ANSI, 1969), and learning abilities.

To simulate the quality of the speech signal perceived by profoundly deaf ears, each observer received amplified speech through a vibrator (Suvag Vibar) which he held in his hand (see Figure 1). To prevent themselves from *hearing* speech, the observers wore circumaural earphones (Realistic Nova-10) to which a low frequency masking stimulus (approximately 90 dB SPL) was delivered from a portable noise generator. Speechreading was their main source of information. They observed activities in progress during two 1/2-hour sessions in each of 26 CID classrooms. The observers both wrote short paragraphs to describe their experiences in each classroom. They compared notes periodically to confirm or question their independent observations.

The observers' primary intent was to try to understand lesson content from the point of view of a profoundly deaf pupil in an oral classroom. Whenever they did not understand the teacher's message, they analyzed the situation to determine the source of their difficulty. Previous research has suggested that the optical environment (Erber, 1974a), the acoustic environment (Erber, 1971), the nature of the speech signal (Berger, 1970; Gault, 1928; Erber, 1972a,b), and the communication strategies used in the classroom (Erber & Greer, 1973) all affect the perception of speech by deaf children. Therefore, the observers attended closely to each of these variables. A summary of their observations is presented below.

environmental conditions

The Optical Environment

The observers reported that with limited sensory input, they noticed

4. EDUCATIONAL RESOURCES

Figure 1 Block diagram of the apparatus used by a normal-hearing observer to simulate profound deafness in the classroom.

(A) In classrooms with wired group systems, the vibrator was plugged directly into an earphone output jack.

(B) In the case of classrooms equipped with wireless or wearable systems, the output of one wearable unit was divided and delivered both to its set of receivers and to a supplementary amplifier which powered the vibrator.

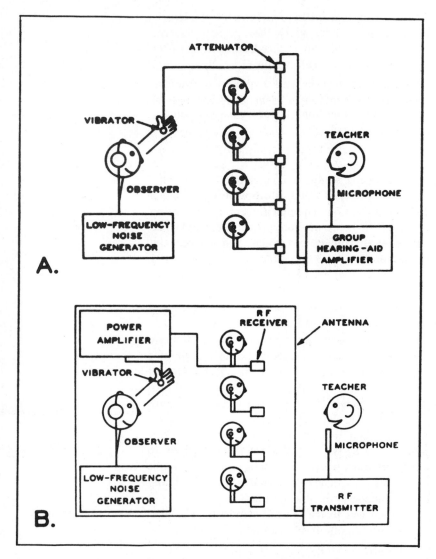

some aspects of the optical and acoustic environments which they had overlooked previously. For example, they found that the optical conditions in several classrooms were not well suited to speechreading. Many of the rooms were inadequately illuminated by their fluorescent tubes, and dull wall surfaces absorbed much of the available light. The window orientation in a few of the classrooms either allowed intense outside light to be directed into the eyes of the observer or caused the interior of the teacher's mouth to be shadowed. It was possible to speechread under these poor lighting conditions, but the task was difficult and fatiguing. On the other hand, when the room was bright and the teacher faced the windows while speaking, speechreading required much less effort.

The use of classroom space and the arrangement of desks also influenced the observers' visual perception of speech. For example, in several classrooms the area behind the teacher was used to present instructional materials, display children's artwork, or store other interesting objects. It was much easier to attend to teachers who sat before an uncluttered, nonreflecting background (e.g., a blank wall or a clean chalkboard) and who referred to materials or objects beside them. The spontaneous movements and gestures of young children also were a major source of visual distraction, which often drew the observers' attention away from the teacher.

The Acoustic Environment

Laboratory research has shown that environmental noise limits the speech perception of profoundly deaf children more than that of persons with normal hearing (Erber, 1971). For these classroom observations, the normal-hearing investigators used a vibrator to simulate the acoustic signals available to profoundly deaf children. Several acoustic signals were found to be very distracting when they were perceived through a vibrator. For example, background noise generated by the children in the classroom often masked the vibratory patterns of speech. These background vibrations were especially disturbing and disorienting when unpredictable bursts of noise occurred. The children produced undesirable vibratory patterns when they tapped on desks to attract attention, kicked a floor microphone or a desk, or spoke spontaneously while someone else was talking. In many cases, the vibratory patterns of these noises were like those of intended speech, and the observers could not distinguish the two stimuli.

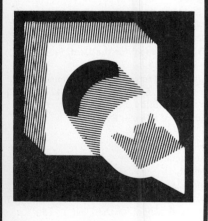

INDEX

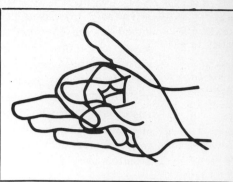

STAFF

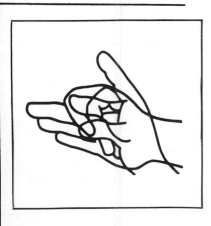

Publisher	John Quirk
Editor	Dona Chiappe
Editorial Ass't.	Carol Carr
Permissions Editor	Audrey Weber
Director of Production	Richard Pawlikowski
Director of Design	Donald Burns
Customer Service	Cindy Finocchio
Sales Service	Diane Hubbard
Administration	Linda Calano
Index	Mary Russell

Cover Design

Li Bailey of Enoch and Eisenman Inc. New York City.

Appendix: Agencies and Services for Exceptional Children

Alexander Graham Bell Association for the Deaf,
  Inc.
Volta Bureau for the Deaf
3417 Volta Place, NW
Washington, D.C. 20007

American Academy of Pediatrics
1801 Hinman Avenue
Evanston, Illinois 60204

American Association for Gifted Children
15 Gramercy Park
New York, N.Y. 10003

American Association on Mental Deficiency
5201 Connecticut Avenue, NW
Washington, D.C. 20015

American Association of Psychiatric Clinics for
  Children
250 West 57th Street
New York, N.Y.

American Bar Association
Commission on the Mentally Disabled
1800 M Street, NW
Washington, D.C. 20036

American Foundation for the Blind
15 W. 16th Street
New York, N.Y. 10011

American Medical Association
535 N. Dearborn Street
Chicago, Illinois 60610

American Speech and Hearing Association
9030 Old Georgetown Road
Washington, D.C. 20014

Association for the Aid of Crippled Children
345 E. 46th Street
New York, N.Y. 10017

Association for Children with Learning Disabilities
2200 Brownsville Road
Pittsburgh, Pennsylvania 15210

Association for Education of the Visually
  Handicapped
1604 Spruce Street
Philadelphia, Pennsylvania 19103

Association for the Help of Retarded Children
200 Park Avenue, South
New York, N.Y.

Association for the Visually Handicapped
1839 Frankfort Avenue
Louisville, Kentucky 40206

Center on Human Policy
Division of Special Education and Rehabilitation
Syracuse University
Syracuse, New York 13210

Child Fund
275 Windsor Street
Hartford, Connecticut 06120

Children's Defense Fund
1520 New Hampshire Avenue NW
Washington, D.C. 20036

Closer Look
National Information Center for the Handicapped
1201 Sixteenth Street NW
Washington, D.C. 20036

Clifford W. Beers Guidance Clinic
432 Temple Street
New Haven, Connecticut 06510

Child Study Center
Yale University
333 Cedar Street
New Haven, Connecticut 06520

Child Welfare League of America, Inc.
44 East 23rd Street
New York, N.Y. 10010

Children's Bureau
United States Department of Health, Education
  and Welfare
Washington, D.C.

Council for Exceptional Children
1411 Jefferson Davis Highway
Arlington, Virginia 22202

Epilepsy Foundation of America
1828 "L" Street NW
Washington, D.C. 20036

Gifted Child Society, Inc.
59 Glen Gray Road
Oakland, New Jersey 07436

Institute for the Study of Mental Retardation
  and Related Disabilities
130 South First
University of Michigan
Ann Arbor, Michigan 48108

International Association for the Scientific Study
  of Mental Deficiency
Ellen Horn, AAMD
5201 Connecticut Avenue NW
Washington, D.C. 20015

International League of Societies for the Mentally
  Handicapped
Rue Forestiere 12
Brussels, Belgium

Joseph P. Kennedy, Jr. Foundation
1701 K Street NW
Washington, D.C. 20006

League for Emotionally Disturbed Children
171 Madison Avenue
New York, N.Y.

Muscular Dystrophy Associations of America
1790 Broadway
New York, N.Y. 10019

National Aid to the Visually Handicapped
3201 Balboa Street
San Francisco, California 94121

National Association of Coordinators of State
  Programs for the Mentally Retarded
2001 Jefferson Davis Highway
Arlington, Virginai 22202

National Association of Hearing and Speech
  Agencies
919 18th Street NW
Washington, D.C. 20006

National Association for Creative Children and
  Adults
8080 Springvalley Drive
Cincinnati, Ohio 45236
(Mrs. Ann F. Isaacs, Executive Director)

National Association for Retarded Children
420 Lexington Avenue
New York, N.Y.

National Association for Retarded Citizens
2709 Avenue E East
Arlington, Texas 76010

National Children's Rehabilitation Center
P.O. Box 1260
Leesburg, Virginia

National Association for the Visually Handicapped
3201 Balboa Street
San Francisco, California 94121

National Association of the Deaf
814 Thayer Avenue
Silver Spring, Maryland 20910

National Cystic Fibrosis Foundation
3379 Peachtree Road NE
Atlanta, Georgia 30326

National Easter Seal Society for Crippled Children
  and Adults
2023 W. Ogden Avenue
Chicago, Illinois 60612

National Federation of the Blind
218 Randolph Hotel
Des Moines, Iowa 50309

National Paraplegia Foundation
333 N. Michigan Avenue
Chicago, Illinois 60601

National Society for Autistic Children
621 Central Avenue
Albany, N.Y. 12206

National Society for Prevention of Blindness, Inc.
79 Madison Avenue
New York, N.Y. 10016

Orton Society, Inc.
8415 Bellona Lane
Baltimore, Maryland 21204

President's Committee on Mental Retardation
Regional Office Building #3
7th and D Streets SW
Room 2614
Washington, D.C. 20201

United Cerebral Palsy Associations
66 E 34th Street
New York, N.Y. 10016

1978 Catalog
SPECIAL LEARNING CORPORATION

1978 Catalog
SPECIAL LEARNING CORPORATION
Programs in Special Education

Programs in Special Education

Table of Contents

Basic Skills

● special education ● learning disabilities ● mental retardation
● autism ● behavior modification ● mainstreaming ● gifted and talented
● physically handicapped ● deaf education ● speech and hearing
● emotional and behavioral disorders ● visually handicapped
● diagnosis and placement ● psychology of exceptional children

Special Learning Corporation
42 Boston Post Rd. Guilford, Connecticut 06437 (203) 453-6212

Special Learning Corporation's
For: Mainstreaming Special Education Teachers

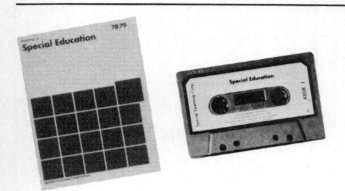

SPECIAL EDUCATION
This seminar provides an overview of special education.
1. Special Education: An Historical Perspective
2. Methodology
3. Mental Retardaton
4. Emotional and Behavioral Disorders
5. Physically and Sensorially Handicapped
6. Learning Disabilites
7. Psychology of Exceptional Children

$24.50

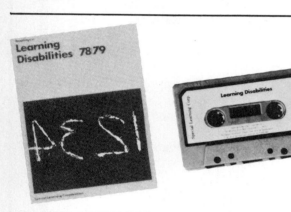

LEARNING DISABILITIES
Discussion of learning disabilities and physical neurological approach to education.
1. Dimensions of Learning Disabilities
2. Diagnosis and Assessment
3. Perceptual Disorders
4. Motor Activity Disorders
5. Language Disorders
6. Reading Disorders
7. Social Emotional Problems of the Learning Disabled

$24.50

EMOTIONAL AND BEHAVIOR DISORDERS
Understanding the difficult child.
1. Emotional Disorders:
   A Perspective
2. Emotional and Behavioral Disorders in the Classroom
3. Hyperkinesis
4. Deviant Behavior and Juvenile Delinquency
5. Behavior Therapies

$24.50

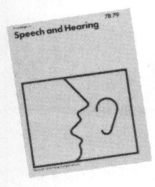

SPEECH AND HEARING
The remarkable ability of brain, tongue and ear in use of speech.
1. Physiological Auditory Impairment: Diagnosis and Assessment
2. Speech Disorders: Pathology and Classification
3. Linguistic Development
4. Cognitive and Communicative Skills
5. Educational Services: Resources and Therapies
6. Research and Rehabilitation: Medical, Technological and Psychological

$24.50

Teacher-Training Series

Administrators, PL 94-142, Special Schools

VISUALLY HANDICAPPED EDUCATION

A discussion of 4 phases in blind and visually handicapped education.

1. Education of the Visually Handicapped: Historical Overview
2. Etiology of Visual Impairment: Research
3. Cognitive and Communicative Skills
4. Perceptual Disorders
5. Vocational and Educational Support Systems
6. Socialization and Rehabilitation

$24.50

AUTISM

Hostile attitudes, interpersonal relationships with emphasis on clinical problems.

1. Concept of Autism: History and Theory
2. Prospectus on Causes
3. Development of Perceptual Skills
4. Behavioral Therapy
5. Language Development

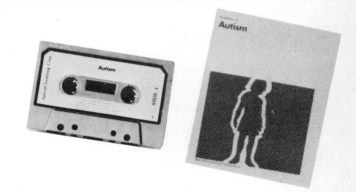

$24.50

GIFTED AND TALENTED EDUCATION

The subject of identification, leadership, creativity, guidance and educating promising youth.

1. Perspective on Gifted Education: Identification
2. Programming for the Academically Talented
3. Curriculum and Materials....Methodology
4. Placement: Mainstreaming vs. Special Programming
5. Community Resources and Support Services

$43.50

DIAGNOSIS AND PLACEMENT

1. Current Testing Procedures
2. Personality Assessment
3. Cognitive Assessment
4. Medical Assessment
5. Placement: Self-Contained or Mainstreamed

Individual intelligence testing is discussed as well as identification of children in need of special help and of gifted, mentally retarded and emotionally disturbed.

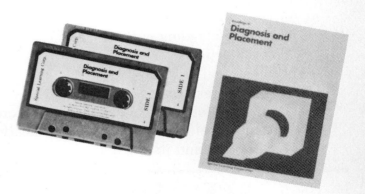

$43.50

COMMENTS PLEASE:

SPECIAL LEARNING CORPORATION

42 Boston Post Rd.

Guilford, Conn. 06437

SPECIAL LEARNING CORPORATION

COMMENTS PLEASE:

Does this book fit your course of study?

Why? (Why not?)

Is this book useable for other courses of study? Please list.

What other areas would you like us to publish in using this format?

What type of exceptional child are you interested in learning more about?

Would you use this as a basic text?

How many students are enrolled in these course areas?

_____Special Education _____ Mental Retardation _____Psychology _____Emotional Disorders

_____ Exceptional Children _____Learning Disabilities Other _____

Do you want to be sent a copy of our elementary student materials catalog?

Do you want a copy of our college catalog?

Would you like a copy of our next edition? ▱ yes ▱ no

Are you a ▱ student or an ▱ instructor?

Your name _____ school _____

Term used _____ Date _____

address _____

city _____ state _____ zip _____

telephone number _____

D/E